the concrete wave

the history of skateboarding

the concrete wave

the history of skateboarding

michael brooke

Warwick Publishing
Toronto Los Angeles
www.warwickgp.com

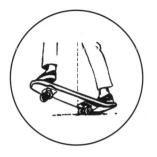

Fourth Printing, October 2000

We acknowledge the financial support of the Government of Canada through the Book Publishing Industry Development Program for our publishing activities.

ISBN: 1-894020-54-5

Published by Warwick Publishing Inc.
162 John Street, Toronto, Ontario M5V 2E5

Design: Kimberley Young/mercer digital design
Cover Photo: Roger Muller, Los Angeles, CA, July 4, 1990 by Scott Starr
Back Cover Photos: Chad Muska, Santa Barbara, CA, 1998 by Scott Starr/Michael Brooke, Toronto, 1998 by Michael Belobradic
Editor: Melinda Tate

Printed and bound in Canada

**This book
is dedicated to
Skateboarders
past,
present
and future**

inside

inside

The Fourth (Permanent?) Wave (1993■ now)

Appendix

Acknowledgements

My deepest thanks to Nick Pitt, Jim Williamson, Kimberley Young, Melinda Tate, and Diane Farenick at Warwick Publishing. All of you have been tremendous during the creation of this book.

There are a number of people within the skate world who have been incredibly helpful with the creation of this book. My thanks go out to these people:

Kevin Harris, Scott Starr, Todd Huber, Pete and Joyce Weldrake, Tony Alva, Norm MacDonald, Tony Hawk, Craig Stecyk III, Jim Fitzpatrick, Frank Nasworthy, Larry Stevenson, Hobie Alter, Larry Balma, Fausto Vitello, Stacy Peralta, Jim Gray, Steve Rocco, Darrel Delgado, Rodney Mullen, Dan Gesmer, Rene Carrasco, Chris Carter, Tim Puimarta, George Powell, Dean Marttinen, Tannis Watson, Mark Waters, Chris Miller, Bob Schmidt, Mike Belobradic, John Falahee, Per Welinder, Jeff Klindt, Larry Gordon, Sean Cliver, Willi Winkel, Jeff Gluck, PD, Dave Hackett, Brad Bowman, Rick McCurdy, Russ Howell, Tom Browne, Stefan Akesson, Bob Burnquist, Dean Hunter, Skip Engblom, Richard Jones, Miki Vuckovich, Mike Bramston, Brad Dorfman, Mark Richards, Richard Neuman, Paul Schmitt, Chris Long, Jack Smith, Paul Romo, Jason Greenridge and Jim O'Mahoney.

A special thank-you to my wife Michal for her support and patience with this book. One day, she will get on a halfpipe! I'd also like to acknowledge my two children, Maya and Jonathan, who enjoy watching skate videos as much as their dad.

Finally, a thank-you to my parents who bought me that first clay-wheeled skateboard in 1975 and have supported my passion for the sport ever since.

Foreword by
Rodney Mullen

What Skateboarding Means to Me

From what I understand, Alexander the Great died in Babylon of drunkenness and obesity shortly after his vanquishing days were over. The spoils of war apparently paled in comparison to the actual act of conquering.

I'm no Alexander, but I can't deny a little of that spirit. None of us can. I figured a decade's worth of trophies might quench my thirst, so that's where I fixed my sights. I defended my world title over 35 times, and I recall being genuinely happy about it only twice. The rest were hollow victories tainted by playing it safe; I did just enough to "win." The media told the world of my greatness, while I felt like a fraud. I was Cowardice wearing a crown.

After 10 years of psychotically striving for some arbitrary goal, I found myself moping around that spent and littered arena, finally waking up to the fact that even if everyone on the planet cried out my name at once, it wouldn't be enough. I had erected this wall between me and happiness by setting my sights on recognition and titles, instead of realizing that what drove me all along was the happiness I got from the endless hours of pushing my own limits, of actually doing what I thought could never be done. I'd toss and turn all night, waiting for daylight so that I could try out my next idea. That breathed life into me almost on a daily basis. And no matter how old and decrepit I get, I will never forget that feeling of being alive.

Skateboarding has been my battlefield, my personal proving grounds — spectators or not. It has been the arena where I could stake my claim, the play where I would contribute my verse, and even the pen with which I write. There is no price that could ever be paid for what skateboarding has meant to me.

Rodney Mullen
1999

What
Skateboarding
Means
to Me

11

Preface

In the summer of 1975, I took my first ride on a skateboard. It's now almost 25 years later and I still feel the same enthusiasm for the sport. For me, this book serves two purposes: for older skaters, my hope is that it will conjure up some great memories; for newer skaters, my goal is to provide you with an understanding of why the sport is so special and where its roots lie.

The roots of this book lie in two events: the emergence of the Internet and a chance remark to a publisher by the name of Nick Pitt. My interest in the Internet was fueled when I visited the Dansworld Skateboard Site on the World Wide Web in 1995. I wrote a piece detailing my 20-plus year history with the sport. It was posted to the site and I started to receive feedback immediately. Numerous e-mails filled with passion were arriving daily from people all over the world, and I knew I had hit a nerve. Readers were excited and eager to add their comments to my story. From this humble start, I approached my brother, Andrew, to start up the Skategeezer Homepage — a page dedicated to the history of skateboarding. Thanks to Andrew's hard work, the site started to grow and gain a following.

My work in the summer of 1997 led me to a meeting with Nick Pitt of Warwick Publishing. At the time I was selling office products to publishers and printers. During the meeting with Nick, I happened to mention that I was running a web site on the history of skateboarding. He responded, "That's interesting, we're thinking about doing a book on skateboarding." In less than two months, I had a book publishing contract. What you are holding in your hands is the result of that chance remark.

Before you start to read the next pages, allow me to relate one other detail. Chronicling the history of skateboarding was an ambitious undertaking. So many things have happened in the past 40 years that to try to document them in 200 or so pages is nearly impossible. With that in mind, please don't get too upset if we've missed something. I have striven for accuracy, but a lot can happen in 40 years and sometimes the line between fact and fiction gets blurred. If we've missed something, don't freak . . . just wait for the next edition!

As well as my own research, this book contains contributions from skateboarders from around the world who posted items to my "Skategeezer" website. Some of these have been edited for the purposes of the book, but can be read in full on the site.

Although most writers hope their books are so compelling that readers "can't put them down," my hope for *The Concrete Wave* is that it gets you so fired up to go and skate, that you *have* to put it down!

Keep skating and have fun,

Michael Brooke
Spring 1999

P.S. E-mail me at:
mbrooke@interlog.com

or write me at: Concrete Wave,
1054 Centre Street, Suite 293,
Thornhill, Ontario L4J 8E5

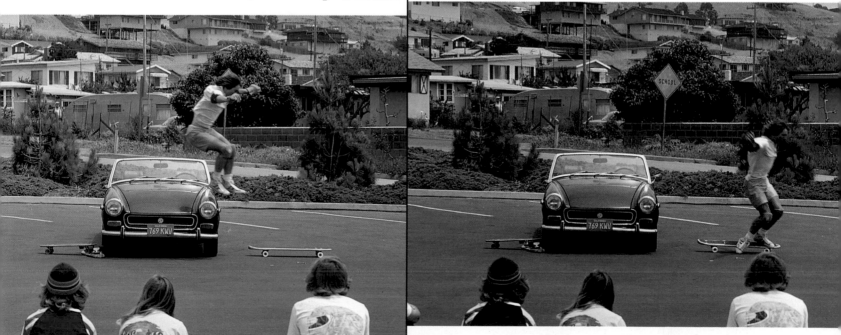

For the past 40 years, skateboarding has rolled in and out of the public's consciousness. It's a sport associated with youth that combines agility, speed and sheer guts. It's not a sport for everyone, and that's just the way skaters like it. At its core, skateboarding is very much an individual sport that can be enjoyed with a group. It's a sport that is continually reinventing itself. Like a hyperactive seven year old, skateboarding will not be pinned down. And like that hyperactive child, skateboarding can be both exhilarating and maddening. On any given weekend huge numbers of people cheer on skaters performing unbelievable aerials at skateboarding exhibitions. Then, come Monday morning, these same people can be heard cursing streetskaters for jumping over railings.

Skateboarders come from all walks of life. Rich or poor, west coast, midwest or east coast, American, Brazilian, Australian — no matter who or where they are, skateboarders are bound by common threads. Some of these threads include an energy and passion for something most of the mainstream ignores.

Despite being accorded only a small amount of attention, skateboarding has made a tremendous impact on society worldwide. From music to the Internet to fashion, skateboarders define what is cutting edge. They are always ready to change the status quo and take things in a new direction. Whether it's Tony Alva's break-

14

through advertising in the '70's, or Stacy Peralta's and Craig Stecyk's video work in the '80's, skateboard culture exerts a huge influence. The only problem is it takes the rest of the world a few years to catch up, and by that time skaters are already working on the next big thing.

Unlike most sports, skateboarding has suffered some very strenuous peaks and valleys of popularity. There has been a number of reasons for this rise and fall pattern: In the 1960's, the first skateboard boom was big, but manufacturers couldn't keep up with demand, let alone improve the product. As a result, skateboarders were faced with poor technology (that is, clay wheels) and concerns about safety. In the 1970's the introduction of urethane wheels elevated the sport again, but by the end of the decade, skatepark liability problems and the proliferation of BMX biking and roller skating caused another crash.

The sport receded as it had done in the late '60's, but a hardcore contingent kept the faith. Backyard ramps took the place of official skateparks (most of which had been bulldozed) and skate videos kept the fires burning. By the mid '80's, vertical skating along with streetskating pushed the sport to dazzling heights. Then, again, as the decade closed, the skate industry faced a worldwide recession and was caught with a surplus of product. Coupled with this problem was the extremely negative tone that the industry had adopted. It was like an unruly teenager with the urge to destroy the past in order to create a new future.

By the turn of the 1990's, the skate industry was its own worst enemy. A shake up was needed. But while other skate busts had been brutal, this time the attrition was not so horrendous. Snowboarding's popularity helped many manufacturers and skate shops weather the blows. Finally, by the mid 1990's, skateboarding was on another roll, this time thanks to events like the X Games and a change in demographics. The baby boomers' kids are now a significant force and will continue to push skateboarding to new levels of popularity.

In keeping with this ebb and flow history, this book has been divided into sections according to the successive waves of popularity skateboarding has experienced. We start in the 1950's, when kids made their own skateboards, and go right up to the present day, when skateboarding has become a big industry and a worldwide cultural phenomenon. Interspersed are the reminiscences of skateboarders, famous and not, from all over the world.

Prehistory

Kids have always had an affinity for their own set of wheels. The bicycle is the prime example, but for a long time bikes were out of reach financially for many families. The alternatives were wagons, scooters and roller skates. When these store-bought vehicles didn't do the trick, young people resorted to creating their own conveyances. Some built go-karts or soapbox carts; others made what would end up being the early form of the skateboard.

This first type of skateboard, which dates back to the early 1900's, was actually more like a scooter. It featured roller skate wheels attached to a two by four. Often the board had a milk crate nailed to it with handles sticking out for control. Over the next five decades kids changed the look of these contraptions, taking off the crate and cruising on just the two by fours with steel wheels. Tens of thousands of rollerskates were dismantled and joyfully hammered on to planks of wood.

After the Second World War, North America experienced a booming economy and an expanding population. The baby boomers quickly made their presence felt in the marketplace. The 1950s would see toy manufacturers stumbling over themselves to come up with the next fad to capture the imaginations and piggy banks of kids everywhere. The appearance of television would help them along. Yo-yos, hula hoops and the like would rise and fall in favor on the playground. It was only a matter of time before someone picked up on the potential lying in those roller skate wheels nailed to hunks of wood. The first commercial skateboards hit the marketplace in 1959.

The dawn of the commercial skateboard industry brought new and exciting technological advances, like clay wheels, that made the ride smoother and new tricks possible. But it also signaled an end to a time when kids gleefully and messily and ingeniously devised their own playthings.

There are a few old geezers out here who remember skateboarding in the 60's. My teenage daughter, an avid skateboarder who does ollies and aerials with her board, believes the sport came into existence in California. Well, there I had to differ, because I remember skateboarding on Oahu, Hawaii, the day President Kennedy was killed; the radio was on reporting it while I was attaching a board to a pair of roller skate wheels. Yes, it was kind of crude but we rolled down the hills at high speeds with the wheels nailed onto a small plank, and made the best of what we had.

There were no fancy graphic decks with high-dollar wheels and trucks then; the island kids knew how to make a skateboard before the California dudes. I learned how to make a skateboard from a little Filipino boy who could also make woven baskets from palm fronds. The ingenuity of children back in those days was marvelous. Nowadays, it's "Mom, I nccd $140 for a ncw skatcboard, my deck is all chipped up and the wheels and trucks are shot."

— A.W.

I started skateboarding back in 1964 in Merced, California. I manufactured mine in wood shop while in high school. The wheels then came from the old iron skates, wheels made of steel. Talk about a rough ride. (smile)

Anyhow, the term used by us in '64 was

"sidewalk surfing"

rather than "skateboarding." Some of my buddies then made their boards from a piece of 2X4 wood, can you imagine? At age 50, I still have shoulder-length hair, own a ballet studio with my fiancée, and am in my senior year at a local university. . . .

Later, dude

The Day They Invented the
Skateboard

By Bob Schmidt, Orlando Florida

I was nine years old in 1961, and I was there the day they invented the skateboard, at least in *my* neighborhood.

We took an old metal roller skate and strapped it to a short piece of 2x4, hopped on top and took off. It was wobblier than hell, moved way too fast, and vibrated on the asphalt enough to jar every bone in your body and loosen every tooth. It was more like getting electrocuted than anything else. We're not talking any hundred-dollar baby here — maybe more like a buck ninety-five, figure maybe five bucks today for inflation. These were the days when we had hula hoops, and Schwinn American Flyer bicycles with chrome handlebars, fenders and racks on the back. We had Frisbees and yo-yo's and whiffle balls. But we would have traded in any of 'em for our skateboards.

We had a big old hill on Hatherleigh Rd. in the Stoneleigh community between Baltimore and Towson, Maryland. We all took turns trying it out on that hill. Only a couple of us lived to tell about it. The rest, well, they belong in the skateboard hall of fame. There was me, and Bob Filer, and Hammond Brown, and Barry and Buddy French, Jack Tuttle, and Mike McClelland.

Every one of us fell on our ass and broke at least three bones every year. A leg, an arm, a wrist, a couple of fingers — you couldn't help it. From top to bottom it was a block and a half long. It started out easy, then started curving over until it got a good deal steeper — cars can't get up that hill in the winter after a snow, that's how steep it is.

You had to start down that hill sitting down. There was no way you could go all the way down the first time, even sitting down. You had to get good enough to ride down all the way on your seat, then start at the bottom standing up, working your way up a couple of feet at a time, getting your nerve up. It took at least a good two weeks to get it right 'cause you'd have to heal up for a couple of days every time you tried. After a while, there was always somebody walking around with a cast on and hobbling on crutches and as soon as you saw them you knew it was *the Hill*.

When you went down the steep section, you got to feeling like you were flying. Then you'd hit a little bump. It wasn't anything you'd even notice on a bike or just walking down, but, man, on a board, look out! If you made it over that bump you'd fly up and just about everybody crashed right there. But once you learned how to twist a little to get past it, well, the rest of it was pretty easy. Unless a car was turning into you just as you got down to the bottom. Then you'd have to veer over the curb, bailing out at just the right time so you could run it off onto somebody's lawn.

That hill became the Challenge. You had to beat the Hill. Then you had to beat it three times in a row. And then, if you were still alive, you didn't have to do anything. You were okay. And that's all there was. We didn't jump over curbs. You couldn't anyway, with just a skate underneath. About the only tricks we ever tried was hanging ten off the side or going down on one foot. One guy tried standing on his hands but he fell over and got really messed up by the time he rolled the rest of the way down. A couple of guys tried to be pulled down behind a bike, but they could never do it. Oh, there was a hot dog who tried it every which way — trying to sit on his hands, go down on his belly and stuff — but nobody was impressed.

We were determined to make a faster skateboard that you could stay on. We spent months tinkering, smashing down the metal heel at the back of the skate, pulling apart the wheels and mounting them here and there until we got a better balance front to back. We tried every piece of wood we could find. Everybody who was anybody had one of their own they had made. Every one was different. We tried painting them, then we found out the girls liked 'em that way, so we decided that was for sissies and we soaked off the paint and left them plain. But the girls got mad, mostly because it was usually one of their skates we were using!

We strapped 'em together. We glued 'em. We nailed 'em. We screwed 'em together. We tried everything. Nothing would hold more than a few times without breaking or coming loose.

Wheels? That was whatever came on a roller skate. Strictly metal. And they only went so fast. Going down the Hill, at some points gravity would be pulling you faster than the wheels could go, and half your body would be falling over and that's when you'd get all banged up. Once a wheel was shot, you had to start all over. Just about the time you'd get good, you'd have to put another skate on and start again. And a spare skate wasn't always available. It's not like you could just run up to the store and get one roller skate.

Bearings? What the heck are those? We heard about 'em from somebody's father who was an engineer. But they were kind of sealed into the wheel and you couldn't get at 'em without totally destroying it. But sand and dirt had no problem getting in, and when it did you were a goner for sure. You'd lock up and go flying at the

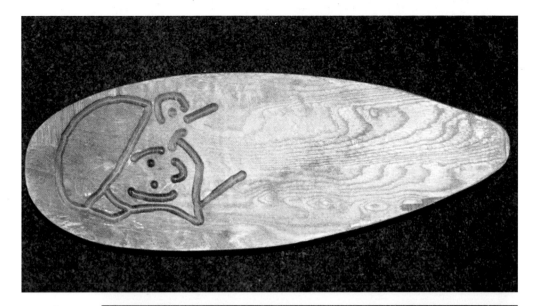

worst possible time, usually just when you were trying to avoid the handlebars of a bike or a parked car. And we didn't have no truck with trucks. The roller skate was its own truck. You were stuck with it. They never wore out, but they didn't have any cushioning in them either.

Halfpipes? What's this wood crap? When we found a halfpipe, it wasn't a halfpipe at all. It was a giant-size concrete sewer pipe, about eight to ten feet in diameter. And when you fell onto that, you knew it. They were hard to come by and we hardly ever got to try one. Even then it would only be for a few days or maybe a week during construction.

There was no such thing as a skateboard park. And it was so new, the parents and neighbors didn't even know what to make of it. But they sure knew we were there. Those wheels made a hell of a racket, especially when they needed oil!

And we didn't have any helmets or knee pads, though we probably would have worn 'em if we had 'em. The only padding we had was our own skin and bones. Yeah, like I tell my son, I was there the day they invented the skateboard, at least in *my* neighborhood.

The First Wave

The late 1950's saw growing commercial interest in the skateboard concept, and by 1959 the first Roller Derby Skateboard had appeared on store shelves. The introduction of commerically produced skateboards coincided with the era of the surfer, and people began to tie riding the waves with cruising on a board on land. By the time the 1960's rolled around, skateboarding had gained a sizable following among the surf crowd.

But it was when Larry Stevenson, publisher of *Surf Guide,* began to promote skateboarding that things really started to take off. Larry's company, Makaha, designed the first professional skateboards in 1963, and a team was formed to promote the product.

Travelling skateboard teams sponsored by skateboard makers would become a staple of skateboard marketing and play a big role in bringing skateboarding to the world. Makaha also sponsored the first skateboard contest, held in Hermosa, California, in 1963. Formal skateboard competitions raised the standards of skateboard performance and gave it its sport status.

More skateboard manufacturers appeared on the scene. By 1965, international contests, movies (*Skater Dater*), a magazine (*The Quarterly*

Skateboarder) and cross-country trips by teams of skateboarders had elevated the sport to enormous heights of popularity. Over fifty million boards were sold within a three-year period. Then, all of a sudden, skateboarding died in the fall of 1965.

The first skateboarding crash was due to inferior product, too much inventory and a public upset by reckless riding. The manufacturers were so busy making boards that little had been done in the way of research and development. Beyond replacing the squeaky steel roller skate wheels with smoother-riding clay wheels and refining the trucks (the devices that hold the wheels), there were few technological advances.

Some companies did develop better-quality wheels, but clay wheels were the cheapest to manufacture. Clay wheels did not grip the road well, however, and skaters everywhere were having some nasty falls. Cities started to ban skateboards in response to health and safety concerns, and after a few fatal accidents, skateboarding was officially drummed out of existence. Manufacturers lost huge amounts of money due to cancelled orders for the Christmas season, and skateboarding virtually disappeared from public view. But a few truly dedicated skaters would keep the sport alive on life support.

Larry Stevenson

The Father of the Skateboard

As a young boy at a State Home in California, Larry Stevenson had no idea the visit from Leo Carrillo in 1939 would have such an impact on his life. Carrillo was a well-known actor who played Zorro's sidekick in the movies. Obviously, the boys at the home would be impressed with this fact alone. But what struck Larry that particular day was what he saw coming out of Carrillo's green Chrysler Convertible. It was a scooter with a handle attached to it. Carrillo would give these scooters out to children at orphanages and state homes during Christmas time. Twenty-four years later, Stevenson would be inspired by these scooters that Carrillo had delivered to the children.

In 1961 Stevenson was busy publishing *Surf Guide.* At the time, the California surf scene was exploding and the guide covered the sport in great detail. He promoted the surf films of Bud Brown and had on staff a writer by the name of Bill Cleary. As Stevenson says, "I realized that with the *Surf Guide* I had a unique capability to promote something." That something was a scooter minus the handle: the skateboard.

It was Stevenson who had the insight that skateboarding could be a part of surf culture. *Surf Guide* laid the foundation for the roots of surfing to mesh with skateboarding. Cleary began to write articles on skateboarding and this in turn got surfers interested. Surfers were the first to embrace skateboarding and realize its potential.

In 1963, Larry Stevenson created Makaha Skateboards. The name came from the Makaha Surfing Championships. Production started up in June 1963 in Santa Monica. Shaped like surfboards, the Makaha Standard was 29 inches in length and the Malibu was a pretty tight 18 inches. The fact that the boards were shaped like surfboards further strengthened the tie-in with surfing. Wholesale cost was $7.77 and retail was $12.95.

Larry Stevenson experimented with a variety of materials to make skateboarding better, including plywood and foam, and even nylon wheels. In the fall of 1963, Makaha sponsored the first skateboard contest, held at the Pier Avenue Junior High School in Hermosa, California. The contest focused mainly on tricks (i.e., nose and tail wheelies, handstands, and high jumps). Brad "Squeak" Blank took first place.

There were other areas in which Larry Stevenson was an innovator. For example, Makaha was the first company to sponsor a skateboard team. Riders like Squeak Blank, Danny Bearer, Woody Woodward, Terry Spencer, Steve Tanner, and John Freis would travel to various places and give exhibitions.

All of Larry's hard work paid off: as the boom progressed, Makaha saw their orders grow to over 10,000 boards per day. From mid 1963 until the end of 1965, Makaha sold $4,000,000 worth of boards.

But despite skateboarding's incredible rise in popularity, there was an immense amount of trouble brewing. The boards, while fun to ride, could not really grip the road well. The clay wheels were too hard. The trucks were also fairly poor in design. Skateboarders were dodging cars and pedestrians. There were numerous accidents and sometimes skaters wound up with broken bones. There were even reports of skaters being killed. The California Medical Association called skateboards "a new medical menace." Worse still, police chiefs were telling stores not to carry skateboards in the interest of public safety.

As a result of these problems, cities and towns began banning skateboards. By August of 1965, 20 cities had banned skateboarding from sidewalks and streets. The hysteria continued into the fall of 1965. In some cities, skateboards were simply confiscated.

All of these problems led to the horrendous skatebust in the late fall of 1965. According to Larry, who was quoted in the *Skateboarder's Bible*:

I can just about recall the week, if not the day. It was mid November 1965, when things just died. One week I was getting so many orders, people were leaving them on my doorstep so I'd see them when I left for work in the morning. The next, I was getting 75,000 in cancellations in a single day!

As a result of the skatebust, Makaha was left with considerable unsold inventory and enormous financial losses. Larry went back to lifeguarding, an occupation he had had prior to publishing the *Surf Guide*.

Nineteen sixty-six is the official year that skateboarding died on a national level. However, there were a number of people in California (specifically the San Fernando Valley) who kept up with the sport. These included skaters like Torger Johnson, Ty Page, and Bruce Logan.

Then, in the late 1960's, Larry came up with something that again would have an enormous impact on the world of skateboarding: he invented the kicktail. "At first it was not accepted," remarks Larry. In time and with a bit of radio advertising, skaters became interested. In 1969 he was awarded the patent for the kicktail.

Other manufacturers soon copied the kicktail design and Larry asked them for a royalty. But the manufacturers didn't want to honor the kicktail patent and pay a royalty to Larry. The exception was Gordon & Smith

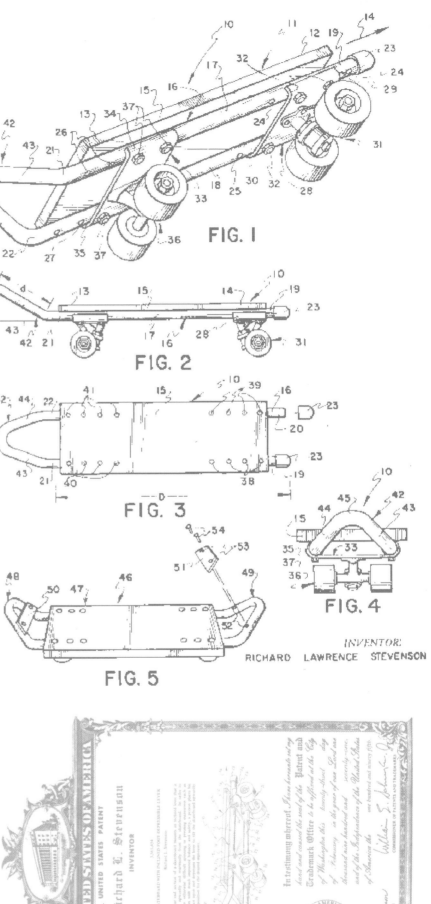

Skateboards, who did pay a royalty for the use of the kicktail. Larry began a three-year battle with the justice system to have other manufacturers honor his patent. In a landmark case, the judge didn't agree with Larry, stating that "the kicktail was an obvious idea." What this meant was that no manufacturers had to pay a royalty to Larry for his invention.

While dealing with the legal problems, Larry continued to promote the sport of skateboarding. In 1969 a new Makaha team was formed to try to revive the sport. Freestyle wizards Bruce and Brad Logan along with Ty Page and Rusty Johnson achieved some success with their exhibitions and fifty thousand Makaha skateboards were sold.

When skateboarding was fully revived in 1973, Makaha rode the second wave. Larry more than recouped his losses from the first skatebust. Over time he slowly moved back behind the scenes of the industry. In January of 1988, he joined up with Curtis Wong to publish *Power Edge* magazine.

Nowadays his son Kurt is heading up Makaha and the company offers a full lineup of surf-inspired skateboards, just like it did more than 30 years ago. Although he's no longer active in the skate industry, the skateboarding legacy Larry Stevenson has left is truly extraordinary.

FIG. 1

FIG. 2

FIG. 3

FIG. 4

FIG. 5

INVENTOR:
RICHARD LAWRENCE STEVENSON

The First
Retail Skateboard Shop —
VAL SURF

If you've ever wondered what was the first "real" store to sell skateboards, then you have to go back to 1962. On October 6 of that year, Val Surf opened its doors in North Hollywood, California. Headed up by Bill Richards and his two sons Mark, age 15, and Kurt, age 18, Val Surf was the first shop to offer skateboards as more than just "toys." Although Val Surf was primarily a surf shop, they began to realize that the skateboard might have some merit. They went to the Chicago Roller Skate Company with the idea of buying just the truck assemblies. At first Chicago was reluctant, but eventually they decided to sell the trucks to Val Surf.

High school students would shape the boards and mount the trucks. In the beginning, Val Surf sold only small numbers of complete boards — fewer than 10 a week. However, everything they made, they sold. It didn't take long for their business to take off. Besides walk-in customers, Val Surf offered skateboards by mail.

Val Surf also joined up with surfboard maker Hobie Alter. Hobie had started making surfboards in 1950 in his garage and went into business in 1954. His name was synonymous with surf culture. Originally, Hobie focused on his surfboards, but when he saw how popular skateboarding was becoming he went back to Val Surf in 1964 and together they designed a line of skateboards. Very quickly, these boards became popular. However, things really took off when Hobie hooked up with the Vita-Pakt Juice Company.

Mark Richards (left) age 15 and Kurt Richards behind the counter at Val Surf in 1962. Notice Val Surf Skateboards on the right hand side.

LIFE

Pat McGee

Hailing from San Diego, Pat was known as a trick rider of the highest order. Pat was featured on *Life* magazine's cover doing a handstand in May 1965.

The craze and
the menace of

SKATEBOARDS

San Diego's Pat McGee,
national girls' champion,
does a handstand on wheels

MAY 14 · 1965 · 35¢

Hobie Alter and the Vita-Pakt Juice Co.

It's hard to imagine a juice company becoming an enormous force in the world of 1960's skateboarding, but the Vita-Pakt Juice Company was no ordinary business. Two events led to Vita-Pakt's involvement with skateboarding. Ed Morgan worked in the sales department at the Vita-Pakt located in Covina, California. Although their primary business was juice, Morgan realized that the company could expand into other profitable areas. He had seen people skateboarding at the beach and came up with an idea for Vita-Pakt.

Vita-Pakt had recently purchased a roller skate manufacturer. Morgan took a set of trucks from the roller skate plant along with a piece of a juice crate to illustrate the skateboard concept to the company brass. The other executives at Vita-Pakt liked his idea and decided to get into the skateboard business.

Around the same time that Ed Morgan was thinking about moving into the skateboard business, the owner of Vita-Pakt was looking into things for himself. Vita-Pakt was owned by none other than Baron Hilton, of Hilton Hotel fame. His two sons, Davey and Steve, were avid skateboarders and were anxious for their father to get into the business of skateboarding.

In late 1964, Vita-Pakt and Hobie Alter joined together and formed a manufacturing/marketing agreement. The Hobie name carried a huge amount of weight within the surf industry and it was natural for a company to market a line of Hobie skateboards. A large publicity effort was put forth to spread the word on the Hobie skateboards. A Hobie Super Surfer team was put together with top notch riders, including Dave Hilton. Interestingly enough, many of these

skaters were taken from the Makaha team. This is a practice that still continues to this day!

Now that there was a team in place, ideas were formulated about how to best promote the Hobie brand. Hobie Alter saw an opportunity. "Bruce Brown was working on the [surfing] film *The Endless Summer* and he would run sections of the film for people. I realized that the film was really hot and I talked Bruce into doing a trip."

Hobie rented a bus (it slept nine people) and filled it with surfboards and skateboards. Starting out in California, they drove to New York. The trip featured surf and skateboard demos along with showings of *The Endless Summer* in cities down the east coast. There were eight screenings of the film and each had an audience of a thousand people. Hobie remembers the impression the film left on viewers: "When people saw the film they'd tell us they were going to return the next day with their friends. We'd be gone by then and off to another town. Believe it or not, people actually followed us as we went from each city."

Crowds for the skateboard demos ranged from two to three thousand people. The surf demos were even more of an event. "We had 10,000 people show up at Gilgo Beach!" recalls Hobie. The entire trip cost about $5,000 but it paid off for Hobie and Vita-Pakt. There was an enormous amount of press about the team. In 1965, The *Quarterly SkateBoarder* interviewed surfer/skater Mike Hynson about the trip:

> We drove across the country in a big bus that Hobie chartered. We all had skateboards, so stopping at a gas station was quite an event. We would pull into a gas station in some small inland town and yell, 'Fill 'er up.' Then the entire crew would burst out of the doors with their skateboards and go rolling off around town exploring . . . The local population just couldn't believe the rolling invasion. In some places we looked like the pied pipers with all the local kids in town following us along.

Baron Hilton also owned the San Diego Charger football team and during a Thanksgiving game, the Hobie Super Surfer team performed a skateboard demo at half time. Through Hobie and Vita-Pakt's work,

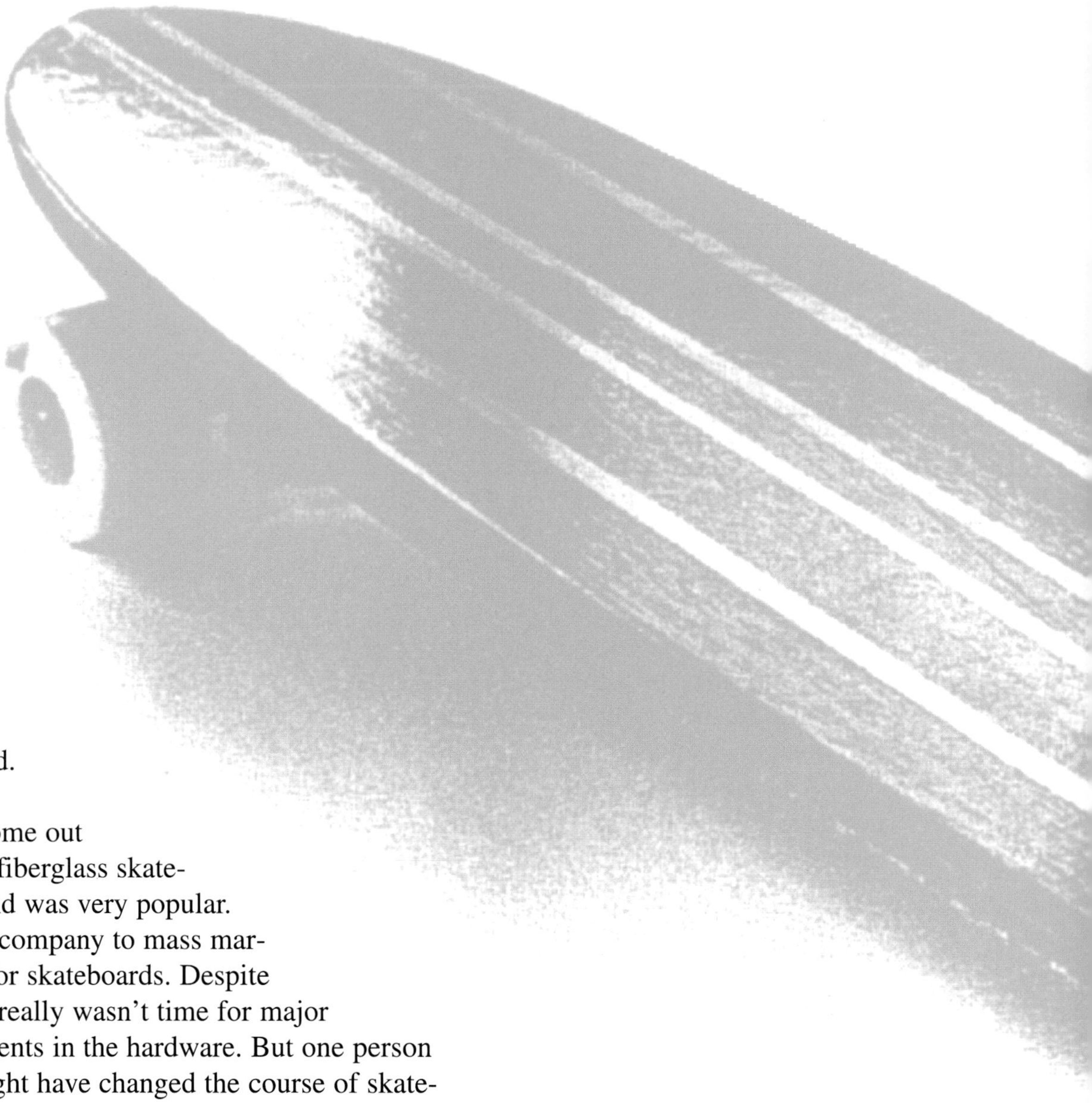

the skate-
board divi-
sion began to
really take off.
By 1965 Vita-Pakt
had orders for
20,000 skateboards a
day and still couldn't
keep up with the demand.

Hobie was the first to come out
with a pressure-molded fiberglass skateboard. It had a rocker and was very popular.
They were also the first company to mass market a truck exclusively for skateboards. Despite
these innovations, there really wasn't time for major
technological improvements in the hardware. But one person
did come along who might have changed the course of skateboarding history.

Wheels at the time were clay or metal and they had a no grip. In 1965, Hobie
Alter was approached by a company called American Latex. The son of the company's president was a surfer and skater. He had cast a set of urethane wheels and
machined their surface. Hobie remembers dropping in the bearings and putting them on a
board. "I took them out to let some of our pro riders try them. Their response was immediate
— they thought the wheels were fantastic."

Hobie then went to the executives at Vita-Pakt with the idea for the urethane wheels. But they were not
willing to market the concept because they felt the price for the skateboards would be too high. At the
time, Hobie Super Surfers retailed for under 20 dollars, and by adding urethane wheels the price would
have more than doubled. "They thought the more expensive urethane-wheeled boards would denigrate
their cheaper boards," recalls Hobie. It would take eight more years for urethane wheels to come to mar-

ket. Who knows how different the skateboarding world would have looked if Hobie had been able to convince the Vita-Pakt executives.

As it turned out, things kept rolling along and demand was strong for what was ultimately a flawed product. After all, there was only so much you could accomplish with clay wheels. At the 1965 Toy Show in New York, buyers for stores went out and placed a tremendous amount of orders with all the large skateboard companies. They knew that no one could keep up with demand. Hobie has not forgotten the buyers' strategy: "The buyers ordered huge amounts knowing that they could cancel their orders if the product wasn't received by a specific date." Vita-Pakt geared up and went full steam ahead with production. Other manufacturers did the same. As Hobie says, "The pipeline was filled up with product."

Unfortunately, it was at this time that police chiefs started calling for the prohibition of skateboards. Most of the public felt skaters were a nuisance and cities began banning skateboards. As a result, demand for skateboards died fast. Enormous inventories coupled with waning interest led to the big skatebust of November 1965. Vita-Pakt were caught with too much product and suffered immense losses. Hobie recalls they even tried to sell skateboards for one dollar each. It was to take almost eight years before things would start rolling again for skateboard riders and manufacturers.

Contests and Championships

by Paul Fisher

Most skaters don't need a formal competition to push one another — they're happy just skating with their friends and trying to see who is the first to attempt or actually land a certain trick. In most cases, the accent is on fun rather than bloodthirsty competition. That's not to say, however, that skaters don't love to compete and win. Since the first formal skateboard contest in 1963, skateboarders have entered tens of thousands of competitions. Some of the contests have gone off without a hitch, while others have had their share of judging problems, disorganization and general chaos.

Over the years attempts have been made to formalize competition within skateboarding. Some people see this as quite noble, others just want to keep things as loose as possible. Whatever the case, skaters will continue to compete and enjoy the contest atmosphere. Paul Fisher recounts his participation in one of the earliest skateboarding competitions:

In 1966, at the age of 16, I entered the National Championships, a combination of downhill, freestyle and flatland slalom. The overall best score determined the winner, and the freestyle was judged by Hobie Alter, based on a one-minute routine without music.

The event was held at a new skatepark in Orange County that was one of the first parks of its kind to be built. The most striking feature was a large, blue, concrete hill that had waves from top to bottom and side to side that created the image of low undulating moguls. The vision of this hill was more than sufficient to strike awe and excitement in those days of few exotic sites, no pools or pipes.

I had won the regional contest held at the same park going into the Nationals, so I had some confidence I had a chance of placing. Most likely there would be few, if any, contestants from anywhere but southern California. I doubt that much effort was made to advertise the event on a truly national scale, so calling it the "National Championships" was perhaps a little inflated. Adding to the excitement, the "thrill of victory, agony of defeat" ABC sports crew was there shooting the event for posterity.

The first event was the downhill. I was using a Dewey Weber model, the stuff of dreams in those days. It was a flexy thin black deck maybe one quarter of an inch thick. We were still on clay wheels in those days (roller skate technology!) Scores were based on the average of two runs. I had the fastest single run but placed second in the event because of a slower second run. I had a mediocre performance in the freestyle and placed fourth. The flatland slalom was a ride through the orange cones on blue concrete; I placed 7th or 8th.

The thing I remember most about the contest was the way I felt at the awards ceremony. Most of our parents were there and we had gotten dressed up for a banquet and the awarding of the $1,000 first prize, quite a chunk for a kid back then. The winner was also to be given a place on the Hobie Skateboard Team. Now, I may have been only 16, with the gullibility of youth, but by my calculation, and I must say that I later majored in math for my first two years in college, I should have won the overall title since the guy who won did not get higher scores overall. I was awarded second place and given a tiny trophy that held about as much esteem for me as a Cracker Jack prize.

I felt betrayed but I couldn't muster the courage to complain to anybody but my parents. Somehow standing up in front of the throng and accusing the officials of fixing the contest or showing favoritism seemed too intimidating.

Guy/girl skaters take up the hobby for different reasons, only they know why. In my own case, I lived in the foothills above Pearl Harbor on an island & most of the Hawaiian and Filipino kids skateboarded for a hobby. Back then, in the late 60's, you couldn't go to a skateshop and buy a custom board, you had to build one yourself & have it aerodynamically designed to travel fast down steep hills.

Fortunately, my brother built me a skateboard and I skated with him and his friends. In doing so, other girls copied me to have their brothers and friends build a board for them to skate. We all skated together. There was no great bickering, criticizing of skating skills, name calling, but we DID try to outdo each other in being the best skater. That was the late 60's, the good old days.

■A.W.

The Quarterly SKATEBOARDER

The grandfather of all skateboard magazines was started by Surfer Publications in 1965 and was originally called *The Quarterly Skateboarder*. The cover of the first issue featured Dave Hilton of the Hobie Super Surfer Team. This first editorial gives real insight into the foundations of skateboarding as a sport and where publisher/editor John Severson felt it should and should not go:

Sidewalk Surfing?

Whenever a new sport comes into existence or an existing sport suddenly gains popularity, its thrills are often compared to other sports. People compare the thrills of surfing to skydiving, bull fighting, skiing, and other exciting individual-participation sports. These same comparisons will be made and are being made in the sport of skateboarding. It's similar in many ways to surfing and to skiing, not only in maneuvers and techniques, but in many cases, in terms as well. Many of the same surfing positions are used in skateboarding, as evidenced in our "SURF/SKI/SKATE" article in this issue. Several months ago LIFE Magazine ran an article entitled "Sidewalk Surfing." Sure, that's what it is, but we predict a lot more for skateboarding. We predict a real future for the sport — a future that could go as far as the Olympics. It's a much more "measurable" sport

than surfing and therefore lends itself more to competition. In the slalom, there's no question about who the winner is — the fastest time through the gates. Flatland stunts and performance will be a matter of judgement, but at least the asphalt isn't moving — everyone gets an equal opportunity. Competition should be big in skateboarding, but it's going to take organization and support from the participants.

Today's skateboarders are founders in this sport — they're pioneers — they are first. There is no history in skateboarding — it's being made now — by you. The sport is being molded and we believe that doing the right thing now will lead to a bright future for the sport. Already there are storm clouds on the horizon with opponents of the sport talking about ban and restriction. Skateboarding is not a sport of speed; it's a sport of skill. It's not a sport of destruction — of others or yourself. It's a sport of control. It's up to you to see that skateboarding does not become a sport of rebels and radicals. It's a sport for young sportsmen. We look forward to a great future in skateboarding and we ask you, the pioneers, to make it great.

Unfortunately, this particular incarnation of the publication only ran for four issues and was promptly folded after the first skateboarding boom ended.

Who could have predicted that the sports of archery and skateboarding would one day connect to create one of the most popular skateboards ever produced: the Fibreflex.

The Fibreflex was manufactured by Gordon & Smith. The roots of Gordon & Smith go back to the late 1950's. Surfer Larry Gordon was studying chemistry in college when he joined up with Floyd Smith. The two began making surfboards in the corner of the Gordon Plastics factory run by Larry's father and two uncles. Eventually Larry and Floyd moved out of Gordon Plastics and into Floyd's garage. In 1962, Larry left school and went into manufacturing surfboards full time. The company was known as Gordon & Smith Surfboards.

In the summer of 1964, Larry's cousin Mike returned home from college where he had been studying business and chemistry. At the time, skateboarding was gaining in popularity and Larry came up with a brilliant idea. He took a material called Bo-Tuff and combined it with a wood core to create a skateboard deck. Bo-Tuff was a fiberglass-reinforced epoxy that was used to make bows for the archery industry. Bo-Tuff had some amazing physical properties. For example, a bow that incorporated Bo-Tuff set a world's record for shooting an arrow — it went over one mile!

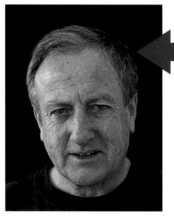

Larry Gordon

By utilizing Bo-Tuff along with a maple wood core, Gordon & Smith developed a skateboard that gave an extremely responsive ride. The camber or arc of the board also added to its responsiveness. If you pushed down on a Fibreflex, it would spring back into place immediately. This was the first laminated skateboard.

In an interview for *SkateBoarder* magazine in 1978, Larry Gordon described the skateboard atmosphere in the mid 1960's. "Slalom racing was the most exciting aspect of the sport at that time, and we felt we had a better idea for a skateboard design."

Larry teamed up with friend Jim Hovde and formed a company to make Fibreflexes. They made a few at a time and eventually produced a thousand boards using a hand-screw press. Over time, a Fibreflex slalom team was put together. Surfers like Skip Frye, Willie Phillips, John Haywoods,

Gordon & Smith

Tommy Ryan, Denis Shufeldt, and Mike Hynson dominated the First Annual Skateboard Contest held in Anaheim in May of 1965. But most skateboarders in the mid 1960's were content to ride on wooden boards that gave little to no flex. The highly advanced technology of the Fibreflex was lost on most skaters, who were still trying to deal with the challenges of clay wheels.

When the skateboard craze died in late 1965, so did production of the Fibreflex. It would take close to 10 years before another one was manufactured. Larry and Mike decided to resume production in 1974 in a garage with the same equipment that had been used in the sixties. On average, Mike was producing about 25 boards a day. Eventually, Mike decided to join his uncle back at Gordon Plastics. He also moved his Fibreflex equipment from the garage to the factory where there were more presses.

The introduction of the urethane wheel in the early seventies brought with it a number of skateboarders who were enthralled by slalom skating. The speed and the smooth, flowing motion that could be achieved on a Fibreflex made it an extraordinary skateboarding experience. The skateboard magazines featured numerous ads and articles on slalom pros Paul Engh, Henry Hester, and Chris Yandall (who of course, were winning contests on Fibreflexes).

By the mid 1970's the factory was churning out 500 Fibreflex boards day, which was still not enough to meet the demand. Dave McIntyre, head of the sales division at that time, vividly recalls having six months' worth of back orders!

On the basis of the success they had with the slalom skateboard, Gordon & Smith soon introduced other models of Fibreflexes. There was a freestyle model that came with a rocker (the reverse of a camber), and a 25–27-inch kicktail model that proved to be very popular. In 1977 they released a stiffer model called the Bowlrider which offered the flex of fiberglass and the stability of a wood board.

Soon after the introduction of other Fibreflex models, Gordon & Smith came out with a solid wood board (which, according to their ad copy, was made from ash or oak, depending upon what was available!). There were two models — a flat wooden board and the Stacy Peralta Warptail model. In the course of 18 months, 110,000 Warptails were sold. The Warptail II model, which incorporated layers of maple veneer, was significantly

lighter. Gordon & Smith also marketed the "Rockit" deck, similar in construction to the Warptail II. In 1978, after their success with both fiberglass and wood models, the company introduced the Teamrider, the widest and largest Fibreflex they had ever made. It was one of the most versatile boards, and countless photos displayed it being used in both vertical and freestyle riding.

Over time however, skateboard manufacturers like Gordon & Smith moved away from fiberglass. Slalom riding took a backseat as more skaters became interested in halfpipes, bowls, wooden ramps and, of course, concrete skateparks. By 1979, the Fibreflex line was replaced by strictly plywood-type boards (although the Teamrider model was still available). The G & S Proline, Dennis Martinez "Flying Ace," and Doug Saladino "Pine Design" were all vertical boards.

Finding an original Fibreflex board nowadays is difficult. The ABC Company licensed the Gordon & Smith Skateboards trademark and is now reissuing Fibreflexes, allowing riders to once more experience the ultimate cruising and carving experience. However, in 1998 Larry Gordon decided to begin production of a longboard Fibreflex that is an incredibly responsive ride, making "Fibreflex" one of the most enduring names in skateboarding.

Four Decades of Skating... And Still Rolling

By Cliff Coleman

Skateboarding is usually thought of as a youthful activity, but there are "first-generation" skaters out there who have kept up with the sport — maybe it's the key to keeping a youthful outlook. Cliff Coleman is a perfect example of this. Here he looks back on his 40 years of the skateboarding life.

I was given my first skateboard by a guy on the UC Berkeley crew team in 1960 or '61. It was a two by four with a steel skate nailed to the bottom. The first time I stepped on it I immediately fell on my tailbone. Being 10 or 11, I tried again. I had a great time riding that old antique. We also used the old steel skates to make coasters and other vehicles to ride the great hills in Berkeley, California.

In 1963 I purchased a Makaha skateboard with Chicago trucks and wheels. They were as great a change over the steel-wheeled skateboards as the change from clay wheels to urethane wheels. I rode this board and homemade boards at the UC Berkeley campus with the Top Sider skateboard team. I wasn't on the team, I was just a friend of theirs.

In 1964 my friends and I received quite a bit of press in the local newspapers. We had photos taken of us doing tricks like the coffin, high jump, handstands, and 360's. The promoters of the San Francisco Sport and Boat Show read about us and hired the Top Sider team to do demonstrations at the show. I went to watch their performances and was allowed to join them. They were paid $60 each. I skated for free and was happy to be able to. Also demonstrating at this show was the Hobie Skateboard Team. Some of their members were Torger Johnson, John Freis, Danny Bearer, Steve and Dave Hilton, George Trafton and Danny Schaefer.

George Trafton was said to be able to do a headstand. None of us had ever seen this move and viewed it as incredible. George wasn't comfortable trying a headstand at the demonstration because of the riding surface. Nevertheless, just hearing and meeting someone who was said to be able to do it was enough encouragement for me to try, and I became the first in Northern California to do a headstand on a skateboard.

During this show the management of the Hobie team figured we were of equal talent and created a Northern California Hobie Team to travel the northern part of California to demonstrate their products. Throughout 1965 we went every Saturday to do demonstrations. As Hobie team members we received free skateboards, clothes, trips, and custom Hobie surfboards. At many of these demonstrations the local skaters would take us to their hot spots to skate.

We were sent to the first International Skateboard Championships in Anaheim, May 22-23, 1965. Torger Johnson showed me his secret trick, the "pirouette". He used this trick to win the freestyle contest. John Freis won the overall and a $500 scholarship. Torger and John invented many of the fundamental tricks that are now a part of skateboard history. Some of these were kickturns, 360's, etc.

Our greatest rivals in the 60's were the Pipelines Skateboard Team. Overall they were not quite as good as us; however, they had one skater, Rudy Esquer, who was probably the greatest skater of the sixties and certainly the best in Northern California. Rudy and I are still friends and he now resides in Maui, Hawaii.

Skateboarding means a great deal to me! I've been riding for 37+ years now and can't imagine quitting ever. I've tried many different styles of riding. I've done wheelies of all types, handstands, headstands, and I even invented a backflip dismount and used it at the end of my routine in Aptos back in approximately 1976. This is one trick that I believe has never been duplicated. One individual did a backflip off a stationary board but never did one from a rolling skateboard. I rode in the parks in pools and in full and halfpipes. I'll be honest with you — I could reach the coping, grind, do cessslides and fakies, but that was before plastic sliding pads on knee pads, so I didn't try anything beyond those fundamental skills.

Since then I've been involved in downhill activities — racing, both slalom and downhill. There are many other styles of downhill. With the slides I've created with my skating friends in Berkeley I've been able to continue inventing new ways to have fun. With a safe approach I can skate for a lifetime and still skate radically.

Skateboarding has allowed me to travel and meet wonderful people. I have also worked with television media, Columbia Pictures as a stunt man, and governmental bodies regarding skateboard safety. I've developed skills as a videographer and still photographer, and I've approached and consulted with political, business and celebrity communities in the production of events. I've consulted with legal firms and the City of Berkeley at their request on the skateboard issue.

On three occasions I've been driven to the top of the Berkeley hills in a black and white patrol car. Not to be arrested but given a ride so that I could skate down some of the most demanding hills in our area. The officer then followed me to the bottom. I've received notoriety for an activity that I love and that in itself is very satisfying.

Each year on my birthday, November 22, I get together with my skate friends and skate the hills of Berkeley. Everyone capable of the sliding techniques necessary to negotiate steep hills is welcome to come celebrate with me!

deep end guts

— The First Pool Rides

Skateboarders view the world differently from non-skateboarders. An expanse of concrete is just that to someone who has never skated, but to a skateboarder it presents endless possibilities. Skateboarders are always looking for new skating challenges. This seems to have been the case from the sport's earliest days of existence.

The first pool riders were the true pioneers of skateboarding. Imagine being the first person to charge into the deep end of an empty concrete swimming pool, in bare feet, with a clay-wheeled board — now that takes guts! It's not clear exactly who first attempted pool riding, but skate sessions can be traced back to 1963 in Gary Swanson's pool in California.

The first media documentation of this activity was the appearance of Roy Diederichsen's empty swimming pool in the first issue of *The Quarterly Skateboarder* in 1965. The pool was located in Menlo Park. According to the article, the riders discovered the possibility of riding in the pool when one of the boys actually fell in. The skater realized it might be a good idea to try to skate into the deep end on a board. Early participants included Roy Diederichsen, Reed Hutchinson, Chuck Cantwell, Mike Glassey and John Abrams.

Three photos accompanied the article. Although nowadays it seems like second nature to get air on vertical terrain, riders were shown simply carving the pool. However, one particular photo that many present-day riders could relate to was included: it was a shot of "Roy in agonizing pain after a horrible deep end wipe-out."

A pool located just outside Santa Monica in Foxtail Park was another early site used by numerous riders, including Steve and Dave Hilton. Throughout the 60's, pool riding was being done by only a handful of skaters, mostly in the Santa Monica area. This probably had to do with the availability of pools in that part of the world.

When urethane wheels finally hit, it allowed skaters to get the grip they needed to ride past the coping and push out into the air. The sight of this no doubt enticed many more skaters to seek out empty swimming pools in their neighborhoods, so that vertical skating soon became a mainstay of the sport.

Jim Fitzpatrick
Skateboard Ambassador Part I

A number of individuals have had a lasting impact on the sport of skateboarding, and not only in the invention of new tricks. Jim Fitzpatrick is one of them. He has been active in many aspects of skateboarding over the years. In the sixties he made the first of his many contributions to the

sport by being instrumental in bringing skateboarding to Europe.

Jim's skateboard career began in 1957 at the house of one his father's fellow workers — Buster Wilson. It was near San Diego in a place called Point Loma where Jim hooked up with Buster's five children. Buster claimed to have made skate scooters along with skateboards in the mid to late 1930's. In the summer of 1957, the five brothers along with Jim were sitting around bored because they couldn't get a ride to the beach. Jim remembers it well: "Buster said, 'Do this,' and we took roller skates and nailed them onto boards."

After spending Saturday night skateboarding like crazy, Jim went back to La Jolla and over the next several weeks made close to 20 boards for friends. "It was pretty much a summer thing and it repeated itself in 1958 and 1959. In 1960 I moved to Topanga and continued skating." It was to be a full two years later when Larry Stevenson would start promoting skateboarding through Makaha and create the first skateboarding boom.

In 1964, Bill Cleary along with *Surf Guide* magazine put together the European Surfing Holiday. Jim was on the Dave Sweet Surfboard team at the time. "The gig was to charter a jet and take 165 surfers to Europe. Bill Cleary had been to Biarritz in the south of France the year before and realized there was potential for a surfing community there. But they never sold enough tickets, so 85 of us flew on a propeller plane to Europe. I took 12 clay-wheeled skateboards with me."

The trip had enormous impact on the Europeans. "I would just start skating and people would not have a clue — it was inconceivable that I could roll along the ground. I would have these conversations with people and give them a skateboard. It was a goodwill tour and by the end of the trip I had given away all 12 boards."

By the time Jim returned to California, the impact of the trip was reverberating throughout Europe. Biarritz was never to be the same!

Jim would continue his association with skateboarding off and on over the next 30 years. In the late 1980s he became involved with the Bones Brigade and led their tour of Europe in 1989. "It was this amazing continuity to an activity that had literally come full circle," remarks Jim. Twenty-five years had passed since the time Jim had wowed the French with his skate and surf abilities.

The trip was jam packed with memories and filled with emotion.

Today, what with satellite TV and the Internet, it's no wonder that skateboarding has become a worldwide phenomenon. But the roots of that phenomenon go back to the days when television was new (and still a luxury item outside North America), and computers took up a whole room and cost millions of dollars, when people could still be amazed and delighted by the sight of someone, like Jim Fitzpatrick, coasting down a street on a board with wheels.

I'm 35 years old, originally from Scotland, where I started skating in 1975, on something that's probably best described as a small ironing board with metal roller skate wheels nailed to the bottom. Cornering was well nigh impossible but, boy, you should have seen the sparks fly when you tried. I graduated through various, marginally better, bastardized/homemade sticks over the next four or five years, until I ended up with my pride and joy, a 10-inch-wide Alva with Tracker Full Tracks and 65mm Lime Green Kryptonics (which I'd swapped for a set of white yoyos). Oh yeah — and I think it sported a Power Pivot screwed to the kicktail too — remember them?

Skating in Scotland wasn't quite as glamorous as skating in California looked on the pages of the overpriced, imported *SkateBoarder* magazines we occasionally saw, but even the hellish vagaries of the Scottish climate couldn't stop us having incredible fun. We had a dangerously narrow wooden halfpipe, a "ramp" that was more like two tables nailed together and, 45 miles away in Glasgow, there was the Holy Grail — a real cement skatepark, complete with rad locals ripping vert and making us Edinburgh skaters feel sadly inadequate. Some of those guys went on to start Clan Skates, a shop producing its own line of boards and clothing which, as far as I know, is still going strong in Glasgow.

I eventually became distracted by beer and ciggies and other sins of the flesh, and had packed in skating by the early 80's, convinced I was too mature for such childish pleasures. However I always kept an eye on what was going on, guiltily buying the occasional issue of *Thrasher*, and visiting the local skate shop to "check out the T-shirts and shoes" while slyly eyeing up all the decks on the wall, and the wheels and trucks twinkling seductively away in their glass cabinets, secretly wishing I was still 16.

All this was made worse by the fact that my subconscious had never given up skating, and I regularly had skateboard dreams where I'd be transformed into Tony McAlva hurtling through a super-smooth, curvaceous concrete landscape, the board under my feet obeying my every command, on a ride so satisfying it was like, well, a dream. And my skateboarding subconscious altered the way I looked at the world around me. I found myself staring at concrete banks, snaking streets and paved underpasses imagining myself ripping them up on my non-existent board. (I had given the Alva to my younger cousin when I stopped skating, and never saw it again. I'm sure he sold it to buy crack or something.)

Anyway, to cut a long story short, I ended up marrying a native of California, who suffered through three vicious Scottish winters before insisting we move to San Francisco, where we now live. As soon as I got here my skateboarding subconscious had alarm bells ringing. Everywhere I looked I saw skaters, including some who looked as ancient as me, and the whole city looked as if it had been specifically designed as some giant skatepark. I knew I was in trouble. I found myself wandering into skate shops, buying magazines, I knew it was only a matter of time — and it was. First of all I bought an Anti-Hero board, which was cool, but I still felt like a bit of an old fool doing tiny ollies up curbs. This has been put to rights, however, as I recently saw the longboarding light, and I'm now the proud owner of a Sector 9 longboard, which I regularly carve around the city on, feeling not the least bit old or foolish. Thanks to that longboard . . . I love skating now just as much as I did 20 years ago. Now if I could just get those damn dreams to stop . . .

—David F.

Dreaming of a Californi

by Richard Jones

In the mid '60's strange vehicles began to appear in Newquay's (the capital of England's surf culture) largest surf shop. OK, we had vaguely heard about or seen skateboards through US surf mags and books but never seen one in the flesh. Clay composite wheels on decks that showed the joys of surfing — I had to have one. Strange, really — we thought the only possible difference between California and Newquay (apart from the lack of Malibu beach) was the amount of sunshine we got!

Hard-earned pounds passed over the shop bench [counter], and soon after we were to find another (and, for the time being, very important) difference. This was the quality of road and pavement [sidewalk] surfaces. It was quickly and expensively obvious that English surfaces, cracked and rough, ate clay composite wheels! The skateboards, which had only ever appeared in surf shops, disappeared. But the thought lingered on. England is not blessed with clear (what we called "California Skies") sunny days, nor with consistent swells, so the thought of surfing on the land wouldn't go away. Metal-wheeled rollerskates were butchered, alternatives sought.

Very quickly after urethane wheels hit California they hit the surf towns of England. This opened the flood gates; skating took off. Initially confined to surf towns, the English tradition of dragging the family to the coast for two weeks a year soon spread the word elsewhere. Kanoa and Hobie boards with X-cal trucks and Sims or Oj's were the things to be seen with. Soon G&S hit the scene, and off we went!

Newquay was still the epicenter for the present, and the early 70's saw a couple of English firsts for Newquay. Blessed with being built on the flat seafront with one side running into a long steep hill, the main road through Newquay was paradise. Too narrow to hold much traffic it saw much skate action. So history for English skating was made — the local council [municipal government] banned skating on that hill. Newquay also saw the first real big skate contest — freestyle and slalom of course!

The second milestone was the building of the first real concrete skatepark. Obviously modeled on the images of barefeet-clad Californians riding mellow waves (OK, so we didn't know they were just school banks), it consisted of a steep shaped run (some of it banked like a snake run) down into a mellow bowl. Set behind the major surf beach called Watergate, it was well sessioned. The official opening day saw a demo skate team (made up mainly of holidaying Australian surfers, one of whom now makes all-terrain Grass Sole boards) going wild. Much to the delight of the local press there were limbs broken and general rowdiness as befitting a crowd of surf-starved surfers!

The other growing centre of skating was London. Transported back by returning holiday kids, skating gave them a way to imagine they were still in Newquay trying to stand up on their rented surfboards. Corporate bodies began to take note, companies were growing up. Up until about 1972/3, the only real stuff available was imported from the States. Now a few companies began to compete for the growing demand. A British Skateboard Association sprang up from the British Surfing Association, and Skuda skateboards hit the scene. Everyone I knew had a Skuda. Real trucks and loose-bearing wheels — the roads were ours. The original decks were made of a steel plate covered in a sort of colored fiberglass, textured on top to help you stay on in the rain (big joke) — they were the works. The latest models were prized items: plastic decks, then one kicktail, then two kicktails (we have come full cycle, eh what?) — Skuda were it. Don't really know what happened to them; American stuff became more common and of course more trendy. Suddenly you couldn't buy Skuda boards, so it was back to the Chicago trucks and wheels.

The news of the skatepark at Newquay spread and people began to follow suit. An early attempt was made by a businessman in Matlock (Derbyshire) to stop people skating his impeccable long driveway. Made of tarmac, it did us proud, and coupled with a homemade ramp that went vert in about three feet and was three feet wide, people traveled from miles around.

England had its share of skate mags from the start. *Skateboard,* the original, was followed in the early 80's by *RAD*

Sky in the Golden Age
— Growing Up Skating in England

("read and destroy"), which grew from a BMX magazine. *Skateboard* had an influence on a lot of skaters; it was good to see homegrown talent, although articles on American fullpipes and ditches had us searching for weeks. A few pipes were found, especially near new dam construction sites . . . the people that were there know where I mean.

The London scene continued to grow. The original skate place, a very wide, very smooth path through a famous park, was fixed with a large amount of gravel. But all was not lost, as skaters who were moving on from catamarans and slalom were blessed with a "natural" skatepark courtesy of the architect of the National Theatre. The South Bank set of banks were a Mecca for skaters country wide. The banks have had a checkered history. Being under cover they were perfect for skaters; unfortunately the late 70's saw an increase in homeless people who also thought the undercover dry area perfect for setting up cardboard homes — often the mix has not been pleasant. Always under the threat of demolition, the banks have withstood attempts to make them unskateable from authority and dossers. Railings were eventually put atop the banks to stop grinds, then ollies became popular — the banks can still be seen cropping up in skate mags today!

Skateparks appeared everywhere, both indoor and out. One park that would have been world famous was the Sheffield Skatepalace. Indoor, huge and wooden, it had a massive banked freestyle area with banked corners and walls merging into the real walls, a wooden pool with coping and a halfpipe run in, plus various mellow bowls and banks. Set to make a fortune, it was spoilt by careless workmen who left their lights on under the pool one night and it burnt down. To cap it off, the guy's insurance hadn't come through.

London saw Skatecity go up and be bulldozed (the day after I got to skate it), apparently because it wasn't safe. The Old Kent Road Mad Dog Bowl replaced it as the venue to be seen. Tony Alva made a few visits and helped its fame. "Meanwhile 1" was a project by skaters to build their own park; it was kind of like an uncovered Burnside, and was hellish and irresistible at the same time. It is still there, although the built-on concrete vert wall has long gone, now just the mellow rolling bowls survive. Property prices in London and a plethora of council parks made the commercial parks' days numbered.

Meanwhile Brighton had its own park built (the Pig Bowl) and heavy sessions went down. A Lord had the right idea and built a skate place at Knebworth Hall. It survived through the 80's with numerous threats of closure and is not supposed to be there to this day. This was the only English park that got the snake run idea right, i.e., a run not a 10-second ride!

The West Midlands had Kidderminster pool and bowl to keep locals interested, although one of the few ridable real pools lay close by in the grounds of a Led Zeppelin member's house . . . needless to say I am glad security systems didn't exist !

Other places got parks, some of which remain today. Skating never really disappeared; it just got less popular and parks that closed were replaced by backyard ramps and a return to street cruising. The 1980's saw little skatepark-building activity apart from a few London public parks made of leftover modular concrete shapes.

BMX infested the public parks (Stockwell has never recovered from this disease). The London scene was concentrated around Meanwhile II and to a lesser extent the South Bank. Gradually it got underground and followed the same trends as in the States. It was hard to buy stuff until a punk record label called Rough Trade Records opened a skate shop underneath its record store. Rough Trade blossomed at the same time as the next 80's craze and they ended up building the Rough Trade Ramp at Latimer Road, which was often infested with local hooligans making skating impossible unless you went in huge numbers, but for a while it gave London a vert venue and enabled the original Bones Brigade to tour.

Since the mid '80's the scene has been the same as elsewhere, but the memory of the Golden Age of English skating keeps me going even now.

The Second Wave (1973–80)

The late sixties seem to have been a less innocent time than the early years of that decade. Legal problems and a lack of innovation in skateboard design were the main factors in the downturn in the popularity of skateboarding that occurred in that period, but it was also a time of great political and social strife worldwide, and carefree activities like sidewalk surfing were eclipsed in the public's imagination by protests, assassinations, and an increasingly controversial war.

Skateboarding didn't disappear entirely, but it certainly entered a dormant phase, until a technological breakthrough would bring it back to the forefront. In 1970, a surfer by the name of Frank Nasworthy began developing a skateboard wheel made from urethane. The resulting ride was magnificent compared to clay wheels, and by 1973 Nasworthy's Cadillac Wheels had launched skateboarding's Second Wave. Truck manufacturers like Independent, Bennett and Tracker began making trucks specifically designed for skateboarding. Board manufacturers sprang up overnight, and suddenly the industry was awash with new products and new ideas. In 1975, Road Rider came out with the first precision-bearing wheel, ending years of loose ball bearings that had a habit of spilling out. Slalom, downhill and freestyle skateboarding were practiced by millions of enthusiasts. *SkateBoarder* magazine was resurrected, and was soon joined by other publications hoping to cash in on skateboarding's comeback. Bruce

Logan, Russ Howell, Stacy Peralta, Tom Sims and Gregg Weaver were featured heavily in these magazines. The sport was on a roll once again.

The first modern outdoor skateboard park was built in Florida in 1976 and was soon followed by hundreds of other parks all over North America. With all the new possibilities the skateparks offered, skateboarding moved from horizontal to vertical and slalom and freestyle skateboarding gradually became less popular. The width of skateboards also changed from six to seven inches to over nine inches. This increase in size ensured better stability on vertical surfaces. Top riders of the Second Wave included Tony Alva, Jay Adams and Tom "Wally" Inouye. Wes Humpston marketed the first successful line of boards with graphics under the Dogtown label. Soon, dozens of board manufacturers were putting graphics under their boards.

Pool skating was hugely popular and as a result of better technology, skaters were able to perform aerials and go well beyond the coping. In the late 70's, Alan Gelfand invented the "ollie" or no-hands aerial, and moved skateboarding to the next level. The roots of streetstyle developed when skaters started to take vertical moves to flatland. Skateboard culture began to mesh with punk and new wave music. Images of skulls began to appear on skateboards, thanks to the creative genius of Vernon Courtland Johnson at Powell Corporation.

But skating's old nemesis, safety concerns, arose once more. Insurance became so expensive that many park owners closed their doors and the bulldozers were brought in. By the end of 1980, skateboarding had died another death and once again, many manufacturers were faced with tremendous losses. As BMX biking became popular and *SkateBoarder* magazine turned into *Action Now,* a lot of skaters deserted the sport. Skateboarding moved underground once more. But even as the skateparks disappeared, a hardcore contingent built their own backyard halfpipes and ramps and continued to develop the sport.

Frank Nasworthy is credited with one of skateboarding's legendary breakthroughs. It was his vision that led to a resurgence of skateboarding in the 1970's. This is the story of how the skateboard wheel went from clay to urethane.

As a teenager in the east coast town of Norfolk, Virginia, Frank got caught up in the skateboard craze that swept the country. He too bought a board with clay wheels. Although Frank remembers the skateboard as a "fun thing," his main passion was surfing. When skateboards died out a few years later, Frank remained a committed surfer. In 1970 he found himself in Washington, DC. In the summer of that year, one of Frank's high school friends, Bill Harward, came around for a visit. Bill mentioned he was going to visit another friend who lived in Virginia. So Frank and Bill set off on the trip to Purcellville.

The friend's father ran a backyard shop called Creative Urethanes. Urethane is a petroleum-based product that was developed in the 1930's in Germany. It has incredible resiliency and is very durable. As Frank was walking through the shop he spotted some large, 55-gallon drums filled with what appeared to be roller skate wheels. When Frank asked what the wheels were used for, the owner explained that he had received a request from a chain of rollerskate rinks called Roller Sports to make a rollerskate wheel that wouldn't wear out. He was making small quantities just for the rinks.

It was at that moment that Frank realized "these wheels would fit our Hobie skateboards." The owner was happy to oblige — the wheels he had seen in the drums were seconds. That day, Frank Nasworthy took home 30 sets of wheels. Frank and Bill headed back to Washington and replaced their clay wheels with their new urethane ones. Magically, the ride became smooth, stable and quiet. As Frank says, "We had free rein over the entire Washington, DC, area." People who tried their urethane-wheeled boards were astounded by the ride. Note that these wheels did not have precision bearings like today's skateboard wheels; they utilized loose ball bearings (16 per wheel).

In 1971, Frank and Bill decided to head out to California. Their sole reason was to go surfing. As they traveled up and the down the coast, they stopped by the town of Encinitas. It was here that Frank decided to stay. He found a place to live, surfed, and got a job in a restau-

rant. Life was going well. But Frank hadn't forgotten about the urethane wheels. He began to think there might be a market for them, and decided to contact Creative Urethanes to see if they could send him some more sets. Their response was that they couldn't sell Frank the other customer's wheels — he would have to design a wheel for himself.

Frank had studied engineering and design in college, so he went about creating his own urethane wheel. After Frank designed the first urethane skateboard wheel, he had to place his first order. "Gotta buy a thousand," was the response from Creative Urethanes.

Although Bill Harward was now stationed in Los Angeles, he had stayed in contact with Frank. On one of his visits down to Encinitas, the two discussed what to name the wheels. As they were talking, a Cadillac dog food commercial appeared on the television, and inspiration struck. They realized that this was exactly what they had done for the skateboard wheel — given it a sense of luxury, a Cadillac-type of a ride.

The first set of Cadillac wheels were sent out to Frank in 1972. He proceeded to load up his car and drive around to two hundred surf shops in Southern California. Although the skateboarding craze had died, there were still pockets of retailers who sold boards. Frank's sales pitch focused on getting people to replace their clay wheels with his urethane ones. Unfortunately, shop owners were not so enthused. As Frank explains, "Shop owners would say, 'I can buy a clay wheel for much less money than your urethane.'" A set of Frank's wheels would retail for $8, a fairly high premium — remember, this was at a time when you could buy a complete skateboard for almost $8. But eventually, Frank was able to find a few customers willing to give his Cadillac Wheels a try.

To create more interest and promote his product, Frank gave a few sets of wheels away. Slowly, more and more people began trying the wheels and the word spread. "It was a classic snowball situation," says Frank. An order was placed for 2,000 more wheels, followed by an order for 4,000 wheels. He took out an advertisement in *Surfer* magazine, and this boosted interest even higher.

In 1974, just two years after he placed his first order, Frank decided to pursue his skateboard-wheel career full time. Cadillac Wheels were becoming extremely popular and orders were reaching tens of thousands of dollars. One company Frank was selling to directly was Bahne Skateboards. Bill and Bob Bahne were brothers who manufactured high-quality surfboards in the same town Frank lived in — Encinitas. Since the Bahne brothers knew how to work with fiberglass and were skilled at lamination, it was only natural that they would take this expertise and start creating their own line of flexible skateboards.

Frank was enjoying the tremendous success of his Cadillac Wheels, but it was also creating a difficult situation for his small business. After all, a $50,000 wheel order can be pretty hard on your cashflow. And by this time the competition had begun to sit up and take notice of Cadillac. Roller Sports, the company that Creative Urethanes had originally manufactured roller-rink wheels for, decided to enter the picture. In fact, Roller Sports didn't merely enter the picture, they bought the entire production of wheels from Creative Urethanes. This was late 1974 and Roller Sports went on a major marketing/advertising blitz to compete with Cadillac Wheels.

When Roller Sports decided to buy the entire production from Creative Urethanes, Frank realized he needed someone else to produce the wheels. "I wanted to continue in the skateboard industry," explains Frank. He decided to join up with Bahne Skateboards, and started working on new wheels.

The Bahne/Cadillac partnering was responsible for some of the most memorable skateboard promotion the world has ever seen. Bill Bahne designed special ramps that were awesome in size. Imagine a ramp made from wood, 150 feet long, 15 feet high, and 30 feet in width. Bahne's ramp first appeared at the Del Mar Championships in the spring of 1975.

Bahne's boards and trucks along with Cadillac Wheels were an enormous success. As Frank recalls, "We put all our money into advertising." There is no question that Bill Bahne's and Frank Nasworthy's fervent promotion of skateboarding in the early to mid 1970's was a major factor in its resurgence. However, the companies' profits were being eaten up by the tremendous amount of promotion. Frank also realized they were reaching a critical point on the manufacturing side of their business. Skateboarders desired a soft wheel but found the bearing

racers would pop out if it was too soft. Conversely, if a wheel held the bearing racers in place, it was usually too hard and wouldn't provide enough traction.

The decision was made to mold a polycarbonate hub to the wheel to ensure the racers would not pop out. "It was a good idea," says Frank, "but we used injection-molded urethane instead of therma set." Injection-molded urethane was not as smooth a ride as therma set. Cadillac also faced competition from Road Rider Wheels. These wheels used precision bearings instead of Cadillac's loose ball bearings. The Road Rider #2 wheel was a premium product and was considerably more expensive than the Cadillac Wheel. In the same way that Frank had replaced clay wheels with his urethane wheels, Cadillac's loose ball bearing wheels were being replaced by premium precision wheels.

"We realized it was a bad decision," says Frank. "Our wheels were dogs compared to Road Rider." Unfortunately, mass production being what it is, Bahne/Cadillac had a million wheels to contend with. In due course, Bahne pulled out of the skateboard industry. Road Rider Wheels went on to become a market leader, along with Kryptonics and Sims.

As things wound up at Bahne/Cadillac, Frank moved to Florida with a new goal: to design and build a skateboard park filled with challenging and imaginative runs. The Cadillac Wheels Skateboard Concourse took a tremendous amount of time and energy to plan and build. Frank again used his innovative mind to come up with something unique. When the skatepark opened in 1978 it was truly state of the art, with impressive 15-foot pools and enormous bowls. However, the park was outside and was constantly being shut down due to heavy amounts of rain. Along with uncooperative weather, insurance for the park was difficult to obtain. Despite Frank's best efforts and the enthusiasm of the skateboarders, the park was shut down in 1979.

Frank eventually returned to school and is currently working for a manufacturer of high-tech printing products. Despite the downturn in fortunes for Cadillac Wheels and the Skateboard Concourse, there can be no doubt about the tremendous debt all skateboarders owe to Frank Nasworthy's ability to see beyond clay wheels.

Cadillac Wheel
A product of Bahne and Company P.O. Box 326, Encinitas, CA 92024

A Quarter Century of Innovation

One of the most innovative and dynamic skateboard companies to emerge in the 1970's was Northern California's NHS. From boards to wheels to trucks, NHS has been at the forefront of skateboard-making. One of their biggest innovations had to do with wheel bearings.

The shift from the clay to the urethane skateboard wheel was a major breakthrough in skateboard technology and led to a revival of the sport in the early '70's. Although not quite approaching the same level of break-through as urethane, when wheels went from 64 loose ball bearings to precision bearings, there was immediate positive impact on the world of skateboarding.

The story of how wheels moved from loose ball bearings to precision begins with a surfboard company. In the early 1970's three surfing buddies, Richard Novak, Doug Haut, and Jay Shuirman, got together to make surfboards. The trio worked out of the back of the Santa Cruz Surf Shop and eventually took the name NHS (from their initials). In 1973, NHS found themselves with a surplus of fiberglass and no customers, so they started to think about other applications. They came up with the idea of making skateboards. Thus, Santa Cruz Skateboards was born.

One day, while Richard and Jay were assembling loose ball bearing wheels onto trucks, something happened that wound up changing the entire skateboard industry. By accident, Jay spilled a wooden cask of nearly 100,000 individual loose ball bearings! After this incident, a man by the name of Tony Roderick walked into the shop. Tony was from a Rhode Island company called Quality Products. Holding a sealed precision bearing in his hand, Tony wondered if there was an application for skateboard wheels. With Quality Products heading up production and

NHS handling the marketing and sales, the Road Rider precision skateboard wheel was born. The year was 1975.

Road Riders started out with their #2 model and progressed to sizes #4, #6, and the Henry Hester model for slalom. Eventually they made harder pink-colored wheels for park riding. Without question, red Road Rider wheels were attached to many trucks during the 1970's. As well, hundreds of thousands of OJ's, Speed Wheels, and Bullets have been purchased by skaters. All of them come from NHS.

But Santa Cruz's innovations didn't stop with wheels. They created graphite-loaded slalom boards, were one of the first manufacturers out with five-ply boards, and Jay Shuirman was instrumental in the development of Independent Trucks. Tragically, Jay died in 1979 of leukemia.

The new person to head up Research and Development at NHS was former skateboard test pilot and freestyler Tim Puimarta. From the start Tim worked on a number of important projects, including the addition of an extra two plys of wood to the five-ply boards and working with silk screen technologies to achieve full images on boards (i.e., the Olson checkerboard design).

In the early 1980's, Tim started working on a variety of board designs. He worked on concave shapes and developed the first upturned nose. "The one thing I never did was copy anyone. There was just something in my nature that said I don't want to ever copy anyone."

Many skaters active in the 1980's remember Cell Blocks — the first stackable, colored riser pads. Black Top skateboards were another of Tim's innovations: "They had black fiberglass on top of laminated wood. Literally, out of the tens of thousands Black Top skateboards we ever made, only one came back broke."

In 1989, Tim took skateboarding to the next level and came up with Everslick, a specific type of thermoplastic that covered the bottom of the board. Tim remembers a pro skater exclaiming, "Oh my God! You can slide over anything!" Santa Cruz Skateboards was fast out of the gate with Everslick. "We got to market first — it took two weeks from concept to production." At first many people thought the idea was crazy, but as Tim recalls, "within six months everyone had copied it."

In 1994, an industrial product designer came to Santa Cruz with an idea for making plastic, injection-molded snowboards. "He had this stuff he'd lifted from Lockheed — definitely Stealth Bomber stuff," recalls Tim. Both Richard Novak and Tim immediately thought "skateboard." From this concept came "NuWood," a board you can drive a car over or leave out in the rain for a thousand years without damage. The interesting thing about NuWood is that it is the world's first truly recyclable skateboard. When a rider is finished with it, they can send it back to NHS, who will grind it up and make a new one.

One of the most recent products to emerge from NHS is grip tape featuring full-color graphics. "Our president, Bob Denike, wanted some sort of innovation to grip tape. We code-named it wacky tape. I found a way to put photos into grip tape." It took about eight months for Tim to develop this new tape, now called Roofies.

Tim Puimarta is humble about the skateboard research and development that he has done for the past two decades. While some of his ideas have failed to take off, most have been incredibly successful. "If I have one strength it is that I can take our team riders' language, emotion, and feedback, and translate it into a three-dimensional object that can be mass produced. If there's a theme to what I've done, it is building value into what a skater buys."

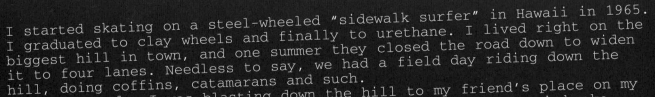

I started skating on a steel-wheeled "sidewalk surfer" in Hawaii in 1965. I graduated to clay wheels and finally to urethane. I lived right on the biggest hill in town, and one summer they closed the road down to widen it to four lanes. Needless to say, we had a field day riding down the hill, doing coffins, catamarans and such.
    One day I was blasting down the hill to my friend's place on my yellow plastic board when the plastic cube enclosing the truck broke open. Needless to say, I messed myself up pretty bad. I was so pissed off that I threw the board down the bottom of a 20-foot excavation ditch and buried it with dirt clods (it was later paved over).
    Someday an archeologist will dig the thing up (no biodegradable parts on these babies). They can have a good laugh at the crappy dept. store skateboards we used to ride. I often wonder how much better I would be if we had had modern gear when we started skating.

Later,
Andy G.

Jim O'Mahoney

Jim was one of the key organizers and players in the mid 1970's skateboard scene. He accomplished a number of interesting things during that time period. He managed and produced a number of skateboard contests and his enthusiasm for the sport extended to every continent.

Accomplishments:

1. Formed the United States Skateboard Association (USSA) which was a sanctioning body of skateboarding. This led to the formation of the World Skateboard Association.

2. Published *Skateboard* magazine and the *Skateboard Handbook*.

3. Helped with the design of skateparks, including The Runway.

4. Involved with a number of skateboard films, including *Go For It*.

5. Submitted the word "skateboard" to the dictionary

6. Involved with Guinness Book of World Records skateboard events.

Jim is still waiting for the US Post office to accept his skateboard stamp.

51

Smooth Moves

The Truck Builders

Three components make up a skateboard: the board, which has been subject to wild variations in shape, size and decoration over the years; the wheels, which have gone from steel to clay to urethane; and the trucks, the metal things that hold those wheels in place. In the '60's the Chicago Roller Skate Company was the main manufacturer of skateboard trucks. They made a few modifications to improve maneuverability, but with the limitations of the clay wheels there was little incentive to explore further possiblities in truck design.

However, when the second skate boom hit with the introduction of Frank Nasworthy's urethane wheel, innovative truck makers like Bennett, Tracker Trucks, and Gullwing were positioned to grab the market from Chicago. They were the ones that saw the potential in the new wheels and were able to respond to the need for new truck designs.

In the initial stages of skateboarding's Second Wave, Bennett and Tracker dominated the truck market. But in the late '70's the alliance of the Ermico Enterprises/NHS/Santa Cruz companies blasted the competition with their remarkable Independent Trucks. The appearance of Independents on the scene sparked further truck innovation. The amount of research and development the truck makers put into perhaps the least glamorous aspect of skateboard design illustrates the increasing sophistication of the whole skateboard industry during the '70's.

Bennett

Ron Bennett was an architect-engineer from Orange County who set out to redesign the skateboard truck and make it more functional. In a June 1977 interview with *SkateBoarder* magazine, it was clear that Bennett understood the problem with the conventional roller skate truck: "In order to get the truck to turn, it had to be loosened up so much that it got speed wobbles."

In 1975 Bennett introduced the Bennett Hijacker. It was truly different from traditional trucks. The kingpin was placed well below the axle. This meant that skaters would not have to worry about the kingpin dragging on the ground. The parts were of high quality: Bennett used aircraft-quality locknuts and a special compound for his "rubbers" (the part that fits between the kingpin and axle). The only area where Bennett's trucks seemed to have a problem were the baseplates — they tended to break. Fortunately, the baseplates came with a guarantee — you could mail them back to Mr. Bennett and he would replace them for free.

Although Bennett's were the freestyler's choice, slalom skater John Hutson also won a number of contests using the quick-turning Bennett trucks. In 1978 Bennett introduced a baseplate and truck designed of "Magalum," a metal compound. These new trucks were called Bennett Vectors. However, as truck competition heated up, Bennett was forced to start promoting other products. Eventually, Bennett concentrated on his Lightbeam and Spacedeck boards and stopped advertising his trucks towards the end of the 1970's.

Tracker

Tracker Trucks began in 1974 when a carpenter named Dave Dominy rode a skateboard that had a set of Cadillac urethane wheels attached. After this, Dave and his friends went to La Costa and started riding the area's impressive downhill roads. When Cadillac introduced their super-wide wheel, "The Stoker," Dave thought traditional trucks looked "really dinky. I decided to modify a set of Sure Grip trucks to make them wider and higher so that they would be stable and strong," remembers Dave, "and I called on Larry Balma to help me build the prototypes." Together, Dave and Larry started working on Dave's concept of a truck that would be stable, controllable at high speeds, and strong.

Dave had long been trying to come up with a small product he could mass produce, and the prototype truck seemed to fit the bill. The trucks' wide axles made for excellent stability and their large size looked perfect with the new large wheels. Another major difference that set Tracker Trucks apart was they did not have a nut below the rubbers — they used just one nut for adjustment.

Although slalom skaters were quick to pick up on the innovations of the Tracker, others were less enthusiastic. As Larry explains, "the Tracker was different. It was wide compared to the Bennett or Bahne. We'd bring it to a shop and tell the guy, 'Here's a new truck.' The response was sometimes, 'It won't work, it won't turn.' Then we'd say, 'Come out in front,' and we'd show them you could do everything on it better." During that first year, shop owners were still cautious; some worried that with the wider trucks a rider's back foot might hit the wheel. "We'd explain to them that boards were going to get wider," recalls Larry.

Eventually, Gordon & Smith started to distribute the trucks and things began to take off. After the initial success with the Fultrack, Tracker introduced the Halftrack and Midtrack for other types of riding, including freestyle and vertical. Their lighter, yellow magnesium trucks introduced in the late 1970's were extremely popular. Throughout the '80's and well in to the '90's, Tracker continues to be one of the most popular trucks.

Gullwing

Skater Mike Williams had already made a name for himself in both downhill and slalom before he approached a manufacturing company about an idea he had for a new truck design. He had been searching for a better-designed axle and would spend his free time thinking of ways to improve upon the skateboard truck. By the fall of 1975 he had determined what he wanted and went to see a San Diego aerospace tooling company called HPG IV. With the help of designers Bill Brawner and Walt Tiedge, Mike Williams greatly transformed the look of the traditional skateboard truck.

Gullwing's "split axle" truck was truly revolutionary. Not only could you adjust the tension of the truck, you could also adjust the turning radius. The trucks became available commercially in January 1976. In the first month HPG IV sold 800 trucks. Eleven months later, sales had increased to 13,000 per month. Mike Williams quit his night job at a shipbuilding company and went to work full time at HPG IV as a pro. Over time, Gullwing modified their split-axle trucks and smoothed out the design. The split axle became a groove and then eventually the groove was replaced altogether.

Despite their popularity, the Bennett, Tracker and Gullwing trucks had limitations in terms of their turning capabilities. In the mid 1970's, Fausto Vitello and Eric Swenson formed Ermico Enterprises with the intention of producing a truck that turned well in the streets.

Fausto's friend John Solomine designed the truck and Eric and Fausto went about acquiring the necessary manufacturing equipment. They purchased welders and drill presses, borrowed a lathe, and set up shop on Yosemite Avenue in San Francisco. The truck was called "The Stroker" and it was rather unusual. While most trucks in the 1970's retailed from $6 to $16 each, Strokers came in at a whopping $26.95 each! The truck had an incredibly complex "steering system" with springs, sockets, and other intricate mechanisms.

Despite the amount of engineering and technology thrown into the truck, it had some major drawbacks. "The problem," explained Fausto, "was that the truck turned too much — it had too many springs. It needed dampners to avoid problems with wobbles. Although we tried to put dampners inside the truck, there was no space."

The Stroker turning system did manage to cause quite a sensation on the downhill circuit, however. Downhiller Terry Nails put a Stroker on his revolutionary aluminum skatecar to compete at the Signal Hill Races. His was the first streamlined skatecar and it turned a lot of heads. "The Signal Hill Race was initially rained out," remembers Fausto, "and we were the only ones there with this streamlined skatecar. When it was rescheduled, an additional four skatecars had been built by other competitors."

There were both good and bad stories at the Signal Hill race. Unfortunately, Terry put his brakes on too late and crashed, but he was still able to place second. The Stroker system had also gained a lot of attention from other competitors and Ermico's name started to spread.

While the Stroker had some partial success, John Solomine went back to the drawing board and came up with the Rebound Truck. Rebounds featured two separate king pins for greater adjustability. Ermico Enterprises manufactured the trucks and they were distributed by NHS (the same company responsible for marketing Road Rider wheels and Santa Cruz Skateboards). It was with this distribution agreement that the seeds of the NHS/Ermico Enterprises alliance would begin.

In the late 1970's, Northern Californian skaters John Hutson and Rick Blackhart were gaining a reputation as masters in their respective fields: John was dominating the downhill and slalom scene, while Rick was known for his incredible vert abilities, which rivaled any pro from down south. "Rick was the ace of Northern California," recalls Fausto.

John was riding for Santa Cruz (NHS) and winning a great many contests on Bennett Trucks. Although pros like Henry Hester were riding Trackers and suggested that he do the same, John had other ideas. "I found Trackers too stiff and I needed the ability to turn. The Bennett Trucks were way more responsive. NHS were interested in developing a new truck that would combine the best design features of both Tracker and Bennett."

John began consulting with Jay Shuirman and Rich Novak of NHS to create a unique steering concept. The idea was to build a truck that provided independent suspension for each wheel. This is similar to the type of wheel suspension you would find on an automobile. The goal was to make each wheel move independently from the other, ensuring a very responsive truck. Over a number of months, Jay refined the truck and eventually three sets were manufactured. According to John, the ride was unbelievable: "They had better turning than Bennett."

At the time work was being done on the "independent suspension" trucks, Fausto Vitello met up with Rick Blackhart and his friend Kevin Thatcher. They too were looking for an alternative to Tracker and Bennett. As Fausto recalls, Rick knew exactly what he was looking for: "He told me, 'Fausto, you produce a truck that turns more and hangs up less, and everyone will ride it.'"

During the late '70's, skateboarders had become more interested in vertical skating thanks to people like Tony Alva. Tony was instrumental in pushing the sport towards a more aggressive edge and moving skaters away from downhill, freestyle, and slalom. This is not to say that downhill, freestyle, and slalom were completely abandoned; while vertical skaters like Rick Blackhart and Steve Olson were involved with the testing of the trucks, so too was slalom rider John Hutson.

After the fourth or fifth prototype and much deliberation, the new truck emerged. But what to call it? Oddly enough, even though the truck had nothing to do with independent suspension, the truck was named "The Independent." Ermico Enterprises started to manufacture Independents in 1978. There were two models available — the 88mm and the 109mm. The success of the truck was almost instantaneous. Recalls Fausto, "At the Newark contest in 1978, Bobby Valdez switched his Tracker Trucks to Independents. He did the first invert, a front side roll in, and won the contest." Within six months, Independent grabbed a 50 percent market share.

While the Independent Truck was a big hit with skaters, it was to have an even more dramatic effect on the skateboard industry. Tracker Trucks responded with their lighter "magnesium" truck along with their plastic white "coper." Indy shot back with the Kevin Thatcher–designed "Grindmaster Device." "This was a spoof of Tracker's coper, and yet it sold millions," recalls Fausto.

Santa Cruz (NHS) enjoyed success three ways — they had a significant share of the board, wheel, and truck market. Tragically, Jay Shuirman died of leukemia at the age of 40 in 1979. As one of the key developers of Independent, he left an indelible mark on the world of skateboarding. One wonders what other things he might have been able to develop had he been given the chance.

If there is one place that most skaters of the 1970's remember, **it's Dogtown** (aka Santa Monica). A number of legendary skaters came out of Dogtown, and collectively they **changed the direction of skateboarding.**

The Roots

Skateboarding may have died in most areas of the United States during the mid 1960's, but it was kept alive in Santa Monica, California. According to Craig Stecyk, this was because skateboarding was ingrained in the Santa Monica lifestyle. "People surfed in Malibu and lived in Santa Monica." When the surfers headed back home to Santa Monica, away from the waves, they got their surfing fix on skateboards. Here riders such as Danny Bearer, Torger Johnson and Dave Hilton would spend hours skating the banks at schools like Paul Revere and Bellagio.

In 1968, a young Tony Alva (he was 10 at the time) started to ride the banks as well. Tony was also very much into surfing at the time and as he recalled in *Thrasher* magazine in May 1984, "by the early '70's I was on all these different surf teams. Back then, skating was just as big as the surfing was, because everyone related their skating to surfing back then," Alva remembers that he and his friends started to progress with their skating and get into "super low speed pivotal moves and slides."

Dogtown was a rough area. There were slums, winos and, as Stacy Peralta remembers, a fair amount of danger: "We would ride our bikes at 4:00 am to go surfing and had to be careful not to be beat up by roving gangs."

The Origins of Zephyr and the Z-Boys

Zephyr was a surfboard manufacturing company started by Jeff Ho, Craig Stecyk and Skip Engblom. Skip and Craig had been hanging out together in the winter of 1968 when they spotted Jeff in his truck.

At the time Jeff was running a company called Jeff Ho Surfboards. It was Craig who suggested that Skip go into business with Jeff. When Skip climbed into the truck, Jeff got quite upset. But shortly thereafter the three were looking for factory space, Jeff's place having been hit by a massive flood.

They found a place on Grandville Avenue, just a few blocks from Santa Monica, renting for 300 dollars a month. In these humble surroundings, they were about to start on a journey that would change the face of skateboarding. Each partner brought different talents and experience to the new company. Stacy Peralta remembers Jeff Ho as a unique individual. "Jeff was incredibly ultra hip. He had multi-colored glasses, drove a 4 x 4 truck back in the 1970's when they weren't popular, and was an amazing surfer. He was what you'd call 'Superfly.'" Craig (CR) Stecyk was an artist with quite a reputation. He had been involved with surfing and skateboarding at a very young age and was the first person to use graffiti as art. Craig was also an accomplished writer and his articles in *Surfer* reached legendary status. Skip Engblom had been riding skateboards since 1955 and at the age of 14 had a job with Makaha branding logos onto skateboards. "I chose the name Zephyr because I wanted to be the last name in the phone book," remembers Skip.

Over time, Zephyr's business grew. Dealers started to carry their boards and Zephyr created their own store. A surf team was formed to promote the company, but the Zephyr surf team was no ordinary team. It would eventually morph into one of the greatest skateboard teams ever assembled: Tony Alva, Jay Adams, Wentzl Ruml, Bob Biniak, Jim

Muir, Nathan Pratt, Stacy Peralta and Shogo Kubo. This group were all strong surfers as well as skaters.

In 1973, Tony Alva and Jay Adams approached Skip and showed him the new Cadillac urethane wheels. Skip realized how good the wheels were and started buying them for the shop. Jay Adams' stepfather, Kent Sherwood, owned a fiberglass shop and a decision was made to have Kent and his partner Dave Sweet start manufacturing skateboards for Zephyr.

As Skip recalls, "We looked at the Bahne skate decks and we knew we could make something better." But the first prototype wasn't as successful as might have been expected. As soon as Skip stepped on the board, it broke in two. This problem was fixed by incorporating a rocker design into the board.

Now that the riders had skateboards from Zephyr, the only thing left to do was enter a contest.

The Contest that Blew People's Minds

The 1975 Skateboard Championships held at Del Mar was the first opportunity the whole skateboard world had to see the Zephyr team in action. Before the contest, Skip had made the "Z-Boys" practice after school. He also made up some shirts that in his words "would make the group look more intimidating." The Z-Boys' moves were completely different from those of the other competitors; they had an intense style that was all their own. As Nathan Pratt explained in a June 1977 *SkateBoarder* interview, the Zephyr team blew a lot of people's minds: "Our concept of freestyle was entirely different; nobody did handstands or wheelies or any of that kind of junk . . . it was a performance style, not a trick style. We said we're going to skate our way, not their way. We went into that contest and did full-out, high-performance, aggressive skating."

Skip took his past experiences with carnivals and put together an image that rocked skateboarders everywhere. He felt like he was staging a movie: "I had Stacy as the serious skater, Jay the natural, Tony as moody, Shogo being Zen-like and Nathan as geeky. The chemistry for the situation was so perfect. You couldn't have asked for a better mix of people."

After Del Mar, Skip would play his part to the hilt when it came to registering at competitions. "I would dress up in a sleazy shirt with dark glasses and carry a briefcase." In the briefcase he would have all the Zephyr team's entry forms filled out along with the entrance fee. "I'd come up to the registration desk, hand over the stuff and say, 'We're the Zephyr team and we're here to win.'"

The Breakup

The amount of attention generated by the Del Mar contest and other subsequent events was enough to ignite the legend of "Dogtown." Unfortunately, things were not running so smoothly at Zephyr. Kent Sherwood had a business disagreement with Jeff Ho and decided to leave and make his own boards. His son, Jay Adams, went with him, as did Tony Alva and Jim Muir, and thus the company Z-Flex was created. This left Stacy, Wentzl, Bob and Shogo on the Zephyr team. The breakup had a devastating effect on everyone. "It was really awful," recalls Stacy. "There was a contest in Los Angeles at Cow Palace. We were riding as Zephyr and the other guys were Z-Flex. It felt really wrong."

At that contest Stacy took third place in the freestyle event (Tom Sims took second and Bruce Logan got first). He was the first skater to show up the '60's skaters and it made a huge impact. "I realized, however, that there was no real future with Zephyr, " recalls Stacy. Most of the Z-Boys scattered to different teams. Stacy wound up at Gordon & Smith Skateboards and Tony, Jay and Bob went to Logan Earth Ski. Shogo stayed with Z-Flex. Jim Muir teamed up with Wes Humpston to start Dogtown Skates.

Although Z-Products are still available today, sadly Zephyr folded after the split. Craig Stecyk would go on to work in many areas of the skateboard world, including Powell Peralta. Skip Engblom got involved in skateparks and skate stores before starting up board manufacturer Santa Monica Airlines.The legacy the Z-Boys left the world of skateboarding cannot be understated. Their intense, aggressive style paved the way for generations of skaters. It is this foundation that people are still riding on today.

Wes Humpston
—Graphically Different

Most skaters today would have trouble envisioning a time when there weren't graphics under a skateboard. However, for many years manufacturers were content just to affix their company's logo to their boards. They weren't really interested in cultivating or developing a more impressive graphical look to the board. But Wes Humpston had other ideas. For him the bottom of a skateboard was to become a wooden canvas, and it was his creativity that would forever change the look of skateboards

At the age of 16, Wes had a job repairing surfboards. It was here that he got his first taste of working with fiberglass. Wes lived near Santa Monica, California, the epicenter of skateboarding in the 1970's, known as Dogtown. Although Wes admits he couldn't rip as well as some of the other skaters (after all, he was competing with the likes of Tony Alva and Jay Adams!), he truly enjoyed skating.

Jim Muir was a friend of Wes's and the two would skate and surf together. One of the prime spots for skateboarding in the 1970's was the enormous (15 foot) banks found in Beverly Hills. Wes fondly recalls such places as Kenter, St. Clements, Paul Revere, and Sunset Beach.

In early 1975, Jim and Wes decided to make their own skateboards. Their friend Kevin Kaiser had a surfboard-shaping room in his garage with a large assortment of equipment, including jig saws, sanding machines, and air brush gear. "The walls were all covered with graffiti," recalls Wes. This no doubt would inspire Wes's imagination.

Jim and Wes would make boards for friends as well as trade them for trucks or wheels. Wes had studied art at school and had always enjoyed drawing. Consequently, he began to draw on the bottom of the decks. They were truly customized pieces and inspiration came from a variety of sources. On a trip out to skate a drained swimming pool with Jim and friend John Pefferman, Wes remembers that it was a 45-minute ride. "I just started drawing to fill the time." As time progressed, more and more skaters came around asking for his "Dogtown" boards.

"I loved to mix things up. I loved things with wings," recalls Wes. Wes took Craig Stecyk's "Dogtown Cross" and added beautiful red and yellow wings to it. Not only was it a stunning piece of work, but it was actually mass produced. In mid 1978, the only boards to have graphics were those produced by Jim and Wes's company, Dogtown Skates. Wes was truly ahead of his time and extremely industrious. As he succinctly put it, "I painted, airbrushed, stenciled, branded, carved, and hand drew on more boards than I can remember."

Wes Humpston also had another tremendous impact on the look of skateboards, in the shape of boards. Originally, Wes and Jim experimented with wood laminates, trying to achieve the goal of crafting a very light board. In a November 1978 *SkateBoarder* magazine interview, Wes recalled: "We were trying to get them down to a pound a board. We also played around with the kicktails."

Wes and Jim's original boards were light but were roughly the same shape as those of other manufacturers. However, as time progressed they became wider and people started calling the boards "pigs." There were two reasons why the boards became wider. As Jim recounted in the *SkateBoarder* interview: "What happened was a fluke. We'd take our last board and make a template by tracing around the outside edge with a felt pen; the overlap from the pen would give us about a quarter inch extra on each side, so the tails started getting wider and noses started getting wider; that's how it all started. Wes was the first to recognize the wider boards were working better; they were just more stable."

Wes saw the need for the stability that the wider boards offered because, as he puts it, "I have big feet." In trying to make the boards wider, Jim and Wes did run into

some problems. "We would pick up stuff at the House of Hardwood," recalls Wes, "and it would split." The solution to their problem came from skater Ray Flores. Ray had picked up an eight-wheel deck from Canadian manufacturer Willi Winkel. Wes had a radical idea: he decided to cut the shape from the Wee Willi Winkel deck. It worked perfectly. The board was wide and had a nicely shaped kicktail. Dogtown Skates also were one of the first

manufacturers to utilize die-cut grip tape. The "D T" letters were cut out and added to the uniqueness of the board. Soon after their success, other manufacturers began selling wider decks.

Dogtown Skates continued to release wider and wider boards, culminating in a 12-inch monster that bore Wes's name. Gradually, boards started to acquire different

shapes. They became less wide and more angled, eventually morphing into the "Popsicle stick" shape of the 1990's, bearing an upturned tail and nose. Ironically, most of the boards in the '90's have very similar shapes and are differentiated only by their graphics. It was Wes Humpston's imagination that paved the way for other skateboard companies to become more creative with their graphics.

In 1996, Wes joined up with another Dogtown legend, Ray Flores, and once again began making boards. The Street Legal lineup of boards features the same type of hand-drawn art that was on the original Dogtown skateboards. Not only are these boards wide, they are also quite lengthy and can reach up to 54 inches. This means there's lots of room for your feet, no matter how large.

Wee Willi Winkels

— Board Innovator

If you weren't skateboarding in Canada in the mid to late 1970's, you may not have heard of Willi Winkels. However, his innovations and inventions have had a remarkable impact on skateboarding, along with many other industries.

Like many people, Willi Winkels (yes, that is his real name) began skateboarding in the 1960's on clay composite wheels. Willi was also an enthusiastic skier who would later gain legendary status in the sport. He enjoyed skateboarding, but it was only when he experienced urethane wheels in the 1970's that he got really interested. Willi tried these new wheels when he visited Whistler, British Columbia. He was so impressed with the ride that he asked a friend who was vacationing in Florida to pick up a complete skateboard for him. However, the boards were so expensive that his friend only brought back a set of wheels and trucks.

At that moment, Willi decided to make his own board. His father owned and operated a door manufacturing company and had the necessary equipment and supplies to create a deck. As the 1970's skateboard boom progressed, Willi got more involved in skateboarding. He started entering contests and winning in freestyle and slalom competitions.

Willi also got more involved with manufacturing skateboards and started to devote less time to making doors. His first boards were like every other manufacturer's — solid wood. But unlike other solid wood boards, which had a wedge of wood glued on for a kicktail, Willi utilized a special process. He cut out both the nose and tail and joined pieces of wood together, to create what was called a "wedge tail." The board had a more professional look than other skateboards. But this process was time consuming, so he asked his father for advice on how to save time. He suggested Willi use a wood laminate.

The year was 1976 and no other manufacturer was using maple laminates to make skateboards. A buzz about Wee Willi Winkel skateboards was starting to build. Collegiate Sports in Toronto took an order for 200 boards. Willi's father went on a business trip and before he left he wondered if he would be able to sell all 200 boards. In two days, all the boards were gone.

It's important to note just how different Wee Willi Winkel boards were. Most skateboards in the mid 1970's were simply shaped from a wooden plank or used a wood and fiberglass laminated combination. Well-known wooden board marketers included Logan Earth Ski, Makaha, Gordon & Smith (the Stacy Peralta Warptail model), and Maharajah. Just for the record, Santa Cruz's "5 Ply" and the Gordon & Smith-distributed, Tracker-developed "Rockit" skateboards didn't come out until 1977.

In order to promote his boards, the Wee Willi Winkel Skateboard Team was formed. They would do demos at special events. Besides freestyle and high jumping, Willi would demo his motorized skateboard. Willi had one model with a chain drive that hit over 60 miles per hour at an airport runway.

In 1976, Lonnie Toft, a pro skater for the Sims Team, visited Toronto to perform at the Sportsman's Show. Willi showed Lonnie his laminated plywood boards and Lonnie showed Willi a template he had designed for a new, wider skateboard shape. Willi immediately cut out the design in his shop. At the time, Willi probably could not have imagined the enormous consequences that Lonnie's visit would have on his life.

Lonnie took this Wee Willi Winkel/Toft Design skateboard back to the Sims manufacturing shop and silk screened a Sims logo on it. A week later he entered a contest and won first place. Everyone noticed this "new" Sims deck and wondered where it had come from. The wider, fuller shape was radically different from most of the needle-nose, skinnier boards of the time. The next day, the Sims company was overwhelmed with phone calls — people were trying to find out about Lonnie's new deck. Tom Sims quickly found out what Lonnie had done, then went to the phone and called Willi. Willi recalled the moment as being rather surreal, as well as quite funny: "Tom Sims phoned during dinner time. He asked me if I could make thousands of the boards that I had just made for Lonnie. I told him that it was my dinner time and that I would get back to him. Not less than five minutes later, Tom called back; 'Screw your dinner,' he said. 'I'm taking a plane up there to see you tomorrow.'"

After Willi showed Tom Sims his factory in Brampton, Ontario, things kicked into high gear. Willi began making boards for Sims, and soon other manufacturers began placing orders with him. Although the factory was making plywood boards, Willi was constantly trying to stretch the boundaries. He began experimenting with carbon graphite boards (super light) and also began producing Lonnie's original idea: the eight-wheeled skateboard. In an interview with *SkateBoarder* in April of 1979, Lonnie explained that the evolution of the eight-wheeled skateboard began with his brother, Dan. In 1973, Lonnie cut out an eight-wheeled deck in his garage. He then went out to a swap meet and picked up some rollerskates and clay wheels. By 1975, he was riding the "Outrageous" eight wheelers on vertical. Willi picked up on the eight wheelers too, and would demo them every chance he could.

Although Willi was involved with skateboard promotion and production, he also worked on developing

skateboard ramps — including pioneering work on the halfpipe. As he explained, "I saw Jay Adams and Tony Alva skating back and forth between two quarterpipes and it occurred to me that these two pipes could be joined together to make a much smoother transition." In 1977, Willi created a halfpipe from wood and then went on to create a mobile halfpipe that was pulled by a truck. And unlike most ramps of the 1970's, Willi's were modular — they were easy to assemble and takedown.

Willi's association with Lonnie Toft didn't stop with the skateboard; the two were also pioneers in the sport of snowboarding. Willi modified a product called the "Flying Yellow Banana," which at the time was a plastic, shaped board that could glide on snow. The idea was to strap your complete skateboard down to the board and go. Unfortunately, the design didn't work well. Willi came up with a better idea. He attached only the deck to the Flying Yellow Banana and added plastic hooks for the riders' feet. In 1978, he took the product, dubbed the "skiboard," to Blue Mountain ski hill in Collingwood, Ontario. Needless to say, the sight of Willi bombing down hills facing sideways blew many people away. Soon after his expedition to Blue Mountain, Lonnie Toft and Tom  Sims hooked up with Willi at Mammoth Mountain in California. This was the start of Sims/Winkel involvement with what was to be known later as "snowboarding."

Willi got out of manufacturing when the second skatebust hit (this was in the early '80's). However, in the mid '80's Willi received a call from someone who asked if he could make skateboards. Willi told him what it was going to cost and the gentleman produced a cheque the next day. Production began almost immediately and Willi was back in the skateboard business again, making boards for a number of well-known firms.

After all that Willi has contributed to the sport of skateboarding, it is ironic that in 1997, Blue Mountain ski/snowboard resort named a run after him. He is now involved with a new prototype ramp that will enable skaters to achieve "huge air."

skateparks:
the skater's refuge

The problem of finding places to skate safely and without the interference of cops and angry drivers, pedestrians and property owners has been a recurring theme in the history of skateboarding. The inability of the skateboard industry and local governments to come up with a solution to the conundrum of finding a safe place for an admittedly potentially dangerous sport has resulted in several crashes of the industry over the years.

One approach to the problem was to build facilities specifically dedicated to skateboarding. But the creation of skateboarding parks was only partly a response to safety problems associated with skateboarders using public streets as their playgrounds. It was also another way to make money off the sport; and it also grew from the desire of skateboarders to have more challenging terrain to play with and conquer.

Contrary to popular skateboard historian belief, the first skateboard park opened in 1976 in Port Orange, (Daytona) Florida, not in Carlsbad, California. Skateboard City was open a week before the Carlsbad park, but of the two, Carlsbad is more well known. It was built by Skatepark Constructors, a company headed up by two of the most famous skatepark designers: John O'Malley and Jack Graham.

In July 1977, John O'Malley, then aged 23, was interviewed by Warren Bolster of *SkateBoarder*. John grew up in New York and started skating at the age of 11. There was a really nice place to ride called Salisbury Park and John and his friends would skate on the asphalt runs that wound through trees and down by a lake. At the age of 18, John moved out to Carlsbad, California.

John explained how his experience of riding in New York became the seed for designing skateparks:

When we were younger, we would sit around and fantasize about how nice it would be to have runs like we had used to ride in Salisbury Park, in a park atmosphere, down through landscaped places, in your own backyard, you know, if you were the son of a rich millionaire or something like that.

Jack Graham was at one time a next-door neighbor to O'Malley. After seeing skaters being arrested on television for skateboarding on a concourse, Jack approached John with the idea of using a piece of land "for some sort of a place to come and skateboard." John was pretty excited about the idea. Besides his background in skating and surfing, he had been involved with construction.

The two began researching the idea in their spare time. But a horrific incident would accelerate their focus on the project: Jack's son was skating with friends when one of them skated out into the middle of the road and was killed by a car. After this, both Jack and John began devoting their full time to the project.

Jack was a long-time friend and business associate of Larry Grismer, the owner of the Carlsbad Raceway, so this was chosen as the site for their skatepark. The area had natural terrain and, most important, as John pointed out in his interview, "it had proper zoning. It was already zoned as a commercial property."

Carlsbad became a very successful skateboard park, and soon after it opened other parks in Florida, Australia and even Japan sprung up. Most of these early skateparks featured flowing snakeruns, freestyle areas and bowls constucted from concrete, although the Ocean Bowl park in Maryland was made of asphalt. The costs associated with building a skateboard park were quite significant, but few matched the budget of the Carlsbad Park, which came in at $250,000 (these are 1970's dollars don't forget!)

But it seems the investment paid off for many skatepark owners. By the mid seventies, the sport was booming again and businessmen everywhere were set to cash in on the craze. In their April 1977 issue, *SkateBoarder* reported the following:

- In its first week of operation, the Wizard Skateboard Park in Wilmington, North Carolina, grossed a reported $7–8,000. The park had a maximum capacity of 70 skaters at a time.

- The Solid Surf Skateboard Park in Fort Lauderdale had a paid attendance of 3,200 skaters over a four-day holiday weekend.

- Skatepark engineers O'Malley and Graham disclosed that their firm, Skatepark Constructors, had to stop signing contracts in the fall of 1976 in order to gear up for the demand.

Despite the enormous interest in building skateparks, however, there were two thorny issues that business people had to deal with. One was the difficulty in getting proper zoning for the parks. In some cases, city councils took months to make a decision. The other problem, which was to have enormous consequences, was obtaining adequate insurance. For both private and public skateparks, the possibility of a parent or skater suing the park was of great concern. As John O'Malley pointed out, "The biggest danger to skateparks are people who are getting into it, or have been into it — skatepark development, that is — and don't have the all-round input, the all-round understanding of the skatepark concept and all the implications thereof."

These legal issues persisted despite the boom, so that by the late seventies, the extinction of skateparks was being predicted. The September 1978 issue of *SkateBoarder* contained interviews with a number of skatepark developers. Among them was Robert E. Spence, owner and operator of a skatepark in Florida. When asked about the future, most respondents discussed skatepark construction and design. Spence, however, realized what the real issue was: "I feel that the sport is at a critical point at this time and, unless some insurance carrier can be found to write liability insurance for the owners at an affordable price, we could see the demise of this industry that we love so well."

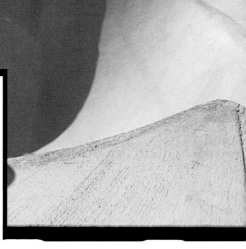

Legal action was the furthest thing from skateboarders' minds when they got to skate in these parks. Most were delighted to be free of the hassling they got when they skated the streets, and they enjoyed the new challenges offered by the landscapes specifically designed with them in mind.

But parents, lawyers and city councils were another matter. In the final analysis, skateparks closed because the insurance became too high for owners to pay and there were just too many lawsuits. A few parks, like the Pipeline, remained open during until the late 80's, but most were bulldozed by 1981. When skateparks began to close, the sport went underground and into people's backyards. Hardcore skaters began building ramps and took the sport in a completely different direction. As we will see, skateparks would be revived once the legal issues began to be dealt with in a serious and innovative manner.

skateparks

During the First Wave of skateboarding little, if any, attention was paid to safety equipment. Things changed in the 1970's, however, when skater/designer Mike Rector went into business with Bob Wolfe. Mike had been a skater during the First Wave, and when urethane hit, he immediately picked up the sport again. Mike's skateboarding led to a new product innovation. As he wrote in *SkateBoarder* in their August 1978 issue, "I experienced the classic creative 'flash.' I envisioned a pair of protective gloves which would protect the hands and wrists of a skateboarder." At the time, most skateboard gloves were really no better than the ones used for gardening.

Mike Rector —
Skateboard SAFETY Equipment

Mike test marketed the gloves and quickly realized that he had a very worthwhile product. He went about the process of getting the gloves patented and setting up the business. The Rector Palm Pads Glov combined pigskin palms with a foam pad. They also featured suede cowhide on the outside along with rainbow-colored wrist straps. The gloves were a combination of style and ruggedness. They did, however, tend to leave your fingertips stained with an orange color.

Shortly after the introduction of the Palm Pads Glov, Rector and Wolfe were faced with a number of companies copying their design. Ever the innovator, Mike Rector created new products: Skatepants, which featured removable padding and elbow and knee pads that were much more flexible than traditional padding. The Flex*Line design featured three pads that were stitched into individual pockets, allowing a lot more freedom to move.

Skaters weren't the only ones picking up on Mike Rector's ideas: New wave band Devo used Rector pads when they went on stage — they found it very useful for ensuring that no one got hurt!

Mike Rector also developed plastic cups over knee and elbow pads to improve their sliding capabilities. He also improved and modified the wrist guards that Hobie had first introduced. If you could add up the number of times that Rector protective gear has helped skateboarders when they have fallen, the sum would now be in the tens of millions.

Don "Waldo" Autry

A legend in the 1970's, Waldo ruled vertical terrain — especially pipes. "At first skateboarding to me meant that the waves weren't very big, so we'd ride the drainage ditch with our clay-wheel boards. Then we moved to handstands and eventually the Pipeline. Twenty years or so later, I'm riding luge. Imagine what it's like to go 65 miles per hour standing up on a skateboard at 41 years of age. Who would have figured."

Ty Page

"Mr. Incredible" was known for his fast footwork and astounding pirouettes. Ty would do high jumps or carve up steep banks and turn 360 degrees with amazing height. He rode for California Free Former and had one of the first signature models. Page is best known for the "Ty Slide."

John Hutson

Sponsored by Santa Cruz, John is best remembered for his speed, both in downhill and slalom. He won numerous contests, including first place in the downhill event at the Catalina Classic held in 1978. John was known for his "hut tuck" fairing stance which helped him achieve speeds of well over 50 miles per hour standing on a skateboard. John was also test rider in the development of Independent Trucks.

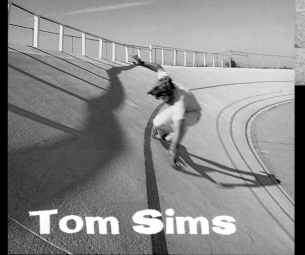

Tom Sims

As the father of the longboard, Tom combined his love for surfing, skiing and skateboarding and had tremendous impact on the sport. He was also an early promoter and developer of snowboarding. Starting in the early 1970's, Tom made enormous skateboards for himself and friends using water skis. Eventually his company, Sims Skateboards, marketed wheels along with boards and became a giant in the industry.

A SURFER PUBLICATION

SkateBoarder

Vol. 2, No. 1 · $1.00

CDC 00147

Hot Action
High Speed
Radical Runs
Slalom, Tricks
Freestyle
Equipment Info

8

SkateBoarder Returns

In 1975, Steve Pezman, then publisher of *Surfer,* resurrected *The Quarterly Skateboarder* as the Second Wave began to gather steam. The glossy magazine, now just plain *SkateBoarder,* covered skateboarding with a great deal of style. The photographs were often stunning and the editorial content ranged from brilliant to bizarre.

Although the focus was primarily California, occasionally articles would appear on other places in the skate world. As the sport gained in popularity, the magazine grew in size, hitting a record thickness in 1978. At one point, *SkateBoarder* was the most popular action magazine at the 7-11 convenience store chain. Contributing to SkateBoarder's success were a number of talented people such as C.R. Stecyk III, Brian Gillogly, Warren Bolster and brilliant photographers such as Jim Cassimus, Glen E. Friedman, Craig Fineman and Jim Goodrich.

While *SkateBoarder* did much to promote the sport and convey to people outside California what was happening, it had to contend with two key issues. Firstly, most people who read *SkateBoarder* were lucky if they lived near a skatepark of the quality featured in the magazine. In most cases readers were treated to images that did not reflect their true skating environment. Secondly, as skateboarding peaked and then started to decline, the magazine had to deal with the attrition of readers. In trying to combat this problem, *SkateBoarder* started to include photos and stories on roller skating. It then followed up with articles on BMX. For many skaters, this lack of focus on skateboarding was unacceptable. They wanted *SkateBoarder* to be only about skateboarding.

As punk and new wave music began to fuse with the "outlaw" or underground image of skateboarding, it started to dramatically change the entire sport. As skating moved from horizontal (slalom, downhill, freestyle) towards vertical (pools, parks, ramps, pipes), it assumed a more aggressive style. There has been much debate about whether this fusion was good or bad, but the fact is that it happened and *SkateBoarder* had a hard time deciding how to handle the sport's more aggressive turn, which was unappealing to some advertisers.

As skateboard parks began to close and skaters headed out onto the street or backyard ramps, *SkateBoarder* decided to change its direction completely and incorporate a variety of sports. In August 1980 it renamed itself *Action Now* and for many readers, this was the final straw. *Action Now* lasted until 1982 (Vol. 8 #6), then promptly folded.

The Evolution of the Ollie

Although there have been several key skateboard tricks over the years, the ollie has dominated skating for the past two decades. Popping the board with your back foot and flying over stairs, rails and other objects has made the ollie the fundamental trick of present-day skateboarding. Many would call the ollie the greatest skateboard trick ever invented. Whatever you think about the ollie, its roots are extraordinary.

The ollie was originally developed not on the west coast, but in Florida by Alan Gelfand in the late '70's. Alan's nickname was "Ollie" and he had started skating at the age of 12. When he was 13, he decided to try something different and began experimenting with lip slides. Alan found he was able to achieve a small amount of air when he popped his board during the lip slide maneuver. From this came the "ollie" pop and then finally the "ollie" aerial.

In 1977, top skate pro Stacy Peralta visited Fort Lauderdale while on a tour of Florida skateparks for Gordon & Smith. "I remember vividly how a guy came up to me and said, 'Ya gotta see this kid!'" Stacy recalls that the kid had a puny little skateboard with the trucks set three inches from the back of the board. "There was hardly any tail, but he was able to get a small amount of leverage from the board and pop it. Somehow, skateboarding worked for him this way."

Alan, the "kid," and Stacy hit it off immediately. When Stacy went back to California, he tried to get Alan onto the G & S team, but things didn't work out. After several months, Stacy left G & S and joined up with George Powell and formed Powell Peralta. Alan was one of the first people Stacy called and he immediately put him on the Powell Peralta team, which became the Bones Brigade.

Stacy recounts the next part of the story: "I brought Alan out to California and he stopped by a practice at the Winchester Skatepark. He was doing ollies and people were impressed. I told him, 'Go home and practice so you can do this trick off a ramp.'" Alan went back to Florida and within two weeks he called Stacy with the news that he could pop a two-foot ollie off a ramp.

Skate/surf photographer Jim Cassimus was brought in to shoot Alan's breakthrough trick, now being performed on a ramp. The ollie moved from being known by a few people to international exposure in *SkateBoarder* magazine. Over the years, many people have modified the ollie and taken it to the next level. But it is thanks to Alan Gelfand and his unique way with a board that skateboarding has entered areas previously unimagined.

73

Most skateboarders, no matter how good they become, usually start their career on a mass market board bought at the local department store. Their parents are not really sure if skateboarding is merely a fad and worry if spending over a hundred dollars is worth it, so they opt for the low-cost alternative. Here is a list of low-budget boards that most skaters will remember from their novice days:

Nash. Spanning four decades, many skaters got their start from this mass producer of skateboards. Prices weren't always low budget either! Wherever there's a department store, you'll find Nash . . .

Skee Skate. Over 500,000 sold by 1965! Painfully small metal wheels. Suggested retail price: $3.00 Now highly collectable.

Roller Derby. Imagine, a skateboard for $1.99 — used at your peril! These boards now sell to collectors for over $500!

Newporter Continental. The Jaws kick-tail model was a particularly interesting graphic.

Shark Board. Working off the same groove as the Jaws model, the ad copy told the whole gnarly story: "engineered with torso-flex . . . scientifically designed flex for optimum handling even on the most radical runs." Just beware of the water!

Cal 240. An immensely popular plastic skateboard that came with Universal Grabber wheels.

Gren Tec. Ask yourself: "Did you go for the GT Spoiler or were you the GT Coyote type?" A mass marketer that produced skateboards on the level of Nash.

Hang Ten Sportsboards. Lots of funky designs on these fiberglass babies! Wood models also available

The 01' Mersedes Bends. It might sound like a fine upscale board, but this was plastic throughout.

California Free Former. Boards for every budget — from plastic to wood.

Ampul. "Still the best for less" — a wide assortment of boards starting at $12 complete!

Jay Adams

Jay Adams' legendary status in the skateboard world stems from his exploits both on and off a board. A skater and surfer since the age of five, Jay was successful in both freestyle and vertical riding. His aggressive surf style coupled with his wild image garnered him many fans. An original member of the Zephyr surf and skate team, Jay influenced a generation of skaters.

Steve Alba (Salba)

A huge force in both pool and pipe, "Le Machine" dominated the Upland Skatepark along with Mt Baldy. Known for his awesome feats in the desert pipes of Arizona (some over 20 feet in diameter), Salba would kickturn over the vertical part.

Brad Bowman

Brad rode for Sims Skateboards and was heavily featured in many skate magazines during the 1970's and early '80's. He was a major threat in pool competitions. "Skateboarding means to me INDIVIDUALITY, FREEDOM and FUN!!!"

Steve Cathey

Steve's style was surf inspired and extremely smooth. He rode for Gordon & Smith Fibreflex and was the innovator of many freestyle tricks. Steve was also pictured on *SkateBoarder's* subscription envelope inside the magazine. More recently, Steve's image can be found on logos from longboard manufacturer Sector 9. "For me, skateboarding came about as a mode of transportation, it was a reflection of surfing. When the surf wasn't good, we skateboarded. For me, being a pro was the best experience I could have had. It was an opportunity that any kid would have loved."

Chris Chaput

Chris excelled in freestyle and was known for numerous handstand variations. He appeared on a number of televised skateboard contests. Originally sponsored by Logan Earth Ski, he went on to ride for Belair.

Eddie Elguera

"El Gato" is credited with a number of amazing vertical moves. Originally sponsored by Variflex, he was the first guy to pull frontside rock and rolls, frontside inverts into fakie (later called the Elguerial), and fakie ollies. He was an outstanding vert rider in both the '70's and '80's.

Henry Hester

Nicknamed "The Bad H," Henry was one of the kings of slalom skateboarding. Hester had his own deck on Gordon & Smith along with his signature wheel marketed by Road Rider. As vertical riding became more popular in the late '70's, Hester started a series of skate competitions that were the foundation for vertical contests.

Skitch Hitchcock

Known as an innovator and master craftsman, Skitch designed and made his own decks. He was also an excellent freestyle skater and blew people away with his gorilla grip. This trick consisted of Skitch skating barefoot and grabbing both ends of the boards with his toes and leaping off ramps. He could spin a complete 360 mid air with the board gripped by his toes. A health food nut, Skitch once said that drinking carrot juice made him jump higher.

Tom Inouye

"Wally" was one of the premier vert riders of the 1970's. He was one of the first to get air out of a vertical ramp. Wally was the designer and builder of the Del Mar Skatepark. Also known primarily for his company, "Inoyoue's Pool Cleaning Service." Possessed one of the smoothest riding styles of any skater.

Shogo Kubo

An original Z-Boy from Dogtown, Shogo was known for an incredibly smooth style. He was an immensely popular skater and went on to become the resident pro at the Cherry Hill Skatepark in New Jersey.

Steve Olson

"Bulky" dominated vertical skating in the late 1970's. In 1978 John Krisik, director of competition for Santa Cruz Skateboards, summed up Steve's talents in the magazine, *Wide World of Skateboarding:* "I believe that Steve is the number one bowl rider in the

Laura Thornhill

A graceful freestylist who rode for Logan Earth Ski, Laura was known for her space walk 360's. "Skateboarding was it for me. It was my way of life for many years. I have a collection of longboards in my garage along with a Laura Thornhill model and now I just ride for fun."

world today. He has so many strengths: He's physically sound, well coordinated, and has a great sense of spontaneity. He can walk into an unfamiliar bowl and begin to rip it right away." Steve rode for Santa Cruz and was on the original test team for Independent Trucks.

Stacy Peralta

Original Z-Boy who went on to more fame with Gordon & Smith (his Warptail model was a best seller). A master of both vertical and freestyle skating. When Stacy joined up with George Powell to create Powell Peralta it became one of the biggest skate companies of all time.

Doug Saladino

Nicknamed "Pineapple," Doug was one of freestyle's greatest talents in the mid to late 1970's. He started skateboarding in 1971 and at the age of 13 was sponsored by Gordon & Smith Skateboards. Pineapple also became an accomplished vertical rider, placing in the top five in numerous contests.

Denis Shufeldt

One of the pioneers of skateboarding, Shufeldt was known primarily as a speed racer and downhill master. At one time he was the team captain for Bahne. He utilized yoga and stylized fairing techniques to attain speeds of 50+ miles per hour. Even at these speeds Denis would maintain flawless control.

Gregg Weaver

Gregg wound up on the cover of *SkateBoarder* magazine's vol. 2, no. 1 — their first issue since the 1960's. His smooth, surf-like style influenced a generation of skaters. Gregg was also featured in the Cadillac Wheels print advertising campaigns and became known as the "Cadillac Kid."

Chris Yandall

One of the world's most famous slalom riders, Chris rode for Gordon & Smith. Included in the sponsorship was his own "honey-colored" Yandall wheel. Chris is credited with inventing the Samoan Squat. This trick took a regular nose wheelie one step further. To pull it off, the rider had to squat down while maintaining a wheelie.

70s Legends

My Skateboard Story

By Tannis Watson

As a teenager, skateboarding was a passion, an all-consuming activity. When I was not on that plank with four wheels, I was thinking about it, often dreaming about it. The friendships I made, the adventures we had, will stay with me forever. This is my story.

I grew up the son of a United States naval officer, in itself a big adventure. We traveled the world, from the tropical islands of the Philippines to the Pacific Northwest of the U.S. In March of 1974 we found ourselves in Long Beach, California. It was there, not long after the urethane wheel was invented by Frank Nasworthy, that my introduction to skateboarding began. Interestingly enough, my first skateboard came to be in much the same fashion that the very first skate-

board came about — an old steel-wheeled roller skate was sacrificed to the "cause." Nailed to a two by four, it provided a few hours of amusement and a number of bumps and scrapes to me and my compatriots. My friend Bobby, my brother Perry and myself quickly graduated to clay, and then plastic/urethane wheels (Super Surfers) with X-Caliber trucks. The only reason I know this is because I still have a pair of each wheel style and a couple of sets of the trucks!

With the acquisition of my first set of urethane wheels, "Roller Sports Racing Slicks," and the absence of the tooth-rattling, bone-jarring ride of the previous wheels, my skating really took off. I found that I had the natural sense of balance to skate, and with the advent of

the urethane wheel the ride and traction problems were laid to rest. At this point the focus became learning and practicing tricks. Freestyle streetskating was the rage at this time. The big tricks I worked on were 360's, handstands, and nose and tail wheelies. We built little launch ramps, and fooled around with slalom as well. Our time in Long Beach was brief, and in July 1974 we moved to Alameda, California, in the San Francisco Bay area.

Skateboarding in Alameda was a great time with great friends. My freestyling was refined, and we became creative, inventing new tricks and refining our style. Skateboarding was really hot during this period, all the kids in the neighborhood were on skateboards. Just as quickly, it seemed to lose popularity, with just a few of us hardcore skaters staying with it. Frank Mixon, Lowell Stephenson, and my brother Perry were among the few that kept skating.

It was about this time that I saw the first issue of *SkateBoarder* magazine. This magazine became our bible, it was vital to our learning new tricks. One of the tricks I saw in *SkateBoarder* was the "Gorilla Grip." This trick just blew my mind! Created by Skitch Hitchcock, mastered by Ed Nadalin, it was a trick that I became obsessed with learning. I bought a thin, fiberglass deck equipped with X-Caliber trucks and small Power Paw wheels. This became the vehicle for learning this awesome trick. I spent hours tearing my bare toes up, repeatedly trying it over and over again. Eventually I got it, but it was one of the toughest tricks I ever did.

Lowell Stephenson was a tall, athletic African American kid who was one of the hottest freestyle skaters I ever knew. We spent hours skating together, building boards, and perfecting a freestyle routine that intertwined with each other's individual tricks. It culminated in a trick where he came at me doing a "plange" and I "Gorilla Gripped" over him! It was an awesome trick that always brought a cheer from the crowd watching. Skating with Lowell was always a blast, and my memories of this time are very fond.

In September of 1976 we moved to Mira Mesa, California, in the San Diego area. It was here that my skateboarding ability reached its pinnacle. Initially, my brother Perry and I continued to street-skate, but when Carlsbad Skatepark opened, the whole complexion of skateboarding changed. It was there that vert skating came to be for me. There was no looking back after that — vert was where it was at!

At this same time we began surfing; our parents, always supportive of our endeavors, bought us used surfboards and new wet suits. Our lifestyle, everything we did, was focused on surfing and skateboarding. We were total grems, and we had found Mecca! Surfing and skateboarding in San Diego was great, and the fondest memories of my youth are centered on this time. When the waves were flat, we skated; when we could get to the beach, we surfed; we hung out with our friends and just had some good times.

We moved onto the Naval Air Station at Miramar in February of 1977. On the base we made new friends and sought new venues for skating. Now, military bases offer interesting and diverse terrain to skate on; unfortunately most of those places are off limits! The Navy finally agreed the skaters needed a place of their own to express themselves, and area next to the Teen Center, on an old building foundation, was set aside to build some ramps on. The Navy had its own carpenters build the ramps — we, of course, modified them later. These ramps were the catalyst for some of the best skate sessions I ever had. And always with great friends, like Gerald Russell, Rob Davies and Scott Davidson. It was there that my skating style became very refined. At that time I felt I was among the best there was at skateboarding. It was the peak of my skating ability. They called NAS Miramar "Fightertown USA"; we renamed it "Skatertown USA"!

In late January of 1978 my dad retired from the Navy, and we moved to Kearney, Nebraska, of all places. In Kearney, my brother Perry and I were the new hot shots. We brought the hottest new tricks and styles with us from California. We even caught the attention of the local news and were interviewed for TV! Before long my attention was diverted away from skateboarding, mostly due to girls and cars! The intensity wasn't there any more, probably because the environment was not the same as it was in California. Whatever the reason, I let skateboarding, such a vital part of my youth, slip away from me.

But one night, in 1982 or 1983, I reached back to that time of a few years before. A girlfriend and I were just cruising around town one night, we went by a sweet little motel swimming pool. I had noticed it before, but every time we had checked it in the past it was half full of water, or full of debris. A perfect key-hole-shaped pool — it was a skater's dream! On this night it was empty, dry and had been freshly painted. I couldn't resist! Back to my apartment we went to retrieve my skateboards and to change into my trusty Birdwells beach britches. We spent the next two hours, Suzie softly singing in the shallow end and me shredding the coping and carving the tile. It was after midnight, and I figured we would be busted at any minute. We weren't, and it was a magic night, one that I think of often.

After that I drifted completely away from skateboarding, going on to other thrills, like motorcycle drag racing. But that period of my life was a great time with good friends I will never forget. Now, 15 years later, I find myself being drawn back into the sport. The longboard revolution has really caught my attention. I have quickly joined this new skate movement, my particular focus being downhill, and vert. I am enjoying it as much this time as I did as a teen. Married now, my two daughters too are coming along with their skating ability. I hope my experience and joy of skateboarding will carry on with them.

We were not famous, we did not win contests, we simply skated for the pure love of it. We were soul skaters, and that attitude and feeling will stay with me for all of my life. I will always be proud to call myself a skateboarder.

Tony Alva

In His Own Words

Tony "Mad Dog" Alva, legendary skater and bad boy of the '70's skate scene, has had an enormous influence on skateboarding. His radical, aggressive style changed skateboarding forever, and his ability to tear up both vertical and horizontal terrain made him the superstar of the '70's. Alva also enjoyed tremendous success with Alva Skates. In these excerpts from an interview with Tim Chiappetta, first printed in *The SkateTrader* magazine, he recalls his skating career and the philosophy behind his skateboard venture.

When did you start skateboarding?
I didn't really get serious about skating until I was about 10 years old and that was about 1967. Basically, it was all based around sidewalk surfing.

Is surfing what drew you into skateboarding?
Yeah, as far as what my style was all about and my attitude towards skating. It was all about taking the moves that we were doing in the water, surfing, and putting them on concrete, which was so accessible to us living and growing up in Santa Monica. A lot of concrete to ride.

So it sounds like surfing also influenced your style of riding?
Most of the guys who influenced my riding were guys that had been skating in the '60's, guys like Torger Johnson for example. They were freestyle champions that were surfers. Their cross training and their influences was surfing to begin with. So that's why my style and a lot of my influence comes from the same medium, from the water.

What was the skate scene like in the early '70's?
It was pretty groovy. It was real low prof and to be a skater was really, really unique. It wasn't like every other kid nowadays that has skateboard out doing flip tricks. It was an old school surf style. Back then the skate community was real small and tight. Everybody knew everybody. The competitions were based around hot dog and freestyle tricks, stuff like that. What we started to do was to take the flatland onto the vert, on banks and in pools.

When was that?
That was in the mid '70's, so skating took a huge jump from, like, 1967 to 1975 or '76. That's when vertical started to come in; that's when the scene really started changing. The aggressiveness, the style and the terrain obviously presented more risk to your body. So that's when it really started to evolve, in the mid '70's.

So before vert what style of flatland riding was being done?
It was like slalom and freestyle and a little bit of downhill, stuff like that. That's when bank skating came in, and as the bank skating got more radical it evolved into vertical. Like backyard pools and ramps. People didn't even know how to build a ramp back then, let alone one with a flat bottom. They were emulating building a fullpipe with no roof.

Did fullpipe skating play a big part in skating then?

Fullpipes came into view with a lot of the water projects that were going on back then. Drainage projects from the Colorado River. There was a lot of guys that were searching and finding a lot of huge underground pipes. So in the mid '70's things were transforming from a flatland sidewalk surfing style to a hardcore vertical approach to skateboarding.

So why did vertical become its own thing in the mid '70's?

Vertical skating let people realize that they weren't limited to just skating on the walls; you could actually come out off the lip, get air and basically do things that were impossible to do before.

Skateboarding tends to have a bad name nowadays; how was it viewed back then?

It was always a real rebel sport, we were always looked down on because of our aggressiveness and our attitude. It became commercially acceptable in the late '70's and early '80's because anything and everything skateboarding was so popular. Back then everywhere you looked there was skateboarding. There was a skateboard on a billboard, there was skating in commercials and in movies. It got to the point where it became such a part of society that it got right to the edge of being commercial, but not quite because the skaters were so hardcore it was hard for society to accept them. Especially guys like myself because we always had such a hardcore attitude. Our attitude was like, "We skate — f**k you!" We are what we are because we skateboard and that's it. I think that attitude still carries on even today. If you don't skate, then you can't relate, and that's all there is to it.

What were some of the places that you were skating back then?

There were a lot of parks in the '70's, so I skated a lot of them. Whenever I toured other countries like England and Europe I was basically transported from park to park. I was just doing the skatepark tour, but that wasn't what I really enjoyed. The thing that I enjoyed most was skating natural terrain like I still do today. That's like banks, pools and pipes. Stuff that's built by man to serve one purpose, but when you have the mentality of a skater and you see this terrain, you can see moves that these people that built it never saw. Basically, that's your canvas, as far as what skating is to me, it's all art form. It's a release of all your energy out on the terrain, your canvas and creation of your own art.

What was the style of the parks then compared to the parks of today?

Parks were different. They had a lot of snake runs incorporated in them. They basically had the old school vert terrain, which was pretty cool, and some of that stuff is coming back in some of the parks going up in the north. The older-style parks have definitely influenced the parks of today. Back then there was a big demand for cement parks and I think that made skating grow. The best park that I ever rode was in Cherry Hill, New Jersey. They had the best pool ever.

They had a pool called the Egg Bowl and that was probably the best pool built by Wally Holiday, an old friend of mine. That would have to be the best pool I ever rode. I heard there's one down in Brazil that's pretty good. The one in Rio De Janeiro which looks real similar to the one I'm talking about. Cherry Hill was indoors and they could slide all the doors

It's a release of all your energy out on the terrain, your canvas and creation of your own art

open to let air in. Cherry Hill had a really good atmosphere and a really good local scene. I have friends from back then that I met at Cherry Hill 15 years ago and still stay in contact with and occasionally still see at trade shows and different skating events even to this day. That spirit of the skating of the '70's still lives with me today.

It's funny being involved in the industry as long as I have because you shoot more photos and people just want to take pictures of you being part of the scene with skating. I enjoy more than anything, just getting out there and just skating, not skating for the cameras, just skating for myself; if the cameras are there, cool.

Is the enjoyment of just skating for yourself what kept you active with the sport so long?

Yeah, it's like with surfing and snowboarding. To me it's a way of staying healthy and staying in tune with what's going on with the youth because I'm totally into working with the kids and sharing some of my experiences with them. It's important that they know where skating came from, but I don't stress that on them. Kids just want to do their own thing and that's cool with me, because when I was a kid I was just as hardcore and hardheaded as these kids want to be. But I think that they should realize that if it wasn't for guys like me and all of my bros that broke the ice, like when I jumped on that ramp during the Rollerblade demo — all the Rollerbladers were dissin' us skaters. Somebody has to break the outer layer to show what can be done. If nobody is willing to push the limits then nothing ever happens. You've got to school a little bit, but not force feed them. If you do that they get turned off. Give it to them in small doses and if they dig it, cool — it works out.

How old were you when you started Alva?

I was 19 years old and basically I built a

reputation as Men's Overall World Professional Skateboard Champion. I had the world's record in the Guinness Book for barrel jumping and just doing crazy s**t. Obviously some of the stuff I did was spur of the moment, I never practiced jumping barrels, that just happened, but with that reputation under my belt is when and why I started Alva, my own company.

What were early Alva Skateboards like in comparison with today?

They evolved from a basic seven- or eight-inch laminated wood kicktail to what you see today. We were one of the first manufacturers to come out with a kicktail and laminated boards. I still have some of the old boards with the die-cut grip tape that I just keep for memorabilia. Some people have a horseshoe over their door, I've got one of my old boards. I'm not a pack rat so I don't collect a lot of this stuff, but everything started with the seven-inch kicktails, then we went into the 10 inch, the really big, fat, pig-shaped boards. Then it transformed and went to a lighter beam board, called the "light beam." We did that board for a while. We were still doing wide boards geared for vert, but we started experimenting with strange shapes. Using fish tails, money bumps on the sides of the rails. Everybody on my team had a different personality, so we tried to design a board to fit their individual personality. We came up with a lot of pretty wack ideas. Now the boards have gotten streamlined again, like 60's surfboards. Back to the rounded dual tip boards.

As far as Alva goes I'm still manufacturing a board for the old school pool riders and for guys that want to ride bigger boards. I've got two longboards, I've got a 34-inch longboard and a 36-inch longboard, they are no wider than nine inches. They look a lot like surfboard shapes, but the wheel bases are customized, set up not only for vert skating but street too. The board I'm riding now is a 34 -¼ inch with a 17-inch wheel base. It's the kind of

board that you can haul ass down a hill on, ride street on, skate in pools and still be happy with just that one board. My goal is to have a board that you can use for everything, that's not just limited to street or vert. For Alva, that's really important because when I see somebody riding one of my boards I don't want them to be a stereotypical streetskater or vert skater. I like to see a person who has an open mind and likes to skate everything. The boards have evolved from a primitive design to a very modern technical design. For Alva, it's a natural progression.

Being such a veteran, do you have any comments on the evolution of the industry?

I think some of the things are gimmicky and nonsense, like the big baggy pants and all the skinny little street boards. That s**t's gonna come, gonna go, but everything has to go through a phase. From one extreme to another to get where function is really incorporated into the design. Like I was just saying, it's more important to have something that works for everything. A person anywhere from a beginner to advanced can go out and use it on any kind of terrain and just have a good time.

As far as clothing and dress, it's just fashion. Skateboarding has always been pretty fashion conscious. I think that skateboarders are the first ones to come out with the new ideas, make them evident on the street or wherever. I'm not saying that snowboarding or surfing bites off skating, but it is definitely influenced by skateboarding.

Skateboarders are usually the trend setters, the guys that are actually out on the street skating. They are the ones dictating the styles. A lot of people would argue that with me. Dedicated snowboarders say that they have their own style, which I think is starting to come of age, but basically all the stuff that's being done in the water and on the snow all carries from skateboarding.

As a person born in 1960, I literally grew up during the introduction, evolution, and refinement of "sidewalk surfing". Yes, I owned a clay wheel board in the late 60's. Yes, I spent more time on the ground than on the wood (due to the incredible unpredictability of clay wheels, which I now refer to as, "Flintstone tires"). Then in 1972 the world changed for me: I obtained a Banzai aluminum board (twin kicker) with composite wheels! The wheels would stick well in hard turns, hold well in vert situations, and were relatively predictable in terms of performance. I rode everywhere, to school, to my girlfriend's house, to football practice… Life was good.

In the late 1970's we discovered the lazy man's guide to skate happiness; yes, we found multi-level parking garages. Seven to ten stories high, great concrete, and no walking (for there was an elevator system)! Until the law caught on to what we were doing, each Friday and Saturday night was "Autotopia."

— Anonymous

autotopia

Russ began skating in 1958 at the age of nine. He kept skating throughout the 1960's, but it was only in 1974 when he really got serious about skateboarding. When the Bahne/Cadillac contest took place in 1975, Russ dominated the freestyle event. He was known for his gymnastic moves (including handstand jumps and three-finger handstands). However, he is best remembered for his incredible spinning ability. Russ Howell can spin 360's for a long, long time. His personal best is 163. Russ was sponsored by Vans, Power Paw and Pepsi. He even managed to venture out to Australia in 1975 for six months with Stacy Peralta to promote skateboarding in the land down under.

Russ Howell — Gymnastics Meets Freestyle

Interviewed by Dan Gesmer

What was the skate scene like when you started? How does that compare with the skate scene today?

Skateboarding was just being invented. When companies figured out there was market, products started showing up in the stores. Roller Derby and Chicago (both rollerskate manufacturers) made most of the stuff we were using back then. The early equipment was terrible, but we were young kids having fun and didn't know any better. Better equipment was introduced from companies like Hobie and Makaha. Surfing was still a major influence. We skated with our friends and made up tricks as we went along. The skate scene today is much more technical, but friends still gather together to push each other's limits.

Were you strictly a freestylist, or did you do other kinds of skating as well?

My surfing interest kept me riding skateboards throughout the years. I've always been interested in freestyle, but I also enjoy slalom racing and riding halfpipes. The halfpipe in my backyard is 10 feet high with various other heights. Competing in the old "Specialty Events" of the mid '70's was also fun: 360's and high jump.

How did you prepare for a contest?
Long hours of practice (6–10 every day)

helped make skating a reflex. I used to make maps of what tricks and lines I'd use during the freestyle event. Having the right music play helped me to remember that I was supposed to be having fun.

Did you get nervous during a contest, and if so, how did you deal with your nerves?

I remember competing in my home town at the Long Beach World Contest. Many of my friends were there, and I didn't want to disappoint them. My nerves were going crazy as I walked out onto the floor. I yelled at the top of my lungs, and the entire arena went silent. It helped, I wasn't thinking about my skating anymore.

How do you feel about flatland freestyle these days? Is there a future for it at all?

Skateboarding has always been a sport enjoyed primarily by youth. The young are often influenced by friends and the media. Streetstyle has become the #1 choice of most skaters. Too many of today's streetskaters have changed the old "Skate & Create" philosophy to "Skate & Destroy." The skate magazines don't promote flatland freestyle because they see no profit in it. I think freestylers will have to carry the burden of organizing their own events. I still prefer "old school" freestyle, but am eager to learn the new tricks. Can't we just all get along?

Why do you think freestyle died? Did it really die?

Many of the freestylists left the sport during the late '70's because their sponsors saw no profit in keeping them active. Only a handful were able to make the transition to the "new school" form. But I still get a lot of requests to teach "old school" freestyle to other skaters at the skatepark.

Have you invented any original tricks?

Freestyle had five main categories: footwork, spins, handstands, aerials, and multiple board tricks. I introduced many of the handstand variations.

Do you have any advice to both the newcomers and more experienced freestylers?

Never skate with the attitude that the sport or somebody else owes you something because of your efforts. Skating is its own reward. Being a better skater doesn't automatically qualify someone as being a better person. Strength isn't shown by pushing others over, but rather by lifting others up. Enjoy what you have and help others when you can. Poverty isn't the diminishing of one's possessions, but rather the increase of one's greed.

Pepsi Pro Skateboard Team Memories

PEPSI·COLA

By René Carrasco

I was honored to be a captain of the Orange County Pepsi Pro Skateboard Team from 1977 to 1981. There was a Los Angeles team and a team from San Bernadino. This was skateboarding's most prestigious pro team at the time. Pepsi demos always began with a skateboard safety speech geared to enlighten the public about skateboard safety equipment. We would do a safety inspection and display the newest boards and wheel designs. The presentation was done with a sense of humor, and we even performed a skateboard safety skit.

When the safety part of our presentation was finished, the Pepsi pro skaters would explode into the most exciting skateboard demonstrations to music. During the weekday school demos, the team would provide the students with refreshments (Mountain Dew, as I recall!)

Weekends and grand openings were a special time when the famous acrylic "Pepsi Ramp" was used to let the pros demonstrate their radical tricks on vertical. Another treat for the spectators was the demonstration of launch ramps. My brothers and I used "Sky Hooks" which attached to the board and enabled us to reach over seven feet of air. The Los Angeles team had two brothers, Dave and Paul Hackett, who used Velcro suspenders attached to their boards to get air.

My years on the team were definitely some of the greatest and happiest of my life. It was really an amazing and very gratifying feeling to be able to teach, share and help out young children to better their lives through skateboarding! I'd like to thank the Pepsi Cola Company for the generosity and to all the children (now adults!), skateboard fans, and those fortunate enough to witness skateboarding's most famous team, "the Pepsi Pro Skateboard team." It was truly a pleasure to entertain you.

85

Tony Magnusson, "Eagle Rock Ramp", Eagle Rock, California

Swedish Style

By Stefan Lillis Akesson

The very first "skateboarding boom" in Sweden was around 1977. A few boards had been sold before that, but 1977 was the year everyone got to know about skateboarding. One could read about it in newspapers, magazines and see it on television.

Almost immediately the media stated that skateboarding was a very dangerous sport, both for the skaters themselves and for pedestrians. Many cities banned skateboarding, but did not build any skateparks, as they claimed skateboarding was just one of those trends that would disappear in a year or so.

However, a few ramps and skateparks were built. New Sport House in Stockholm was one of the most attractive indoor skateparks in the late 70's. It was built in a former movie theater. The place was ruled by famous skaters like Tony Magnusson and Per Viking. Per was the very first Swede to have a "Who's Hot" profile in *SkateBoarder* and the first one to be on the cover. (Per tragically died in 1997.) Tony Magnusson moved to California in the early '80's, went pro, and now works in the industry.

Swedish freestyler Stefan Akesson executes a 50/50.

Another skatepark was Skateland, located outdoors in Gothenberg. Due to the long winter months Swedish skaters have always looked for indoor alternatives. Skate Saloon was an indoor skatepark, built in a former movie theater in a little town called Smedjebacken, located a few hours north of Stockholm. Skaters from nearby and far away towns went there in the winter months. A few names were Hans Gothberg (still skating and competing), Hans "Puttis" Jacobsson (still skates now and then), Mikael "Slappo" Adolfsson and Tarmo Salo. Although these skateparks are now gone (New Sport House is now a church), Swedish skaters from the '70's and early '80's will never forget them.

As there were not many indoor ramps, eager skateboarders tried to find places to skate and even built small ramps. It was not an easy task, basements and parking houses were usually the only good alternatives. But these places were perfect for freestyle! In Stockholm subway systems freestylers such as Per Welinder and Hans Lindgren perfected their freestyle tricks on the platforms. They were usually kicked out by security guards. A few hours north of Stockholm, in a town called Falun, I found a basement called K2. I was able to get my own key and practiced alone for many hours during the winter months. Now and then I would session with freestylers like Per Holknekt, Stefan Johansson and Uffe Hansson. Stefan Johansson perfected some of his stationary tricks in his own too-small basement in his hometown of Grängesberg. Stefan Spång skated indoors in Borlänge on an indoor asphalted soccer court. Very small, but large for a freestyler.

Some of these freestylers became very successful. Per Welinder moved to California, got picked up by Powell Peralta, did some stuntskating in *Back to the Future* and competed as a pro for many years, being the only one to beat Rodney Mullen. He also became a very good streetskater and ripped jump ramps and toured all over U.S. Per now runs Birdhouse with Tony Hawk, and occasionally pulls off some freestyle moves. Per Holknekt spent a few years in California and got his own signature model from Tracker. Per along with people such as Garry Scot Davies, Neil Blender, Larry Balma and Peggy Cozens helped form "The United Skate

Mike McGill

Front" and this eventually resulted in the magazine *TransWorld Skateboarding*. Holknekt now lives in Stockholm and runs a few skate/snowboard stores and Streetstyle Distribution. He does a few freestyle tricks a few times a year. Stefan Spång is seen on a miniramp now and then but can do double and triple kickflips anytime. Uffe Hansson quits and starts in a never-ending cycle, but only gets better. I have moved away from my lovely K2 basement, but wherever I have lived, I have so far managed to find an indoor place to skate. In the mid 1990's I formed the International Network for Flatland Freestyle Skateboarding and started to produce the newsletter *Flatline*. In 1998 the online version of *Flatline* appeared. Swedish skaters have done well in slalom, producing such

champions as Jani Söderhäll, Fabian Björnstierna and Peter Clock.

In the early '80's skateboarding lost the interest of the youth and was considered dead by most media. When the third boom hit in the mid '80's, the Swedish Skateboarding Association took form, and contests and the Swedish Cups were held all over Sweden. Sweden started the concept of a skateboard summer training camp. The first ones were held in Rättvik, a little town a few hours north of Stockholm out in the beautiful Swedish countryside. Skaters from all over Europe attended and the camps had trainers from the U.S., such as Mike Weed, Bob Skoldberg, Alan Gelfand, Stacy Peralta, Mike McGill and Stevie Caballero.

A few years later the camps moved to Stockholm (always to be missed by the girls in Rättvik . . .) and trainers were Rodney Mullen, Billy Ruff, Neil Blender, Mike McGill, Lance Mountain and Tony Hawk. Top skaters from all over Europe and the United States showed up.

In 1987 Swedish youths watched *Back to the Future* and skating made a big comeback. Camps became popular again, with both U.S. and Swedish trainers, but now only Swedish kids attended. Eventually, streetskating became popular and many talented streetskaters popped up from all parts of Sweden. Today, some of the new big names in Swedish skateboarding are Mattia Ringström, Ali Boulali, Pontus Alv and Chris Åström.

In the '90's, indoor skateparks are being built all over Sweden. Some are very small and of varying quality, while some are very good. Once again, the two most famous are located in Stockholm and Gothenburg – Fryshuset in Stockholm and Galaxen in Gothenberg.

Skateboarding Across America

I rode my first skateboard in 1964 in the small town of Sweetwater, Texas. My dad made that first board from some scrap plywood and a pair of steel-wheeled shoe skates. I also have a vague memory of what I think was the Hobie team performing a demo in our town. I didn't really skate again until 1969 when I found that same board in an old chest in our garage, at this time we were living in Anchorage, Alaska (I was a military brat).

My real involvement with skateboarding began the day after I graduated from Morro Bay high school in 1974, when I found an old Hobie laminate in my best friend's backyard. At this point I wasn't even aware of Cadillac wheels. So me and my pals put together some clay-wheeled wonders and began skating the local hills. After seeing a Bahne/Cadillac ad featuring Gregg Weaver in *Surfer* magazine, we jumped in a car and drove 150 miles to a surf shop that sold these new "wonder rollers."

Skateboarding soon became my life. My very first contest was the Bahne/Cadillac Nationals held at the Del Mar fairgrounds in 1975. I entered the slalom event, placing 18th. More importantly I got to meet skaters like Denis Shufeldt and Chris Yandall, and to feel the tremendous energy of this new sport. I soon began organizing contests in my local area. In 1976 myself and two friends decided to become the first skaters to cross the country by skateboard. We sent a letter to Roller Sports asking for sponsorship. They responded by offering us all the equipment we needed, t-shirts and $500 each if we finished the trip. Well, to say the least, we were stoked, grabbed an old road atlas and mapped out a route from Lebanon, Oregon, to Williamsburg, Virginia.

Three weeks later found us somewhere in eastern Oregon wondering what in the hell we were doing. The trek took 32 days and was full of adventures and wonderful people.

After the cross-country trip, I continued to compete in local contests and organize shop teams. I was also working for Good Clean Fun Surf and Skate at this time. In 1978 I helped to design the Solid Wave skatepark in Arroyo Grande. In 1977 I had attended the Signal Hill downhill race; after seeing the skatecars I knew this was something I had to try. With the help of Vetter Motorcycle fairings, Independent, Santa Cruz and *Cycle* magazine the Vetter Streamliner was born (this skatecar is

now on display at the HB Surf Museum). In the '78 Signal Hill race I tied with Henry Hester for second place; two weeks later at the Akron Soap Box Derby track I placed second to Nick Leonard in a race that was filmed and aired by CBS Sports Spectacular. I also raced slalom and stand-up downhill that summer on the Another Roadside Attraction Pro Tour in Colorado.

About this time I was being sponsored by Flite Skateboards; they happened to send me one of their early snowboard designs, with which, along with my friend Gary Fluitt, I proceeded to our nearby sand dunes. We totally immersed ourselves in the

development of sandboarding.

Some of you may remember our articles in *SkateBoarder, Action Now* and *Surfer*. We used to joke that we were the only professional sandboarders in the world. We were featured in surf movies, a television commercial for Arnold Palmer Sportswear of Japan, "That's Incredible" and some lame kids' show called "We're Movin'" featuring Willie Ames. We even started a little sand/snowboard company called A-Team (we had the name before the stupid TV show). I remember being at some of the early snowboard events and seeing Jake (Burton) Carpenter trade boards for his motel bill.

In 1984 I once again skateboarded across the country, this time with Bob Denike, Paul Dunn and Gary Fluitt; with the improved equipment and a little training we were able to complete the trip in 26 days.

During the early '90's I was heavily involved in collecting old skateboards and memorabilia. Dale Smith and Todd Huber, along with Stacy Peralta and the guys from Screamin Squeegees now own 99% of my old collection.

Over the years I have had the pleasure of working for/with people such as Dave Dash (*SkateBoarder, Action Now*), Larry Balma, Peggy Cousins (Tracker, TWS), Rich Novak (NHS), and meeting skaters from all over the world, including Beau Brown, who remains a true friend and confidant to this day.

Sometimes it's hard to believe that it's been 32 years since I took that first ride. And now as I turn 40 I look forward to skating with my two sons, and sharing the wonders of that "Magic Rolling Board."

—Jack Smith

The Third (1983-91) Wave

More legal wrangling and competition from other youth pursuits like BMX biking led to a second fallow period for skateboarding in the early 1980s. Although skate contests were held, the turnout was small and the prize money was even smaller. But, as in the past, a core of dedicated skaters kept the sport alive. In 1981, *Thrasher* magazine began publication in an effort to provide hardcore skaters with information on the skateboard scene.

By 1983, skate manufacturers were beginning to see the sport on the upswing and *Transworld Skateboarding* magazine entered the skate scene. Vert riding took off in 1984, followed closely by streetstyle skating. Launch ramps became popular. Powell Peralta created the first "Bones Brigade" skate video, which helped to propel skateboarding to new levels of popularity. Numerous vertical champions emerged, including Tony Hawk, Christian Hosoi, Lance Mountain and Neil Blender. In the street, Mark Gonzales, Natas Kaupas and Tommy Guerrero created new ollie variations. Freestyle skateboarding was also a part of the scene and Rodney Mullen dominated all competition. Board royalties and contest winnings escalated, and some pro skaters pulled down earnings of ten thousand dollars a month. The National Skateboard Association, headed by Frank Hawk, held numerous contests across North America and eventually throughout the world.

Dozens of new manufacturers sprung up, but in the mid to late 1980's three handled most of the skate market — Powell Peralta, Vision/Sims and Santa Cruz. Skateboard shoes from Airwalk, Vans and Vision became enormously popular, along with skate fashion, even among non-skaters.

Toward the end of the decade, the focus shifted to streetskating, and vert riding became less popular. A number of pro skaters decided to leave the larger manufacturers and start their own skate companies. One of the first to do this was Steve Rocco, who started up World Industries. "New school" skateboarding was born. Its focus was on ollies and technical tricks, and it took on a whole new attitude.

By 1991, a worldwide recession hit and the skate industry was deeply affected. As in the past, a number of manufacturers were faced with large financial losses. The industry turned extremely negative and began the process of reinventing itself.

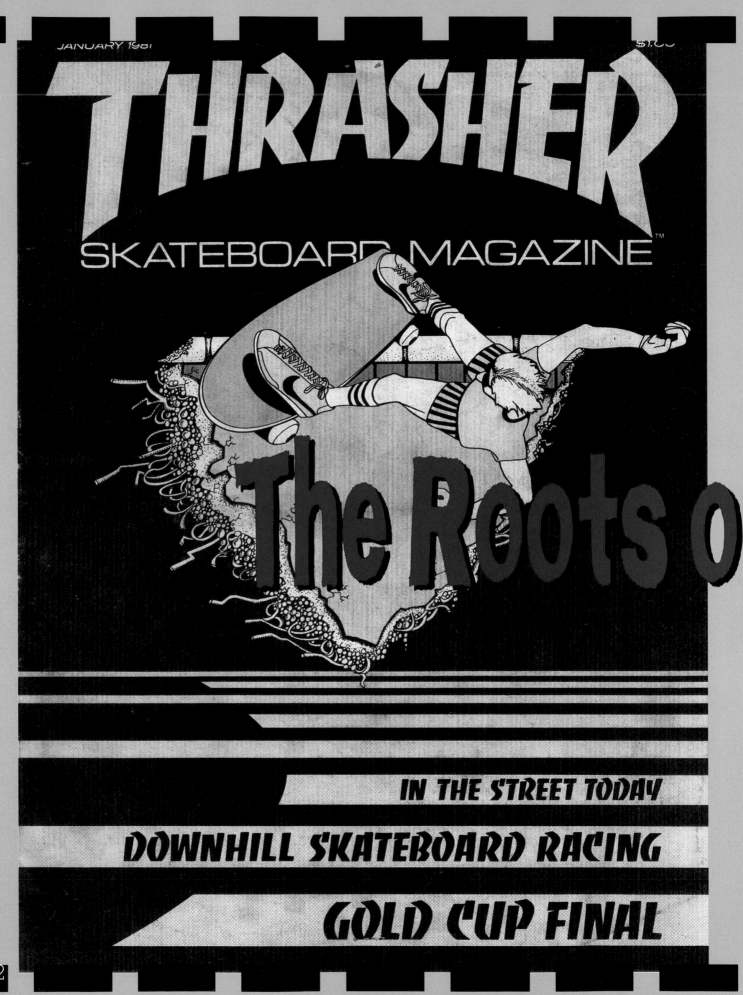

JANUARY 1981 $1.00

THRASHER
SKATEBOARD MAGAZINE ™

The Roots of

IN THE STREET TODAY

DOWNHILL SKATEBOARD RACING

GOLD CUP FINAL

By August of 1980, *SkateBoarder* magazine had morphed into *Action Now* and there were no "skateboard only" magazines left. *Action Now* featured a variety of sports including BMX, windsurfing, and once even featured a horseback-riding photo (page 44, Oct. 1980 issue). In trying to appeal to a wider audience, *Action Now* upset a lot of skaters who wished to have a skateboard-only magazine. As Fausto Vitello, manufacturer of Independent Trucks, explained, "The people who put together *Action Now* thought skateboarding was a fad. Their publication didn't address the skateboard market."

After *Action Now*'s decision to cover more sports, Fausto decided to create his own publication. "I approached the skateboard industry with the idea of a skateboard-only magazine and received a cold shoulder. We had Kevin Thatcher do a mock up and there was no response." It was then that

Skate and Destroy

Fausto decided to get money from other sources. He gathered as much money as he could find, along with some investors, and formed a publishing company called High Speed Productions. *Thrasher* hit the newsstands in January 1981. This was the period when many skateboard parks had closed. Skateboarding's second bust had come, leaving in its wake only the truly dedicated. *Thrasher*'s philosophy from the start was to be a magazine written by skateboarders for skateboarders. The impact on the skateboard community was immediate: "Skaters loved it," remarks Fausto.

The original format of *Thrasher* was much larger than what you see today. It had the same dimensions as the old *Rolling Stone*. "The reason the magazine was originally large," explains Fausto, "was that my friend had a printing press that was set up for that size of paper. We found out, however, that the large size was a problem to distribute and that advertisers had to create special-size ads. Eventually we shrank the magazine down to a standard size."

Thrasher was originally printed on newsprint. Over the years the quality of its paper has improved, but as Fausto is quick to point out, "it's not about glossy stock." In fact the only glossy part about *Thrasher* is the cover. The logo has remained the same since inception.

The two people skaters identify most closely with *Thrasher* are publisher Edward Riggins and editor Kevin Thatcher (who has since become co-publisher). Kevin's artwork graced the first cover and his editorial spelled out exactly the *Thrasher* philosophy. The following is an excerpt from that editorial, entitled "Grab That Board."

The average individual was never properly exposed to the unlimited possibilities of a platform with four wheels under it — a simple, basic, mechanical device which serves as an energy-efficient mode of transportation, a basis for a valid sporting activity, and as a vehicle for aggressive expression."

Meanwhile, at the height of the skatepark explosion, the skaters have been virtually swept off the streets and deposited in the parks, where the action is radical but lacks the inspiration of a knock down, drag-out backyard pool session or a skate cruise down the boulevard with the crew.

There's no rule saying you have to go fast or skate vertical. Just being outside or in the skatepark practicing maneuvers and balancing is a lot of fun. Remember, there are tons of asphalt and concrete being poured every day, so — GRAB THAT BOARD!

From the start, *Thrasher*'s mission was to cover all aspects of skateboarding, from downhill to vertical to street to freestyle. *Thrasher* also put a great deal of effort towards introducing its readership to new music. From Punk to New Wave to Metal to Hip Hop, *Thrasher* has always kept its finger on the pulse of new music. The fact that *Thrasher* happened to be based in San Francisco meant they were able to closely document the California Punk/Thrash scene of the 1980's.

Numerous skaters have contributed their photographs or writings to *Thrasher*. A short list includes people like Brad Bowman, Bruce Walker, Rick "Ask the Doctor" Blackhart, Bob Denike, Stacy Peralta, and Rodney Mullen.

During skateboarding's slump in the early '80's, Fausto Vitello went on the road to promote the sport. He even did backyard contests complete with barbecues. "Whatever it took," recalls Fausto. "It was about pure skateboarding. It was a matter of survival. We were keeping the spirit alive." Fausto's dedication and *Thrasher*'s skateboarding focus played a vital role in resuscitating the sport, building up to its Third Wave.

One very important part of the magazine's history is that well before the Internet and World Wide Web became everyday words, *Thrasher* ran a very popular BBS site. This kept skaters from around the world informed.

While some people have disagreed with Fausto's philosophy, his influence on skateboarding cannot be understated. He has had a dramatic impact on equipment, skating styles and, of course, publishing.

He is direct about his magazine's role in the skateboard world: "Skateboarding attracts a unique person. It influences the rest of society. *Thrasher* is not about hypocrisy or selling out to corporate America. We are about skate and destroy."

Since 1983 *Transworld Skateboarding* has provided the skate world with visually stunning material and a different perspective than *Thrasher* magazine. This perspective comes from *Transworld*'s founder, Larry Balma. In the beginning, Larry was joined by a number of dedicated individuals, including Peggy Cozens, Neil Blender, John Webster, Bryan Ridgeway, Garry Scott Davies, Per Holknekt, and Grant Brittain. Collectively, their organization was called the United Skate Front and it published *Transworld Skateboarding*.

The beginnings:

Larry Balma: When *Action Now* stopped publication, many skateboard manufacturers were frustrated. There was a small group of manufacturers but there weren't enough to start a magazine. *Thrasher* magazine was pretty hardcore at the time. There was sex and drugs and rock n' roll. In the early '80's the skateboarding boom started up again. We had parents going into the stores. At the time there were only a few manufacturers and none of us had the money to print up catalogs for the shops so the ads in the magazine were our catalog.

The shop owner would open up *Thrasher* magazine to show off the product to little Johnny and his mom or dad in Arizona or North Carolina or wherever they are. The parents look at *Thrasher* and see some pretty gnarly stuff in there — a lot of punk stuff, etc., and parent says, "Wait a minute, let's go look at the soccer balls." We were losing our customers. As much as me and the rest of the industry talked to *Thrasher* about making it work for the mainstream a little bit more, they were sold on their part of it. And their part of it has a place. So we ended up doing a magazine.

The editorial of the FIRST edition:

The United Skate Front was formed by a concerned group of skaters consisting of skate greats,

The FIRST issue!

MAY/JUNE 1983
VOL. 1 NO. 1

TRANS-WORLD
SKATEBOARDING

SKATE
CREATE

★ RAMP BATTLE ★
DEL MAR
RUSTY HARRIS SERIES WRAP-UP 1982

COLLECTOR'S EDITION
TWO RAD CENTERFOLDS!

THE G
☆ ★ RAMP

DEL MAR
.......REVISITED
RUSTY HARRIS SERIES WRAP-UP 1982

COLLECTOR

TWO RAD CE

uninhibited artists, radical skaters, old timers, new-comers, and even moms and dads. We are all hard working skater enthusiasts uniting together to make for you, the true skateboarders of the world, a magazine that covers every aspect of the sport of skateboarding — nationally and internationally.

You are the skateboarders and we like you — New Wave, old wave-hip, hippie-hillbilly, rocka-billy-punk, funk-surf style, streetstyle-ski style, freestyle-radical, mellow-mod, rasta-hard rock, cool jazz-country, city-integrated, ethnic-blues, soul-awesome, gnarly . . .

Anyone, anywhere, anytime, anywave . . . We like our sport, we like our world, we like you!

Join us in a United effort to show the world our awesome sport. They haven't seen anything yet!

— The United Skate Front

Question:

Did you ever think that Transworld would become larger than it was in the 1980's?

LB: No, not really. I mean we're just doing it because it's fun and it's what we like to do. My whole philosophy of life here is that we spend more waking hours at work than we do anything else. So you better do something that you have fun doing and surround yourself with people you like to be around. If you can do that, you're doing pretty good.

Since its inception, *Transworld Skateboarding* has consistently come up with an innovative and visually appealing look. Photographers like Tod Swank, Grant Brittain, O, and Lance Mountain have provided readers with a stunning array of images. Contributing writers over the years have varied from industry insiders like Stacy Peralta and Paul Schmitt to pros like Ed Templeton, Tony Hawk, and Rodney Mullen.

As its name implies, *Transworld Skateboarding* has always tried to embrace every facet of skateboarding from every area of the world. Its success shows that this positive, open approach has struck a chord with a wide range of readers.

MAY/JUNE 1983
VOL. 1 NO. 1
$1.75

ARDING

R'S EDITION

ENTERFOLDS!

97

Powell — The Story Behind the Skulls and Bones

Symbiosis has been a hallmark of skateboarding. Skaters push their boards to the limits; skateboard makers constantly strive to remove the boards' limitations. The energy and creativity of both have joined to make skateboarding the incredibly dynamic sport it is today.

It is not surprising, therefore, that the vast majority of those manufacturing skateboards are also skaters themselves. For over two decades, the Powell Corporation/Powell Peralta has provided skateboarders with some truly memorable skateboard products. George Powell began riding a homemade skateboard in 1957 and by 1965 he had an oak board with clay wheels. He studied engineering at Stanford University and occasionally would hop onto a board.

"In 1974, I was working for an aerospace company in engineering sales and my son had come to me and asked for a skateboard. So I pulled one of the Hobie Super Surfers from the garage and he started to ride it," remembered George. The next day George's son came back and said, "It's no good 'cause all my friends have yellow wheels." The yellow wheels turned out to be urethane and George realized this was truly a product breakthrough.

George then went out and bought a pultruded (plastic) board. He didn't like the ride, so he went out and purchased a Fibreflex. He liked the ride, but was caught up with the idea of designing his own boards. As George related to *SkateBoarder* in 1978, "Urethane wheels had turned a toy into a real vehicle with exciting potential. As soon as I discovered this, I wanted to see if my engineering design experience could be used to further improve skateboards."

He then began testing various prototype boards and wheels in his home and really got into things: "I picked up some premixed urethane that I could bake in my oven and I started making my own wheels." Originally, the boards were quite rigid and combined aircraft aluminum and fiberglass skins with aluminum honeycomb, foam, and spruce cores. One day, while testing a board at Pacific Palisades High School's parking lot, he met up with legendary skateboarder and innovator, Tom Sims.

"Tom was doing a commercial shoot and riding one of his longboards. I told my wife I had met up with Tom and she said that her parents lived near him." As a result of this connection, he contacted Tom and asked him if he had any interest in the prototypes George was creating. It was Sims who suggested the idea that was to change George's career. "Although he wasn't particularly interested in my boards, he was looking for something to compete with the Fibreflex because he didn't have a slalom board." Over time, George perfected the combination of fiberglass and aluminum. One of the first test riders of the resulting flexible slalom boards was Stacy Peralta. As George recalled, "Stacy was so impressed with the pumping action of the board, he offered to buy one on the spot."

George had developed a great product but was still working full time in the aerospace industry. He deliberated over whether or not to quit his job and go full time into skateboarding. As a result of being laid off, however, George was given four months' salary, so he decided to take the plunge and become a skateboard manufacturer. He left Los Angeles and moved with his family north to Santa Barbara.

In November 1976 Powell and Sims wrote up a formal agreement and joined together to market the Quicksilver ProSlalom deck. It came with two unique sales pitches. One was that the deck was offered in three combinations depending upon a rider's weight (50 kg, 70 kg and 90 kg). The other innovative feature was that the skater's name could be engraved next to Tom Sims's name on top of the board. George was able to produce anywhere from 30 to 60 boards a day. Initially, the boards were sold by mail order.

Quicksilver

Although both the Quicksilver and Fibreflex offered a terrific snap, there was one key difference with George's board. By incorporating aluminum, the board had better torsional resistance and this meant it could pump more easily than a Fibreflex product.

Soon after its introduction, the Powell Corporation brought out the Quicktail, which was a freestyle/vertical terrain deck with much less flex than the Quicksilver. The board got this name because it came with a kicktail. At the same time, Powell also introduced the first double radial wheel, called "Bones." The white urethane was quite a contrast to other wheels at the time.

"I had looked at the big, wide wheels with big lips. Although they were pretty grippy, they didn't go over bumps very well. I decided to build wheels with hard lips and big radiuses that would enable you roll over the bump better."

George started to experiment with urethane in a quest to produce a fast and highly responsive wheel. Eventually he found a urethane that fit the bill perfectly. The urethane wheels came out a white color, so George decided to call them "Bones."

The wheels were immensely popular, but Powell faced problems filling orders. "The wheels were difficult to pour and there were a lot of rejects. After a bad experience with one supplier, I finally solved the problem, got quality and production in gear, and Bones took off."

As skateboarding began to change from slalom to street and vertical riding, the Powell Corporation began to expand into other areas. As wooden boards became more popular, Powell switched production from aluminum and fiberglass to wood laminates. Their first series of wood boards were called Brite Lites, featuring fluorescent colors. Things really took off in late 1978, however, when

Stacy Peralta joined forces with George. At the time, Stacy had achieved a great deal of success with Gordon & Smith Skateboards. His pro signature models (the Warptail I and II) were very big sellers. But, as he related in a March 1979 interview with *SkateBoarder,* he had his reasons for leaving G&S: "You've gotta move on . . . you can't stagnate. With Powell, I'm part of the company, so financially, if they do good, I'll do good. At Powell now, if I want to change a design, experiment with new materials, or try anything different, he's behind me."

Stacy's original job at Powell was to be the team manager and direct promotions and advertising. Powell Peralta's first model together was "The Beamer." Combining traditional wood laminates and two aerospace strips for reinforcement, the board was extremely popular from the start. More products hit, including the Bones "Cubic" wheel, which was suited for vertical riding.

In 1979, Powell Peralta put together a team of skaters that would have an enormous impact for future generations of skaters. The original rider for Powell was Ray "Bones" Rodriguez. George recalls how Stacy built the team: "He started adding members like Steve Caballero, Alan Gelfand, Mike McGill. He found skaters with a unique combination of grace, style, and charisma. Stacy was very good at finding people." The Bones Brigade was headed up by Stacy and their mission was to spread the word on Powell Peralta and move the sport of skateboarding forward. It's hardly surprising that they succeeded in their mission.

The team was mostly made up of vertical riders, with the exception of freestylist Tim Scroggs (who went on to influence Rodney Mullen in a big way). Ray "Bones" Rodriguez had the only signature model on the team.

By 1980, skateboarding's second bust had hit. The fun aspect of skateboarding seemed to have diminished and in its place was general malaise. Skateboarding moved underground. Powell Peralta was one of only a handful of manufacturers that continued with the sport. "We stayed with it because we loved the sport," says George. But the company was facing financial hardships. "I think at one point in the 1980–81 period we were building five hundred decks a month. They were extremely lean years."

During these lean years Powell Peralta's riders took a cut in pay. Stacy went into acting and ran the Bones Brigade on a part-time basis. Thankfully, skaters rediscovered skateboarding at the end of 1982. "All of a sudden we started receiving triple the amount of orders." Stacy started adding more members to the Bones Brigade. Freestyler Rodney Mullen was asked to join. Soon after, vertical rider Tony Hawk came on board and the third skateboarding wave was starting to build. The following quote is taken from a Powell Peralta ad found in the March 1984 issue of *Thrasher* magazine:

> Hawk seizes the thin line that separates genius from insanity and ties it in knots. Tony realizes that how you get there is more important than where you go. He requires innovative equipment for his unconventional actions. For such a man the choice is obvious . . . Powell Peralta.

Capitalizing on the start of a third boom, George began setting aside more money for production of a video. In October of 1984, Powell Peralta advertised what was to become one of the main ingredients in the launch of the third skateboom — the Bones Brigade Video. Although Powell Peralta had created a 16-minute video in 1981, it had been mostly overlooked during the skatebust. The Bones Brigade Video show, created with the talents of Stacy Peralta and artist Craig Stecyk, was the one that people crowded around skateshops to view.

The video opened with Stacy getting angry at a television host's ignorant comments about skateboarding. Stacy gets so irate that he takes a pick ax, drives it through the TV set and pulls a Powell Peralta board from the mess of electronics. He then utters the most famous line of the entire video: "Now *this* is a skateboard!"

The video featured skater Lance Mountain as the official host who travels around to each skate spot checking out the action. The key members of the Bones Brigade are featured riding in backyard ramps, pools, skateparks and, in one memorable sequence, sliding downhill at tremendous speeds. The video's humor and pace would set the stage for other installments and dramatically boost the sales of Powell Peralta products. The video cost $15,000 to produce and went on to sell thirty thousand copies.

In the second video, additional skaters joined the ranks of the Bones Brigade. Streetstyler Tommy Guerrero stunned viewers when he was featured ollieing all over the streets of San Francisco. Freestylers Rodney Mullen and Per Welinder (who had both appeared in the first video) were joined by Kevin Harris.

Powell Peralta's third video, "The Search for Animal Chin," was the first to actually have a "real" storyline. The skaters featured were Tony Hawk, Steve Caballero, Lance Mountain, Mike McGill, and Tommy Guerrero. The video was a huge hit and still turns heads to this very day. Besides the Chinese imagery used throughout the video, "Animal Chin" is best remembered for its amazing wooden ramp (located in the middle of nowhere.)

Powell Peralta continued to bring additional skaters to their roster of talent, but visuals remained an important element in the company's popularity. Along with the videos, Craig Stecyk's artistry was also applied to Powell Peralta's advertising. The graphics and imagery created by Vernon Courtland Johnson were simply awesome. The Powell Peralta board logos and graphics were reproduced on countless stickers and shirts and filled the magazines. Johnson's image of a skeleton ripping out of a canvas is burned into most skaters' brains from the 1980's. As Powell Peralta's market share grew, so did their manufacturing facilities, eventually culminating in an enormous 185,000-square foot factory/warehouse.

However, something happened to skateboarding in the late 1980's that was to have a dramatic effect on Powell Peralta. Smaller, independent, skater-owned companies like World Industries started to change the game. This is George's take on the situation: "Steve Rocco, the founder of World, empowered himself to start his own company. He also empowered other skaters to do the same thing. Steve pulled all the pro skaters from the larger companies in an attempt to gain a foothold in the industry."

Of course, the phenomenon of pro riders changing teams had been going on ever since the Makaha team was raided by Vita-Pakt/Hobie in 1964–65. The difference this time was that pro skaters who were nearing the end of their careers were now starting up their own companies. This increased competition set the stage for a shakeup in the industry.

Skateboarding's Third Wave had been extraordinary and Powell Peralta had been the dominant player. But toward the end of the decade, things started to change. As Stacy recalls, "When Powell Peralta got successful it damaged our ability to be on the cutting edge. I felt we had to work even harder to maintain our position, we couldn't sit still." It was a difficult time for Stacy and he was at odds as to which direction to take his career. Finally, he decided to change course. "I was done. I felt it was time for a new chapter." He walked away from a life-time job during the biggest season Powell Corporation had ever had — December 1991.

George recalls the period with some sadness. "Stacy was unhappy with the way the industry was going. He wrote me a letter saying he didn't want his name on any of the products we were making. When he left, it set the stage for the newer independents to develop further market share." After Stacy's departure, Powell Corporation faced some extremely difficult financial problems. During the early '90's, George became introspective. "I'd ask myself why weren't we doing well, what was going on in skateboarding, how do I compete against the crap that was being thrown at me. People printed stuff that wasn't true or was misleading in an attempt to slander me and detract from our presence in the industry and what we'd done. I was an easy target, because I didn't fight back — I wasn't going to lower myself to their level. But, I learned my lesson and I'm not going to take it again lying down." George looked at the strengths of the Powell Corporation. He had reinvested a great deal of the profits into the business and realized he could build better-quality products than his competitors.

"Throughout the '90's we were given a bad rap because we had been a really large company in the '80's. It wasn't cool to be a big company. Ironically, most of the smaller companies that complained about the awful practices of the companies that had been popular in the '80's, like telling their skaters that they had to behave themselves, or not allowing everything on a board, or exercising a certain amount of restraint, soon discovered that it has to be done at times. It's kind of like when kids become parents — the shoe is on the other foot. That's all happened now and it's over. We're kind of all on the same footing at this point."

George Powell has lived through enormous changes in the skateboard industry and has created a tremendous legacy through his products. When the creative genius of Peralta was joined with Powell Corporation, the company provided skateboarders with truly memorable products and imagery.

George continues to manufacture with the same attention to detail he used in his garage and kitchen back in the mid 1970's. "What I've come to realize over my 20 years in manufacturing is that **we are here for the skater who use our products,** not for the pro skaters. We have to listen to what our customers want and then try and build the best equipment we possibly can. The pros are there to educate and inspire, but the focus at Powell Corporation is on the consumer of skateboards."

Vernon Courtland Johnson

The powerful graphics that Powell Corporation and later Powell Peralta developed came from the mind of Vernon "Court" Johnson. Court was George Powell's first employee. He had started with the company making Quicksilvers in Santa Barbara. He eventually became shop foreman and ran production. However, as George is quick to point out, "Court had always been a great artist." His first major design for the company was the Ray "Bones" Rodriguez deck featuring a skull and sword. The startling graphic was the foundation for the incredible imagery that would be a trademark of the company for years to come.

The Man Behind the Skulls

"Ray had come to us with this little piece of paper and I didn't even recognize what it was at first. I think he had seen an image from the Emerson Lake and Palmer album, 'Brain Salad Surgery.' Ray wondered if we could make a skull with a sword in front of it," George recalls. "The drawing was not very detailed and only when Ray explained what it was could you see it." Court decided to try his hand at the graphic.

Court experimented with a number of drawing techniques and finally settled on the style of Escher, the Dutch artist famous for his black and white optical illusions. George helped out as art director. The image was to be silk-screened onto the board, and it required a number of attempts to achieve a high-quality reproduction.

It was the first time Court had done a graphic and the entire project took over four months to complete. George fondly remembers the outcome of all their hard work: "We finally got it right and we thought it was great. We didn't know if people would like it. The board turned out to be a big hit."

The board turned out to be a big HIT.

After the success of the Rodriguez model, Court was fully entrenched in the art department and moved out of production. Almost every graphic produced by Powell and Powell Peralta had Court's creativity behind it. T-Shirts, stickers, posters, and decks all carried his VCJ logo. Highlights of his work include The Ripper, featuring a skull peering out of a cloth, Tony Hawk's Bird (which can be found on Tony's own company — Birdhouse Projects), the Steve Caballero Dragon, and the Rodney Mullen Skeleton (dancing with chess pieces).

Eventually, Court moved away from the skateboard industry, and has recently become a spiritual leader. He still lives in Southern California. His legacy is so great however, that if you check old-school skaters' closets, no doubt you'll probably find a few skeletons — some approaching their twenty-first birthday!

5 for Tony Hawk

"Skateboarding to me means freedom, an outlet for any sort of stress and responsibilities. It's my way of expressing myself."

■Tony Hawk

1. What is your earliest skate memory?

My earliest memory is the first time I ever stepped on a skateboard. It was in our alley in San Diego when I was nine. My brother Steve was already an avid skater, so I wanted to try it also. I succeeded in making it to the end of the alley while yelling back to Steve: "How do I turn?" I eventually had to step off and pick up the board in order to turn it around.

2. What is your best memory of the Bones Brigade?

The best memories I have of the Bones Brigade were during the shooting of Animal Chin. We basically lived with each other for nearly three months, all the while feeding off of each other's creativity. All we cared about was skating, so it gave us many opportunities to try out new terrains while learning from each other. I think most of us grew up during that era.

3. Most important contest?

The most important contest for me was the 1988 finals in Dayton, Ohio. I had done well in the two series before, but never skated to my full potential in the finals (both Vision contests). It was the first time that I had ever practiced a line before ever getting to a particular contest, which paid off in the end. I even made a 720, which was rare for me in a competition.

4. What is your favorite trick?

My favorite trick is a backside ollie because it feels like I have so much control of my board by only using my feet.

5. Describe your ultimate skatepark:

Woodward Skate Camp with more realistic street structures.

Rodney Mullen
The King of Freestyle

For someone who has left (and is still in the process of leaving) an incredible legacy to the world of skateboarding, Rodney Mullen's start with the sport was fairly inauspicious. When the second skateboard boom hit in the mid 1970's, Rodney was eager to ride a board of his own. He had been watching the neighborhood kids, envious of their boards. Rodney had asked his father for a skateboard on numerous occasions but every time had been told "no." On New Year's Eve 1976, Rodney decided to ask his father for a board just one more time. In an article written for *Thrasher* (January 1996 issue), Rodney recalls his father's response that evening: "He reluctantly made a deal: the first injury I got, or the first time he caught me without my pads, I had to quit."

With his father's reserved blessing, Rodney wasted no time and marched down to the local shopping mall on January 1, 1977. He picked up a black Banzai Aluminum Board with precision wheels and ACS trucks. Prior to this purchase his father had been concerned that skateboarding was not a very safe sport. In hindsight, he needn't have worried. Quickly, Rodney began practicing and learning freestyle tricks — in full pads. About nine months from the time he received his skateboard, Rodney picked up his first sponsor: The Inland Surf Shop.

He started winning contests in his home state of Florida. In 1978, Rodney blew a lot of the California pros away when he reached fourth place at the Kona contest. In 1979 Rodney took top spot at the Oceanside contest in California and was immediately sponsored by Walker. With all this success,

Rodney's father realized that his son had mastered skateboarding. The only problem was, now his father wanted him to try to master something else. What was the sport Rodney's father had suggested he pick up?: "Golf," says Rodney, with a tinge of disbelief. But Rodney didn't pick up the clubs and he kept training.

In August of 1980, he received a call from Stacy Peralta inviting him out to a contest in San Diego. Rodney remembers the time vividly. "This was to be my last fling." He was 13 years old and would be competing with top Sims freestyler Steve Rocco. The contest was extremely close and the judges kept on awarding the same number of points to both Steve and Rodney. Eventually, on the last runoff, Rodney won the contest. It was then he officially starting riding for Powell Peralta. "After this success," recalls Rodney, "my father was motivated to keep me involved in skateboarding."

In the early '80's, skateboarding was very much underground. The sport had peaked, just like in the '60's, and now there was only a group of hardcore skaters who kept up with the sport. Rodney wrote articles for *Thrasher* magazine that explained, step by step, complex freestyle moves. He wound up in first place in almost every contest. In the mid '80's, the sport picked up again, primarily due to the proliferation of skateboard videos. The Powell Peralta and Vision *Psycho Skate* videos showcased Rodney's amazing abilities better than any sequential photo spread found in a magazine. Viewers were in awe of his command of the board. As Peter Weldrake, owner of Toronto's famous Hogtown Skateboard Shop, recalled, "In the

mid 1980's I had a little black and white television hooked up with a VCR and crowds of people would jam the store in awe of what Rodney was doing. They had never seen skateboarding like this before!"

As the 80's progressed Rodney became increasingly famous. He has some positive memories of the time: "There was so much opportunity. My friends were doing well." Rodney wrote in *Thrasher,* "Skating blew up from around '86 to '91. I felt like a rock star. I flew on the Concorde." Despite all this success, however, Rodney recalled some painful truths about fame: "Each time I thought I got somewhere else, I realized I hadn't gone anywhere."

Slowly, Rodney entered into the world of new school skating. He put away the traditional freestyle board and with encouragement from Plan B's Mike Ternasky and World Industries head Steve Rocco, Rodney started to move into streetskating. His practice paid off and he can be seen in the 1992 *Questionable* video. His blending of new streetstyle skating with his amazingly technical freestyle tricks set a new standard and blew many people away.

There is no question that Rodney Mullen dominated freestyle skateboarding for over a decade. In today's world of streetskating, Rodney is still a major force. Many of the tricks he invented the 1980's are now the foundation of new school skateboarding. He is, however, extremely humble when asked about the tremendous influence he has had on skateboarding. "I was just doing my thing. I didn't think of myself as a pioneer." Rodney works full time in the skateboard industry, and nowadays heads up a division called A Team within the World Industries skate empire.

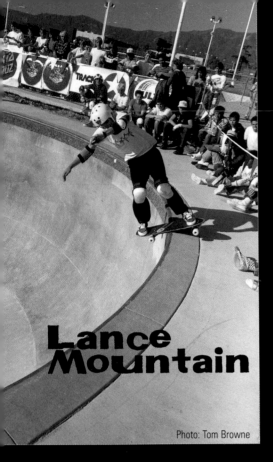

Lance Mountain

Photo: Tom Browne

Originally a rider for Variflex in the late '70's, Lance became one of the key members of the '80's Bones Brigade. Lance can be seen hosting *411 Video Magazine* every month. In 1992, Lance started his own skateboard company called The Firm.

Known by many as a visionary. Invented the "lien" ('Neil' backwards) air, along with pioneering all sorts of difficult lip tricks in the 1980's. In an article in *Thrasher* he foretold the trend of all boards being exactly the same size/shape, and that the graphics would be most important, second only to skate "fashion" (clothing, etc.).

Photo: Tom Browne

Neil Blender

Christian Hosoi

Photo: Scott Starr

Known for his incredibly huge airs, "Holmes" was one of the biggest vert superstars of the '80's. He started life as a pro on the Sims team and eventually promoted his own line of boards, including "The Hammerhead."

"Cab" is one of skateboarding's legends. He was first sponsored by Campbell Skatepark in 1979 (this was a year after he picked up the sport), and later that year got picked up by Powell Peralta. He has been with Powell since that time. Steve invented the "Caballaerial" and was known for huge (11 foot) backside airs. When asked, "What advice do you have about longevity?", Cab told *Thrasher* magazine: "Just having a nice, positive attitude towards everything that has to do with skateboarding . . . Skateboarding is my whole life — ever since I was 13 years old. Basically, I've made a career out of it and I enjoy it as much as I did when I first started."

Photo: John Old

Steve Caballero

Skip Engblom started riding scooters in 1955 at the age of seven. "At some point," recalls Skip, "I got tired of the handles." In 1959 he moved to Venice Beach and started buying old roller skates and making skateboards for himself and others. By the time he hit 14, Skip was working for Makaha Skateboards. In 1968 he teamed up with Jeff Ho and Craig Stecyk and created Zephyr Surfboards. In 1973 Zephyr started making skateboards and had such legendary riders as Jay Adams, Tony Alva, Stacy Peralta, and Shogo Kubo.

Unfortunately, the team broke up and in 1976, Skip left the skateboard world and took up surfing again. He eventually got back into it, getting involved with skatepark construction and skateshop management. In 1978 Skip and friend Jim Shulty started making their own skateboard decks. "I was across the street from the Santa Monica Airport," recalls Skip, "and my intention was to make a very elaborate board in the shape of an airplane wing." The reason for this was to ensure maximum hang time for aerials. The location of the shop, coupled with the imagery of flight, produced the company name "Santa Monica Airlines."

Skip's girlfriend at the time started drawing seaplanes on the boards and the logo caught people's attention. Sims pro Jack Waterman joined Santa

Santa Monica Airlines ■ Flying High

Monica Airlines and became their first sponsored rider. Towards the end of the 1970's–early '80's, skateboarding suffered its second downturn. Skip closed up shop, but thanks to a clause in his contract, retained the rights to the name Santa Monica Airlines.

During the low point in skateboarding in the early '80's, Skip designed customized skateboards for people. But he always knew that skateboarding would return. He kept making surfboards, and over time, he saw his orders for skateboards increase.

Skip had spotted a young skater in his area pulling incredible tricks. "This kid was phenomenal — I had that sense about him. I tried to speak with him, but he was just too quick." While Skip wondered how he was going to find this great skater, the kid showed up at his shop. Skip clearly remembers how the scene went down: "He showed up and said that he won this skateboard at a skate contest. It was one of my decks and he told me 'It's the best board I've ever owned.' I asked him to skate for me, and right there and then I knew I had my skateboard team." The kid turned out to be Natas Kaupas, and he was the only skater Skip needed for his newly reformed Santa Monica Airlines.

In 1987, Santa Monica Airlines entered into a business agreement with Santa Cruz Skateboards and had great success during skateboarding's Third Wave. Skip Engblom's work in manufacturing has touched the lives of skateboarders for over three decades. That's a lot of hang time!

One of the biggest skateboard companies to emerge during the past 40 years is Vision. The company's roots go back to skateboarding's second wave of popularity in the seventies. A woman named Lou Ann Lee began making shorts for skateboarders in her garage. The skate shorts were durable and had the name Mad Rats. Top vertical skaters like Eddie Elguera promoted the shorts and they began to get more popular. From this beginning, Lou Ann's brother, Brad Dorfman, got involved in the distribution of the product.

Brad also introduced a product to the skateboard market called the Space Plate, which was a plastic skid plate placed at the tail of the board. As the Space Plate started to sell, a decision was made to get into manufacturing skateboards. Brad chose the name Vision and his first deck was a fairly non-descript board with two-color grip tape. The second board was called the "Beef Stick" and it was 10-inches x 30-inches. When local Del Mar skater Mark Rogowski got his name on a Vision board, things started to take off. Mark's nickname was "Gator" and his board was extremely popular. He was followed by a host of other skaters, including the extraordinary streetskater Mark Gonzales.

At the beginning of the 1980's, Brad started a licensing agreement with Tom Sims. "Tom wasn't doing much with the brand name at the time," recalls Brad, "so we put together a deal and Vision began producing and marketing boards under the Sims name." The deal proved to be a very wise move — a number of great skaters would join the Sims team, including Kevin Staab and Pierre Andre.

Although Vision was becoming successful with their own boards and those of Sims, what really stood them apart from other competitors was their expansion into what are called soft goods (that is, shoes or t-shirts). "Vision was the first skateboard clothing company," explains Brad. "We had Gator and other riders coming to us and saying, 'Surf companies want to sponsor us, you have to start making your own clothing.'" From this simple premise, Vision

Mark "Gator" Rogowski
Gator rode for Vision and was one of the biggest vert riders of the 1980's. He had a tremendous following and his signature board was extremely popular. Gator received national media attention when he killed his girlfriend's friend and was punished with 30 years to life imprisonment.

Street Wear was born. Vision Street Wear was literally everywhere. Shoes, shirts, hats, pants, jackets . . . the magazines carried numerous ads featuring all the Vision Pro's skating in the product. Vision Street Wear was so successful that mainstream fashion publications started writing about the new look and dubbed it "Mondo Vision."

At a surf show in Florida in the mid 1980's, Brad met up with Paul Schmitt of Schmitt Stix, and the two got together to set up a wood shop in California. Schmitt Stix, Vision, and Sims were three of the top skateboard companies in the 1980's and they were all under the Vision empire. Brad was also producing boards for other companies. It was a huge operation that generated enormous amounts of revenue.

Over the years, Vision has developed a number of unique products. They were one of the first to market a double concave board, and their "Vex Cave" design increased the strength of skateboards. Vision was also one of the first companies to round the rails of their decks. Vision also got heavily involved with video production during the 1980's and formed a successful company called Unreel Productions. Their first video was called *Skate Visions,* but most skaters from that era probably remember *Psycho Skate* best.

Brad Dorfman has many great memories of the 1980's. "Traveling with the team across the United States was great, but the best memory I have was the Vision Pro Contest," recalls Brad. The Vision Pro Contest took place in 1987 and was an enormous event staged indoors, with over 10,000 spectators.

Due to a number of different things happening in the skateboard world, Vision's fortunes began to change towards the end of the 1980's. "One of our problems was that we had all vert riders and the focus shifted to streetskating. We were slow to change," says Brad. Vision had to let a number of riders go and begin rebuilding the team. Vision Street Wear also got a little out of control. Things grew pretty fast in too many areas. However, as the '90's draw to a close, the Vision logo is back and demand for their products is growing once again.

The Four Wheel Wonder Down Under

by Richard Jones

Skateboarding [in Australia] followed the same ebb and flow as its popularity in America. If there is a difference it is that it tended to happen and die more suddenly. Australians always seem quick to jump on a bandwagon and equally quick to swap when something new pulls along side. In the mid '60's there was a skateboard craze of sorts. Confined mainly to the real strong surf areas it died as quickly as it arose. Pre 1975 it was still a surf influenced thing, people made their own [skateboards] or some surf shops imported them. However, between 1975 and 1976 the "four-wheeled contrivance" (as classed by the Australian Road Act) had a booming time. If a kid didn't have one then someone was planning to buy them one for Christmas. This meant that skateboarding became a household word. Skating along on this popularity, American pro's were welcomed to the land of opportunity with open arms. Russ Howell, Stacy Peralta and Torger Johnson were amongst the first. Seeing what the pro's could do just pushed the popularity of the sport higher.

In 1975 it was mainly surfers who were at the forefront of technique. People such as Cheyne Horan, Robbie Bain and Wedge Francis were going off. Some of these may still be seen longboard cruising today.

Late '75, early '76 saw a number of major competitions being held. The venues were mainly multi-storey car parks and major shopping centres. Freestyle and slalom were the order of the day, and the comps had huge attendance and numerous entrants. Team events were prestigious affairs and the teams were from surf shops or companies (many still have sponsored skaters today). Ones that ring a bell are :

The Mcoy team
Golden Breed team
Surf Ski Dive team
Peninsular Surf Shop Team
Trax Team
Saraus Team
Lorne Team

The popularity of surfing in the '70's was immense; with the Australians dominating world surfing, skateboarding became the way that the masses could emulate their world-beating heroes. Skating seemed to be everywhere, things were huge. Corporate sponsorship wasn't found just from surf- or skate-related companies; lots of importing, radio and food companies were eager to share in the pie.

This enabled two home-grown magazines to appear: *Skateboard* and *Slicks*. Unfortunately for these two, the mass, soft-core participation in skateboarding died in June 1976 with the latest must-have craze. Ninety-five per cent of the people who had been so dedicated to the sport were history. So there was the second example of the Australian curse — the craze!

However, these two crazes did leave a residue of hardcore skaters willing to carry the flag. Due to the way local authorities work in Australia and the fact that land is hardly short to come by, even in major cities, they also left a number of concrete parks, many of which are still fully sessioned today.

Hardcore skaters gravitated to these relics, or places like the Manly Corso, the Spillway, Stuart Creek, Hobart bowl, Dolphin Pool, Vandas Pool, Rocia pipes, Wales bank walls and the Fishpond. Spots like these prepared the skaters for the terrain the next late '70's–early '80's craze would produce. On the back of this craze many a council spot was built, not of the size of the '70's maybe and still none of any real functional value, but there were stand outs. These included the commercial fibreglass Manly Skatecity and the Canberra concrete pool.

But the curse struck again, with even most of the hot locals losing interest. Parks closed or turned into parking lots, skating was dying. It had lost its roots and was doomed. But all was not lost; skating went underground and got closely tied to streetskating and thrash music. *Thrasher* was the bible, bringing together the skaters, the music and the attitude. The underground scene began to grow.

Underground skate 'zines appeared; local ones included *Skateboard Australia* and *Skate On*. The skaters that were still involved were few but dedicated. By 1984 Australia looked like it was in craze mode again. Pushed by the emergence of *Transworld Skateboarding* and the skating on show in the new videos (*The Bones Brigade* and *Skate Visions*), skating was once again creating interest in the public. More and more backyard ramps appeared. But perhaps more important for skating in Oz, the reemergence of streetskating style took skating back to where it had started — sidewalk surfing.

After that, skating in Oz never looked liked dying again. During the technical stage of skating little pockets of resistance stood firm. Skaters were still skating hard and fast and the Australian surf style never faded.

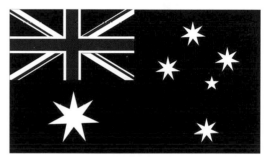

Mainstream skating followed the same trends as elsewhere. However, Australia was eager and quick to grab onto the current diversity found in the skating world. Grass Sole were one of the first companies in the world to reinvent the all-terrain wheel and boards, home-grown longboard labels have sprung up, like Jones Longboards and Topline. Longboard imports have hardly kept up with the demand for people to start street surfing again.

With all the available concrete waves and bio ramps, Australia deserves to be called — The Land of Oz!!!!

The Professor

— Paul Schmitt and the Rise of Schmitt Stix

For nearly two decades, Paul "The Professor" Schmitt has been providing skateboarders with innovative, high-quality products. Paul's history of involvement with skateboarding epitomizes the enthusiasm and dedication that has kept the sport alive during its downswings in mainstream popularity.

Paul started skating in 1973 on a clay-wheeled skateboard his neighbors had picked up at a swap meet for $3. Not long after, he made a visit to a local department store to invest $20 in his very own board with urethane wheels. In 1975 his family moved from Wisconsin to Tampa, Florida, where he skated in the streets until skateparks began to appear.

By 1977 skateparks had sprung up all over, and ramps and bowls were now the focus for the sport. Skateboards had become wider, and to help skaters achieve a better grip as they did aerials, rails were put underneath the boards. In Clearwater, Florida, Steve Fisher made wood rails called Fish Stix. In California Z-Flex made Grabair rails out of urethane. In 1977, at age 14, Paul Schmitt made his rails out of wood and fiberglass so they did not break. However, neither wood nor urethane rails slid well. At Alan Gelfand and Mike McGill's suggestion that rails should slide, Paul started making his rails out of a tough, durable plastic called UHMW polyethylene. His rails were popular with local skaters, who dubbed them "Schmitt Stix". These rails were cut out at the woodshop at school, drilled at a hardware store/woodshop where Paul worked, and then packaged in his parents' living room.

Schmitt Stix rails soon became popular all over Florida and were sold at a number of retail stores and skateparks across the state. In 1979 Sims pro Mike Folmer took them with him on his cross-country road trips. He spread the word about Schmitt Stix rails along the way, and influential pros like Brad Bowman started to ride them. In 1980 Rax Works became Schmitt Stix's first California distributor. Around this time, Paul started to have his rails extruded into a half-round, easy-to-grab, no-hang-up shape. In 1981 Vision began to distribute his rails around the world.

Although rails were his main product, Paul had always liked building things and had long experimented with making his own boards. In high school Paul had the opportunity to gain some real-life work experience building sailboats at a local factory. This allowed him to learn many differ-

ent manufacturing processes, including mold making and working with fiberglass. It was also an important experience in terms of forming his business philosophy. Recalls Paul, "My supervisor, Eric Falago, let me know that it was OK to think differently about a job that Eric had done for 20 years. This was my foundation to go forward in many aspects of life."

By 1981, skateboarding had entered another slump. Only the truly dedicated stayed with the sport. In Florida, as elsewhere, the skateparks had all closed, except for Kona in Jacksonville. Kona held a pro contest each year that brought the California skate pros east and also became a sort of annual convention for every skater left on the east coast. It gave these scattered and isolated skaters a chance to meet and find out what was happening with the sport.

One popular topic of discussion at the annual Kona event was ramp construction. It became clear that in response to the skatepark closings, many skaters were creating their own backyard ramps. Paul Schmitt helped St. Pete locals rebuild John Grigley's ramp, which became the focal point for Florida skateboarding. He also became active in the Florida Backyard Ramp Series. For a few years he organized and promoted the contests, then documented them with photos and articles that appeared in *Thrasher* magazine.

This was the era of punk and new wave music, with its "DIY" (do it yourself) ethos. As with music, communication among the different scenes was maintained through grassroots events like the Backyard Ramp Series, and by enthusiastic, creative people who published their own magazines. St. Pete skaters made a 'zine called Just For Fun, and many other publications of all different shapes and sizes were produced across the country.

During these years Paul Schmitt continued to experiment with skateboard-making. He purchased finished boards from a few California woodshops, as well as blanks that he cut out and painted himself, and started selling Schmitt Stix skateboards. His first board press was his mom's car parked on top of the mold; later he moved up to a press with car jacks in it that he kept in his bedroom.

In early 1983, Paul wanted to go to a skate contest in Tennessee. The management at the boat company he was working for wouldn't give him the time off, so Paul gave them

117

his six weeks' notice. By a twist of fate the contest was canceled. At this point, with time on his hands and no other gainful employment, Paul decided to go into skateboard manufacturing full time. He had not been happy with the quality or designs of the boards he had been buying from the California woodshops, so he used his experience in mold construction

to refine what he thought a skateboard should be. Monty Nolder became the first pro for Schmitt Stix. Chuck Hults started working full time for Schmitt Stix to make Monty's board, along with the Terrampula and the ATV models. The company also began producing foam-core boards, which had fiberglass and foam in them to make them lighter and stronger.

After the summer 1983 edition of the Kona contest, the California pros came to the St. Pete ramp for the informal "Just For Fun" contest. Word spread about the great ramp and good times. Fausto Vitello from Thrasher helped to promote and run a full-blown backyard pro ramp contest over the New Years holidays. Both Thrasher and Transworld Skateboarding were there to cover it, and Monty Nolder's second-place finish gave Schmitt Stix a lot of exposure.

By late '84, Paul had come to realize that Florida was not the place to be for a serious skateboard company. Skateboarding was finally back on the upswing and Schmitt Stix had huge potential for growth, but Paul didn't have the money needed for expansion. A change would have to be made, so in the spring of 1985 Paul packed his shop in a U Haul, and along with John Grigley and Chuck Hults drove across the country to the skateboarding hotbed of California. There Schmitt Stix joined forces with Vision, which had been the largest distributor for its boards and rails. Paul and his friends soon had a 1,000-square-foot shop where they lived and built boards for six months.

The St. Pete ramp had given Paul a reputation for building ramps, so along with his skateboards he ended up building and rebuilding quite a few ramps out west as well. He also coordinated their construction for contests, but when he got too busy with Schmitt Stix, he passed on ramp requests to Florida's Tim Payne. Tim had done jobs with and for Paul and was the best ramp builder. Tim has since gone on to build thousands of memorable ramps for all of the National Skateboard Association contests of the '80's, the Animal Chin Ramp, and many more.

To give you an idea of the phenomenal rise of skateboarding's third wave,

at the end of 1985, Vision's Brad Dorfman walked Paul into a 15,000-sq.-ft. shop and announced it was Paul's new factory. Within a year the factory would be making 50,000 boards a month for Vision, Sims and Schmitt Stix. As Paul explains, "The best thing about the facility was that we could have an idea, build it and test it." It was truly skater-directed research and development, with a staff consisting of Paul, Chuck Hults, Mike Pust, Barry Deck, and Kelly Bellmar. John Lucero and Jeff Grosso joined the Schmitt Stix team in early 1986.

Many of those who started skating in the '80's say that their very first board was a Schmitt Stix. Innovation and maintaining a high level of quality were the two key ingredients in the success of Schmitt Stix. The 36-inch Yardstick, introduced in 1987, is still a highly requested item today. The Chris Miller board introduced in 1988, with its 4.75-inch upturned nose, paved the way for the mold designs and high standards of today's skateboards.

During the late '80's, despite his busy work schedule, Paul Schmitt found the time to help promote and run the NSA amateur series, because he felt the promotion of amateur skating was important. Most of the pros of the late '80's and early '90's competed in those events as amateurs.

As the '80's drew to a close, Paul was feeling a need to move on. Vision had become an enormous enterprise — boards, clothes, shoes, even snowboards — and Paul wanted to get back to basics. He left the Vision empire and started a woodshop called PS Stix. Schmitt Stix Teamriders did not feel comfortable in the shadow of Vision, so in Spring, 1990, the New Deal skateboard company was founded, with Steve Douglas as the team manager and Andy Howell as the artist. This company was an instant success; as the traditional, established companies were falling, New Deal was on the rise due to its positive image and street-skating focus.

After two decades in a chaotic industry, Paul Schmitt remains devoted to the sport of skateboarding. While he may have never gone to college, he will always be known as "The Professor" to skaters of the '80's.

Another Roadside Attraction

— A Contest in the Rockies

Vail Merchants Pro-Am Skateboard Contest, July 9, 1978, Dual Slalom, pro racer John Hutson wins.

Vail Merchants Pro-Am Skateboard Contest, July 8, 1978, Downhill (practice), Tom Ryan

Dillon/Silverthorne Pro-Am Skateboard Contest, August 19-21, 1977, Dual Slalom, Tom Ryan (left) and Bobby Piercy.

Lakewood Merchants Pro-Am Skateboard Contest, June 24, 1978, Dual Slalom, Randy Smith.

By Peter Camann (contest organizer and promoter)

A Professional and Amateur Skateboard Race Series was organized, directed and produced by Another Roadside Attraction, Inc., in the 1970's. The program was designed to naturally promote the skills of racing and the safety of skateboarding from the most accomplished level of experience, that of the professional.

The Pro-Am Race Series toured the Colorado Rocky Mountain communities of Boulder, Lakewood/Denver, Vail, Aspen, Broomfield, Breckenridge, Silverthorne and Dillon, from May through August. The emphasis was on racing, specifically the most popular accepted disciplines in race competition: Downhill, Giant Slalom and Dual Slalom. Special events contested at specific venues were Freestyle and Cross-Country. The race circuit attracted the finest skaters in the U.S., who competed on a regular basis throughout the summer tours of 1977 and 1978.

The tour had eight locations, hosting competitions on weekends, with operations on a bi-monthly schedule. A minimum of two disciplines and a maximum of three disciplines were held at each event site. The cash purse for each discipline was initially set at $3,500 per discipline. The capital value of the entire circuit was set at $63,000. (I don't believe I was able to raise that amount due to a lack of manufacturer support.)

The Business Plan written stated: "Competition is the key inspiration behind goal pursuits and technological advances. Creating an environment strictly for racing, sets the stage for Manufacturers to test prototype equipment under conditions equally the same for their competitors. As a result, race statistics become meaningful scientific data, which lead to industrial discoveries."

Another Roadside Attraction, Inc., Pro Race Series was the culmination of a steady compilation of marketing data, an experimentation for a feasible competitive race format, the development of a rapport for multimedia presentation, and the design of a compatible advertising theme for sponsorship investment. ARA Inc. was the first and only race series to bring credibility to racing skateboard equipment on the streets of America, in a fair and unbiased racing climate. That was then, and it remains so to this day.

The Story of SKULL SKATES

One of the most well-known images in skateboarding is of a skull with the word "skates" underneath it. Most people would be hard pressed to tell you where and how this logo came about. The story begins with two brothers named Rick and Peter (P.D.) Ducommun. In 1977 they founded a skateboard company called "Great North Country Skateboards." Rick had been skating since the mid '60's and P.D. since 1972. Saskatchewan, Canada, might seem like a fairly unusual place to start a skateboard company, but then their story is pretty unusual too.

Great North Country Skateboards was soon abbreviated to "G.N.C. Skates" and their logo changed from a Ying and Yang symbol to a skull in April of 1978. The first version of the skull logo was cut out from grip tape. As P.D. tells it, "it only took about five minutes to cut out the design, but one look at it and we said, 'That's our new logo.'"

Skull Skates, armed with a logo that perfectly mirrored the underground nature of skating in the early 1980's, moved to Vancouver, British Columbia. They opened up a retail store near Stanley Park to do battle with rollerskaters. The Roller Disco movement of the early 1980's is something few skateboarders are willing talk about — mercifully, it didn't last long.

The store moved again to South Vancouver. Thanks to an incident at Marina Del Ray Skatepark, Skull Skates was starting to get better known outside Canada. In 1980, two local skaters, Jimmy Plummer and Billy Yeron, replaced a sponsor's banner with a Skull Skates banner and the company received a great deal of coverage in *SkateBoarder* magazine.

In the mid 1980's, Skull Skates relocated its manufacturing facilities again. It wound up in Van Nuys, California — one of the major centers for skateboard production and marketing. It was here that the brothers got fully involved with sponsorship of skaters and shipping their product worldwide.

Over the years, some of the biggest skaters were connected to Skull Skates. These include riders like Christian Hosoi, Duane Peters, Steve Olson, and Dave Hackett. There are very few people who skated in the 1980's who didn't either own or at least ride a Hosoi "Hammerhead" model, which featured a curved, blunt nose. Skull Skates also got involved in manufacturing boards for rock groups like the Red Hot Chili Peppers, Social Distortion, and the Vandals.

Other images that would come out of the 80's included their infamous "Dead Guys" graphic with coffin-shaped template and the Tod Swank "Moon and Star" deck featuring Islamic flag graphics. This board came out at a time when the United States was having some major problems with Iran.

The time spent in Southern California turned out to be a combination of success and pure hell. At one point, their board shaper torched his factory for insurance purposes and tried to burn Skull Skates at the same time. The brothers also encountered a fair amount of random violence and were shot at for no reason over half-a-dozen times. It was decided to leave the industry in Los Angeles and return to Vancouver. Upon their return, the brothers got back into the part of the business they do best: "quietly continuing along our wayward path, producing a large variety of products in small quantities."

The Sole of Skateboarding
— A Look at the Skate Shoe Industry

Most early skateboarders skated barefoot. The reason for this was simple — the skateboard was an extension of a surfboard, and you didn't need to wear shoes while you surfed. There were of course some downsides to skating without shoes — namely, if you weren't careful, you might possibly shred your feet.

One of the earliest shoes to find its way onto skaters' feet in the 1960's was Converse's Chuck Taylor model. This was a high-cut canvas shoe inspired by one of basketball's earliest stars. Of course, many companies copied the Converse style and knockoffs can be found to this very day. The shoe was available in both a low-cut and high-cut version. In the 1980's, "Chucks" reached their height of popularity and were standard issue for many skaters. Streetskaters and freestylers liked the soft sole of the shoes and the sensation of almost being able to feel the board under their feet.

In 1965, an advertisement appeared in *The Quarterly Skateboarder* for the "Randy 720." It was marketed as the skateboard sneaker for sidewalk surfing and was made with "Randyprene for built in tuffness." It was also billed as the official sneaker of the National Skateboard Championships.

However, to most skateboarders, Vans are the true original skateboard shoe. The Vans story begins with brothers Jim and Paul Van Doren in 1966. At the time, the Van Dorens were already 20-year veterans of the shoe industry. They teamed up with Gordon Lee and Serge D'Elia and decided to build a shoe factory in Anaheim. The factory was capable of producing both canvas and leather shoes in a variety of styles and widths. The plan was to make high-quality shoes and sell them directly to the public. The

Van Dorens soon opened a chain of stores in California and found that people liked their durable, well-made sneakers.

The Van Dorens experienced a great deal of success with the retail shoe outlets, and by 1974 they had almost 70 stores in California. Over the years, surfers had become fans of Vans. When skateboarding's second wave hit, Vans were poised to move their marketing and sales focus to skaters. The campaign to move into the skateboard market was led by Betty Mitchell, who to this day works

in public relations for Vans. Many skateboarders were also into surfing, so the jump was quite natural. The industry magazine *SkateBusiness* summed up the situation concisely: "Many of the popular skateboarders in the early 70's — like Tony Alva, Stacy Peralta and Jerry Valdez — were skating in Vans." There is no question the pros heavily influenced the general skateboarding population to go out and buy "the real skateboard shoe."

Originally, Vans were only available

in three colors. In the mid 1970's Vans went from this plain styling to a red and blue, two-tone look. More padding was added to the shoe for additional comfort. This shoe was called the "Off the Wall" model and it became very popular with skaters. Soon after, Vans introduced both a medium and a high-cut shoe. They even added ankle protectors to their product lineup (called "Van Guards").

Although skateboarding was in a slump in 1982, Vans had major success that year with their black and white, checkered shoe, as a result of Sean Penn sporting them playing the character of surfer dude Jeff Spicoli in the movie *Fast Times At Ridgemont High*.

After this success however, Vans ran into some financial difficulties. Over time, things worked out and in 1988 the company was sold to a venture banking firm. Vans continues to be a major player in the skateboard shoe industry. They have been involved with both professional contests, like the Vans/Hard Rock Triple Crown of Skateboarding, and amateur competitions like those that took place on the Warped Tour.

Vision Skateboard shoes were an offshoot of the immensely popular line of Vision Street Wear and Vision Skateboards. Vision was one of the first companies to leverage their skateboard credibility with a lineup of fashion and shoe merchandise. Brad Dorfman wanted the Vision emblem and merchandise everywhere. As a result of Vision's aggressive promotion, they were incredibly successful in the mid to late '80's. Unfortunately, Vision ran into difficulty when new skateboard companies came on the scene with a more alternative image. Pro riders bailed out and the Vision merchandise and logo were now considered too mainstream by skaters. Of course, while all this was happening, Vision was also facing intense competition from another shoe company called Airwalk.

Airwalk was started in 1986 by George Yohn. Like the Van Doren brothers, Yohn had spent many years in the shoe industry. Prior to launching Airwalk, Yohn had made a number of attempts at capitalizing on the athletic shoe market. He had gone from aerobic to jogging to tennis shoes without much success. As detailed in *Forbes* magazine, "One of his designers noticed a sport that had yet to be exploited by a sneaker company: skateboarding." Yohn quickly designed a specialized shoe with generous amounts of material plastered over it to ensure durability. He named the shoe after a trick called the "ollie airwalk." With this trick, a rider's feet spring off the board and go sideways while he grabs the nose of the board.

Marketed directly to the skateboarders, Airwalks became a hot item. The company remained focused on the skateboard market and featured pro riders like Tony Magnusson, Lester Kasai, and Tony Hawk in their advertisements. The late '80's saw a move to a tremendous amount of ollie-based moves. Jumping with your front foot and scraping it against grip tape led quickly to shredded shoes. Airwalk addressed this problem with additional protection on the front of the shoe.

By 1990, Airwalk sales had reached $20 million, but then the early '90's bust hit. Their sales fell to $8 million and Airwalk was in deep trouble. Yohn then hit upon the idea of taking skateboard shoes outside of the skateboard market. Sales rebounded tremendously as Airwalk went mainstream. Their shoes could be found in places such as Sportmart and Footlocker. However, this newfound success was to prove both a blessing and curse in much the same way it had for Vision.

The skateboard specialty shops, along with their customers — skateboarders — felt Airwalk had slighted them by going too mainstream. The shops were upset that they were now forced to compete with the large chain stores. Some skaters disliked the fact that Airwalks were now becoming a fashion statement for the masses as opposed to being exclusive to the skateboard industry.

While the large chains were selling a variety of Airwalk products (i.e., BMX shoes), many skateshops stopped selling the Airwalk brand. The company was forced to take a hard look at its impact on the skateboard industry. Airwalk's answer to the problem was to give skateshops exclusive rights to sell their skateboard shoes and let other retailers handle the rest of the line. The strategy appears to be meeting with some success.

Changes in the skateboard shoe industry in the 1990's included an increasing number of pro skaters getting their own signature shoes, and the rise of smaller companies to challenge Vans and Airwalk.

Etnies were one of the first shoe companies to take on Vans and Airwalk. Etnies shoes were originally brought over to North America by French pro freestyler Pierre Andre in 1990. Etnies quickly made an impression on the skateboard market with their Natas Kaupas signature model. Natas was a legend in streetskating and had made a name for himself with Santa Monica Airlines. Unfortunately, in 1995 Andre was faced with the potential loss of the Etnies trademark. In response, he launched Sole Technology and went about promoting three new lines — Sheep, Emerica, and eS. Eventually, Andre was able to secure the Etnies name for himself and now the company markets four distinct brands.

Over time other skateboard shoe companies have sprouted up — Simple, DC, Axion, Hook-Ups, Nice, Duffs, Osiris, 2-Fish and Globe are just a few of the many brands available. The skateboard shoe business has become very competitive and in economic terms it rivals the size of the skateboard industry itself. Larger, more traditional sports shoe companies like Nike and Adidas have developed their own skate shoes after seeing the potential of the market.

In 1997, Nike gained worldwide attention for their ads promoting skateboarders in a positive light (i.e., skaters as athletes). Their television spots featured golfers and joggers being hassled in much the same way as skateboarders are. Nike received an incredible response to the ads from both skaters and non-skaters, most of which was very favorable.

Over time, the skateboard shoe industry has carved out a special niche for itself in the world of skateboarding. Whether it's Vans, Simple, DC, or Converse, skaters pick up on a style and make it their own. Others (mostly non-skaters, and sometimes parents of non-skaters) see the benefits (i.e., durability, comfort) and want to be part of the action. Although it might be hard to conceive of now, maybe one day historians will acknowledge skate shoe companies as the bridge builders of the generation gap.

Profile: Lynn Cooper

I'm 36 now and have been skateboarding for the last 22 years of my life. I began seriously skating in 1976, when the first precision bearings and urethane wheels started appearing on the market. My first board was a "Black Night" skateboard with clay wheels. When I would carve fast around a corner, I used to spend a lot of time looking for the little ball bearings that would fall out of the wheels.

I spent the early years building and skating ramps and empty swimming pools in Anaheim, California. Sadlands, The Fishbowl and the Concrete Wave Skatepark were my local hangouts back in the mid '70's. When the Skatepark era hit, I spent every possible moment skating with my friend Terry Jackson (now a legendary stuntman and stunt director) at all the new concrete skateparks all over Southern California. I was really fortunate to have been born at the right time and lived in the right part of the world.

I started competing in vertical and pipe skating back in 1981, under the ASPO (Association of Skatepark Owners) series. I was strictly a vert skater at that time and didn't know much about freestyle. I was very competitive and always going for the overall points. Therefore, I had to also compete in the freestyle, high jump, downhill, cross-country, pipe pasting and slalom competitions as well. It was great to be able to learn all aspects of skateboarding this way. I became a well-rounded skater because of it and was able to learn from the world's top pro skaters, in each specific area.

My first freestyle contest was at Magic Mountain, in 1981. It was the first time I had ever seen pro freestylers. It was the first time I saw Rodney Mullen. It was quite impressive. I didn't even own a real freestyle board at that time. I ended up cutting down my Eddie Elguera pool board into the shape of a freestyle board to enter the contest. I entered the 1A division and earned 1st place in both the freestyle and slalom events and skated to "Just What I Needed", by the Cars.

I'll never forget that contest. Not because I won, but because my truck was almost stolen. John Lucero and I found it at the other end of the parking lot all beat up. Brian Martin helped me to hotwire my truck, so I could get home. The door locks and ignition switch were gone. I had to duct tape a tool socket in the ignition switch hole, so that my steering would turn, otherwise it would lock in place. I'm glad the socket didn't fall out while I was driving through LA's freeways on the way home.

The '80's were an interesting time for me. I had so many vert skating friends that turned pro and so many new friends that were into freestyle. I would spend half my time at the skateparks and the other half freestyling. I competed from 1981–1990 in well over a hundred contests. The only reason I stopped competing is because the skate industry stopped promoting and holding freestyle contests. If freestyle contests were ever to re-emerge, I'd be up to competing for fun again.

I've always valued the experiences and confidence I gained from having competed for so many years. However, what I truly value the most are the great people and close friends that I have had the honor of making through the last 22 years. Skateboarding is the single element that has had the largest impact on my life, in so many ways. Wherever I skate, I end up working with the younger skaters and teaching them old-style my-style tricks, as well as a history of skateboarding, where certain tricks came from, how skating differs today vs. yesterday and how skating can create a positive image in your mind, so that you can remain successful in life. Success is what you make of it!

As long as my health holds up, one day I'll be skating even longer than Russ Howell. I won't be needing Geritol either — how's that for a goal!!!

When I was a kid, I remember a line someone wrote in *SkateBoarder* magazine. It simply said: "Go Where You May!" That about sums it up for me!

—Lynn Cooper

Kevin Harris

One of Canada's best exports in the freestyle market, Kevin consistently placed at the top of many contests during the '80's. He was known for his dazzling array of 360 variations and lightning-fast footwork. Kevin was sponsored by Powell Peralta.

"I will never forget the day, walking though Del Mar Skatepark parking lot, and a voice from a car yelling at me, "Hey you, Lou Wrigley! Lou Wrigley, over here." This was a nickname only one group of skaters knew. They were from Winnipeg, Canada, and told this nickname to the legendary Stacy Peralta. . . . Stacy had developed a team called the "Bones Brigade." This was the top team in the world at the time. Just then a dream was about to come true: Stacy asked me to ride for the team. The year was 1982.

"After this, the years to follow were incredible: tours, demo's, contests, traveling the world and my own pro model. This was all taking place within the company of top skaters such as Tony Hawk, Steve Caballero, Mike McGill, Tommy Guerrero, Lance Mountain, Rodney Mullen and Per Welinder. The company cared very much for the riders and it was a great company to ride for.

"George Powell and Stacy would later set my family up in the business side of skateboarding to distribute their product in Canada. This was another dream that came true and a natural step to go from professional skater to the business end of it. It was an additional gesture I have so much gratitude for. Skateboarding has meant so much to me. It has been a huge part of my life. It is all around our family all of the time. I have been so lucky to have met so many skaters from all over and still keep in contact with a lot of them. I think skating is in your blood, once you start. It is always there in some form. I started skating in 1975 and still have a desire to skate now. I hopefully will pass that feeling to my kids who skate now and have been for some time. I know I will always be involved in skateboarding, as it is such a great part of my life and will be for years to come."

Kevin Harris
POWELL PERALTA

World Industries

When skateboarding hit it big for the third time in the '80's, five major skateboard companies emerged: Powell Peralta, Santa Cruz, Tracker, Independent, and Vision (which also had Schmitt Stix and Sims). Enormous amounts of money were rolling into the industry. It was not unheard-of for professional skaters to be making twice or three times what their parents were earning.

But despite this success, all was not rosy. Most skateboard manufacturers at the time tended to be more corporate and conservative. Skaters wanted to do whatever they felt like doing. In most cases, this led to some friction between the two parties. Many skaters felt that the manufacturers were unwilling to listen and act on their suggestions. The companies, for their part, tried to respond as best as they could within the parameters of standard business practices.

As skateboarding moved from wooden ramps to the street it became increasingly technical, incorporating numerous ollie variations and flips. Pro skaters were the first to start changing their technology. Skaters like Mark Gonzales would take freestyle wheels (which were much harder and smaller than the traditional skate wheels) and use them to achieve higher ollies.

Skaters who had started life as pros in the early to mid '80's were no longer teenagers. They had minds of their own and they disliked not being able to follow through on their ideas. The dream of skaters making equipment for skaters was the catalyst for the rise of the independent skateboard company.

Steve Rocco was the first person to start chipping away at the Big Five's domination of the marketplace. When he started his own company in 1987, people had no idea that within five years, the skateboard industry would be turned upside down.

The Story of World Industries
by Steve Rocco

The Beginnings

When I was about 11, my brother Pat got a skateboard for his birthday. My dad got me one also. There was a curb about 18 inches high near our house. We would spend hours just trying to ride off of it.

The First Sponsor

There was this guy, Jim Drake, who lived near me. His brother owned Tunnel and he just started giving me free stuff. At first I was the worst guy on the team, sort of like a mascot. I wound up on Powell, but I only rode for them for about a month, then Sims offered me a Pro Model in 1979. This was the first freestyle pro model.

The Problems and the Solution

In the early 1980's, Vision took over Sims and it was all downhill. Brad [Dorfman] treated us like bastard step-children while Vision got all the glory. I was very rebellious and in 1987 Brad kicked me off the team. I was living on Natas Kaupas' kitchen floor at the time. I vividly remember having dinner with Natas and Skip Engblom [of Santa Monica Airlines] at a Mexican restaurant. I was 27, with no sponsor. I thought my life in skateboarding was over. I would have to go back to work for my dad in the dry cleaning store. Skip told me not to worry. The next morning he took me to this woodshop and told me if I bought 500 boards he could get them sold for me. I cash advanced by credit card for $6,000 and Santa Monica Airlines: Rocco Division was born.

We've Got a Company, Now What?

From there things just got crazier. I teamed up with John Lucero [from Black Label] and we got a warehouse together. After three weeks, Lucero backed out because I spent $800 on shelves. Once again, I thought it was over. This time rescue came from a very unlikely source — Rodney Mullen. Rodney bought out Lucero for $6,000 and we were partners. This might lead you to believe that Rodney had a keen sense for business and prophetic vision of the future. In reality, I tricked Rodney out of the money and he pretty much figured it was as good an investment as flushing it down the toilet and hoping more would come back up. Which is pretty much true, because at the time, we were broke. I borrowed $20,000 in a paper bag from a bookie. The pay-back conditions were simple: borrow $20,000, pay back $30,000 in one year, or else. Nothing motivates like fear. And with Rodney around, we had plenty of that.

I took my bag of cash down to Vision and waved it around the parking lot. Jesse Martinez was the only one who would listen to me. I offered him $2 a board [royalty], twice the industry standard, and he fell for it.

1988 — Things Start Moving

With Jesse at my side the company started to take shape. He brought in Jeff Hartsel, which now gave us a team of three. For the first time I actually felt like things were starting to go well. The problem was they were going *too* well. We started selling more than anyone had ever anticipated, and before long the eyes of the big [skateboard companies] were on us. The first to act was Santa Cruz. At the time Santa Cruz was licensing the Santa Monica Airlines name from Skip. They got a little annoyed because I ran an ad saying that all wheels come from the same place and were made of the same stuff; hence there was no such thing as "special formulas."

The penalty for telling the truth was to have Skip call and tell me I could no longer use the Santa Monica Airlines name. I was devastated. Next Rodney was told that if he didn't pull out his investment (now up to $18,000), he would be kicked off the Powell team. Rodney came to me and told me he was out. Then another competitor kicked in and tried to stop our mold maker from delivering us the first double kick molds. At this point most people with any common sense would have just given up. [These three companies] had combined sales of over 100 million dollars. I was living off the dollar bills kids sent in for stickers. Fortunately, the only thing I had less of than money was common sense.

Job one was to convince (trick) Rodney into staying. Rodney was trying to figure out where to stay by confronting me and George Powell with worst-case scenarios. He told us both that he was leaving and figured he would stay with the one who handled it better. He asked me if I would pay him back all his money. I told him sure, no problem (even though I would have killed him). He then told George he might be leaving and George told him he was an idiot for considering World over Powell. Rodney came back and said he was quitting Powell and he and Mike Vallely were going to ride for World. I tried to act surprised, but I knew what Rodney was doing all along. Mike and Rodney each put in $15,000, which gave us the money we needed for the double kick molds. We changed our name to SMA World Industries as a joke, but they said we couldn't use the SMA part, so we dropped the SMA and World Industries was born.

The Notorious Nineties

To the skateboard industry World Industries was now an actual, real company with real riders. But to us the company was more like a giant toy. Our company motto was pretty much "Why not?" We would do ads without products, skateboard graphics with cartoons instead of skulls, and skateboard shapes that didn't look like skateboards. Now in the wacky world of skateboarding today this sounds like no big deal, but in 1990 people thought we were out of our minds, and at the time, we were. In fact, only in retrospect can we now look back and see the thin line we walked was closer to insanity than the premeditated genius that people often give us credit for. But success quickly transforms pea-brains into prophets and our success started with the Mike Vallely animal farm board. This board, and the people behind it, would change the face of skateboarding forever. This was Marc Mckee's first skateboard graphic.

The cartoon characters not only represented a clear departure from the usual skulls and gore which dominated the market at the time, but it introduced the element of wit and humor into graphics as well. In the years to follow McKee would set the standard in graphics for the whole industry. This was also Rodney Mullen's debut as a shape maker. At the time almost all large boards were pointy nosed. This looked more like a giant freestyle board than anything else. Though by today's standards it may look funny, this board was the predecessor of modern shapes to come and like McKee, Rodney would lead the way in shapes for the next decade.

Blind, 101, Plan B, Etc.

In 1990, Mark Gonzales approached me after he saw what we were doing. He was pretty amazed that we did whatever we wanted and he wanted to be a part of it. At the time he was riding for Vision and the whole idea of Blind was his idea — "Blind" being the opposite of "Vision." We started up the company together and took our best pro from World, who at the time was Jason Lee, and moved him to Blind. Things just took off from there.

In 1991 we started 101. Natas Kaupas was friends with Mark Gonzales and myself and he saw what was going on and he wanted to do the same thing. It was a real sim-

SUPERFLY

FLAMEE
31.375"

GIGER SLICK
31.875" X 7.875"

TR...
32...

ple, handshake deal. Nothing was ever really planned out.

Plan B was different. In 1992 H Street's Mike Ternasky came to me and said he wasn't happy with the way the owner was treating him. There was some disagreement over money. Mike came to me to help get him started. We were the distributor and manufacturer and Mike worked on marketing out of his San Diego office.

One key thing Mike was able to accomplish was that he got Rodney Mullen, the world's best freestyler, pointed in the streetskating direction. He recognized Rodney's talents and as a result, most of the ollie variations done by today's skaters have their roots with Rodney. Plan B was one of the first companies that was formulated for instant success. Mike was going to call the company Type A (after the personality classification) but eventually decided to call it Plan B.

In 1993 things were going real good until about September. Plan B rider Rick Howard got into a fight with Mike Ternasky over a wheel invoice. It was a completely retarded thing and he got the other skaters all riled up. Rick took seven of our top pros and started Girl.

Mike was devastated after they left. We sat down and tried to regroup — it was like getting suckerpunched. In January 1994, we got hit again when Girl started up Chocolate and took another whack of our riders. Although I wanted to kill these guys, Mike made me promise that we would beat them fair and square. Tragically he was killed in a car accident in 1994. Eventually Plan B broke away from the World Industries family.

In 1995 I realized that both World and Blind needed more cohesiveness — we were doing things and they were okay, but there was no general direction. That's when I picked Marc McKee's "devil man" logo to be the base of World. We saw how well that worked and added the grim reaper to be the focus of Blind.

In 1997 the A Team was developed and it was the first company that was completely thought out. It was aimed at the skaters who were extremely serious about skating. The hardest thing when you go on a demo with the A Team guys is to have them stop once the demo is finished. You can't get them to stop, even after the kids have left.

Our whole company has skateboarding in its roots. Skateboarding is part of the lives of the people who work here. The challenge is to grow the company to make it a different type of organization. But at the core of World Industries, I am just happy to continue to do the fun stuff.

Pooling Your Memories

by Darrel Delgado

I was your typical five year old coming from divorced parents with two older brothers. I grew up for the most part in Santee, California. Santee was a semi-rural town that was really quite nice as I think back on it. I was mainly interested in bikes up until eighth grade, even after I had seen Gregg Weaver on the cover of *SkateBoarder* magazine carving a pool. I remember how that picture blew my mind — I knew that skateboarding was cool and all, but to see that — the whole concept of what was really going on entered my brain. Think about how the urethane wheel invention changed skateboarding forever. You could ride on anything your wheels would grip on, an amazing thought! This cover shot also ingrained in my brain how soulful and incredibly expressive the medium of skating a drained swimming pool actually was. The possibilities are endless, it is just a matter of how long you can hack this truly unique discipline of skateboarding.

In 1976–1977 I was able to witness the art of pool riding at an egg-shaped pool a few miles from my house. It was called the "Tidy Bowl." The guys riding the pool were com-

pletely oblivious to the politics of skating, they were just having fun. I would be at home daydreaming, just imagining them riding this pool. Another session I was fortunate enough to stumble upon being a youngster was at the "Massage Bowl" in El Cajon, CA. This pool was behind a massage parlor. The session was heavy; players included Pat Weaver, Rodney Jesse, Rocket Man, Steve Cathey, Dave Repp, Layne Oaks, Ron Fletcher, etc. Watching this at age 12 again left an impression on me of the raw energy being generated.

Growing up, my friends and I skated everything we could, although the Tidy Bowl was the first pool I ever rode. I was getting more and more out of bikes and started to learn to carve a pool. After witnessing those earlier sessions by the older guys it was time for me to give it a try. The Tidy Bowl scene was mellow for years, a flattened house with a pool next to it, but like a lot of pools it eventually was bulldozed. My friends and I were surrounded by pools at a young age; this is just the way Santee is, a lot of homes have swimming pools.

In 1978 my brother Dave built me a seven-foot-high quarterpipe. Having a ramp at my house, my popularity grew amongst the local skaters and was a turning point for my deeper interest in skateboarding. One day Dave Duncan showed up at my ramp. Dave was a few years older and was heavily into skating. Dave was the new kid in town and our friendship grew as we agreed on what and who was radical in the sport at the time. Our biggest influence was of course Dogtown and anything that had to do with the skaters or style of Dogtown. One entire wall in Duncan's room was covered with pictures of Tony Alva. I had witnessed some radical skating by this time, but I really started thinking more worldly about all the terrain that was before me just by meeting Duncan. Dave had already accomplished so much — he traveled around and entered contests and was sponsored by Pro-Am Skateboards. . . .

With Duncan off to skate contests or traveling, my friends and I kept the scene alive; after my ramp was gone we built at least four more ramps in the years to come. We had the terrain, it was just a matter of picking what we wanted to ride at the time. One day in the neighborhood we stumbled upon a six-foot oval pool. We went to the door and obtained permission to skate, but only if we cleaned the pool. We could ride it for two weeks as payment for cleaning the pool. We found dead frogs in the pool while draining it and named it the "Frog Bowl." This early pool experience spawned many more instigations into the further discovery of drained or ready to be drained swimming pool situations. My friends and I called our town "Frogtown," appropriately named after our biggest influence. . . .

By 1983 the skating possibilities were endless and *Thrasher* magazine was the staple periodical that kept us hyped up on finding and grinding anything in our reach. As time and countless sessions passed, the more I learned that the main focal point of all my skating should be a surfing style. This style to me was and still is the best you could have and nobody looked better doing it than Jay "boy" Adams of Dogtown. Jay [set the standard for] the way skating should look. The low body positioning, looseness, hand placement and snappy body contortions are all part of true surf style. The Dogtowners showed me that style is everything.

By 1984 I was a surfer-skater; it didn't matter that I lived 24 miles from the beach. I was also a control freak of sorts, I made it a point to have a handle on every skate spot in San Diego, my hometown. I wasn't trying to prove anything, I just wanted to know what all my options were . . . I would follow up on any tip, lead or

connection that would get me access to a spot. I wasn't shy when it came to confronting people that I didn't know as long as ultimately I would get in the door to skate. Soon I realized that I had to keep lists of pools in order to remember all of them, which I did.

1987 was another turning point for me. By this time I knew for sure that pool skating was the best discipline of skateboarding there was, so leading up to this year pools had taken more of a precedence over the other

disciplines of skating. When Dave Duncan said that he had met Tony Alva and had skated with him it was a big deal. Alva — an original Dogtowner and one of the true pioneers of pool riding.

After Alva saw me skate at Del Mar's Kona Bowl II pool, he told Duncan that I could get boards, wheels and accessories for free. There was no other company that was more bad ass than Alva at the time. I was honored to ride Alva's products, nothing could compare, especially for a pool rider. I

took my sponsored amateur status seriously, but never wanted to get a big head over the whole deal. I just wanted to be myself and stick to my program as I always knew it. . . .

I had worked full-time for two years by 1987 and was attending college part time. I had to really decide what to do with my life. I was 23 and wanted a decent future for myself. After contemplating everything and everybody I had ever met in the skateboarding world and also trying to be realistic about my skating ability, I decided that I would continue to

work full time and keep going to school and at the same time try to be one of the best backyard pool skaters in the world. I felt that for me this was the only direction that would make sense for me. I knew that I could never be good enough to be a professional skateboarder and that it would be more beneficial and smart of me to just take my sponsored amateur status as far as it could go. I am really happy that I made this decision. I have obtained far more than I could have ever imagined out of skateboarding by simply not expecting too much out of it. It seemed that

once someone went pro, the opportunity to travel and make money did increase, but the turnover rate was high and trying to make ends meet was hard for most. . . .

Maintaining my head and not claiming to be more than I was gave me a beautiful path on which to enjoy skateboarding. In 1988 I seriously hurt myself while skating a backyard pool. My skating has never been the same since that day. I am so happy just to be able to walk again. I broke both bones in my ankle and had a metal plate and ten screws put in my leg. My doctor told me that my ankle could be 90–95% [of what] it had originally been. I took that thought and have been running with it ever since. I know I am not as radical as I used to be, but I have come damn close at times, much to my amazement. I am still rehabilitating 10 years later. I am fortunate to even be able to ride, but now am stoked to just have fun.

I have sometimes felt that I have never met my objective in skateboarding. I mean to obtain credit for what I was trying to do up until 1988.

My main objective was to take pool riding to a more thorough level. I am talking about riding the entire pool, every wall, nook and cranny, shallow end and not leaving any wall unskated. Carving was to be the fundamental base mixed in with any other maneuvers you could do. Picture in your mind a super ball being thrown into a four-wall racquet ball court, bouncing everywhere and in all directions. This was my intended contribution to pool riding. This type of skating takes a lot of work, but once accomplished is very satisfying. I was in the process of show-

ing the world my perception of how a pool should be ridden. I am not sure how many skaters received the message, but I do know that I have ridden with some of the best riders in the world and have met all the skaters I have really looked up to and sessioned with a lot of them, this to me is success. When some bad ass tells me that I have inspired them it makes me feel that I have met my objective in skating. It doesn't matter if you are in the magazines or not, it only matters that you are satisfied with yourself.

Skateboarding in a pool is like being a painter, and every new pool is a blank canvas and you are the artist. Every artist has a different approach and every pool is different, which keeps the intrigue alive. You can go wherever your mind and the transitions will let you go.

Craig R. Stecyk III

Craig R. Stecyk has enjoyed a long career in skateboarding and surfing. At the age of 17 he had his first article published in *Surfer,* and since then he has had a profound effect on the art and imagery of the sport.

Craig grew up on the border of West Los Angeles and Santa Monica. From a young age he skated with some of the best in the world, including Danny Bearer and Torger Johnson. To give you an idea of the extent of Craig Stecyk's contributions, here is just a partial list:

➡ • *Designed "Rat Bones" logo for Powell Peralta* The rat motif arose from an amusement park being pulled down near Lick Pier in the mid 1970's. As the park was being destroyed, the rodent population was being forced from their natural home. Craig and some friends visited the pier at night and were amazed to see groups of rats moving in formation. The image stuck with Craig and he spray painted it in numerous places. Eventually it wound up as a Powell Peralta logo.

➡ • *Skateboard Video.* Craig had spent a lot of time filming skateboarders and surfers in the '60's. By 1974 he was using reel-to-reel video tape (this was before video cassettes!) to shoot skateboarders. He was instrumental in bringing video and skateboarding together, later serving as art director and production designer on a number of Powell Peralta videos.

➡ • *Zephyr Surfboards/Skateboards.* Along with Skip Engblom, Dana Wolfe and Jeff Ho, Craig started Zephyr — one of the most influential surf/skate manufacturers of the 1970's. The Zephyr skateboard team helped move skateboarding from freestyle/slalom to vert in pools and pipes. Their aggressive attitude paved the way for a whole new development within skateboarding.

➡ • *Dogtown — The Name.* A number of stories are kicking around as to how Santa Monica got its skateboard sobriquet. People talk of Chicano gangs in the 1930's coming up with the name, but another legend credits Craig as the originator. Craig recalls that in the late '60's he was sitting on a park bench in Ocean Park and came up with the following sentence: "It's a dog's life, it's a dog's town." And the name stuck.

➡ • *Graphics on Decks.* Craig drew on a lot a boards and was responsible for the Dogtown Cross, along with its "Chicano Style" in the mid 1970's.

Craig has also given the art world a tremendous amount as well. He's known for blowtorching Cadillacs in half and bronzing roadkill for art installations ("Roadrash").

The skateboard is a fantastic transportation medium . . . you've got to give skateboarding props their due, constituting the single most important contribution that post-industrial-evolution society has come up with in the area of high performance, user friendly, easily accessible, adaptable and ecologically oriented transportation . . . an important thing when people worry about automobiles spewing out their own weight in carbon every year or old polyester foam and fiberglass surfboards that clog landfills for thousands of years, never breaking down, while a skateboard consumes no fuel in its use, is capable of providing hundreds of thousands of miles of transport over its life, and is made from materials that are almost entirely renewable and recyclable.

— CR Stecyk, "Sidewalk Surfing," 1997

80's Legends

Eric Dressen
Appeared in *SkateBoarder*'s "Who's Hot" section at the age of 10. Went on to fame as a top streetstyle skater. Originally a rider for Logan Earth Ski, Eric is one of the few riders to span three decades of pro skating.

Mark Gonzales
A streetstyle legend. The first rider to do handrails, and inventor of numerous ollie-based tricks. Originally a rider for Vision, street-skaters the world over owe a huge amount to the Gonz's talents.

Tommy Guerrero
An awesome streetstyle skater who took the ollie to new heights at the start of skateboarding's third comeback in the '80's. Tommy's ollies in the streets of San Francisco on the Powell Peralta videos set the foundation for streetskating to become enormously popular during the 1980's.

Natas Kaupas
One of the major streetstyle skaters of the '80's, Natas' influence can still be felt today. His reworking of the ollie pushed the sport into new areas. Natas rode for Santa Monica Airlines and then Santa Cruz. He eventually wound up with Steve Rocco and creating 101. The first skater to have a signature shoe (by Etnies).

John Lucero
One of the early pioneers of street skating. John was thrown out of a skatepark and began pulling moves in the parking lot to the amazement of skaters. He has enjoyed a great deal of success with his Black Label skate company.

Duane Peters
"The Master of Disaster" was a major innovator of many vertical tricks including the layback roll-out, the sweeper and the invert revert. One of Duane's greatest achievements was the "loop of life," a full, 360-degree rotation in a specially designed loop. A totally committed skater since the mid 1970's.

Jeff Phillips
Originally from Texas, Jeff Phillips was an extremely talented ramp rider. His signature move was the "Phillips 66," a trick very few skaters could do. In 1989 Jeff opened his own skatepark which received rave reviews from all who rode it. Tragically, Jeff took his own life on December 25, 1993.

Rob Roskopp
Originally from the East (he has lived in Michigan and Ohio), Rob moved out to California in the early '80's. Within three months of his arrival he was sponsored by Madrid and after a year wound up riding for Santa Cruz. Rob was a very strong rider in both vert and street.

Per Welinder
Swedish freestyler/streetstyler who incorporated both strength and technical moves into his routines. Rode for Powell Peralta and joined forces with Tony Hawk to create Birdhouse Projects.

Mike Vallely
One of the best streetstyler skaters from the late '80's, Mike was originally sponsored by Powell Peralta. He was known for his innovative style and his riding has influenced a generation of skaters.

"When I was 14 years old I started skateboarding, and my life was changed for the better that day. It was changed because at that time I found a sense of purpose, a reason to hold my chin up. I got an identity and something productive. It was creative, physical activity and I used my entire being to do it. I found my thing, my niche, and up until that time I had been searching. I think it was the most important time to find something like that because I was able to bypass all the bull that you usually have to go through as a teenager. It made my life better and it's now many years later and it still remains what it was that first day. I am very protective of my initial dealings with skateboarding. It's hard, but I try to ensure that other kids who are starting out get that same experience. It's a good thing for young people to do that brings many rewards."

Fourth Wave (1993–now)

Economic recession put a damper on all industries in the early 1990's. Skateboarding also had to contend with a new nemesis — Rollerblading. As in the past, a hardcore contingent remained with the sport, but this time the attrition was not as great as it was in the past. The growth of cable television, satellite TV and the Internet would lead to greater worldwide awareness of skateboarding. The "baby boomlet " — the offspring of the baby boomers — were hitting their rebellious teens. This, combined with their significant spending power, led to skateboarding's fourth, and possibly permanent wave. Those kids who took up skating in the '70s now have kids of their own, to whom they want to pass on the fun and liberation of skateboarding. And many of those young moms and dads are digging out their old boards and hitting the pavement once more themselves.

By the mid 1990's, skateboarding once again reemerged and the fourth wave had begun. In 1995, skateboarding gained a great deal of exposure at the ESPN 2 Extreme Games. Skateboard shoe manufacturers like Etnies and Vans begin selling huge quantities of product and were joined by other soft good manufacturers eager once again to cash in on skateboarding's popularity.

At the end of the 1990's, skateboarding's focus remains streetstyle and the industry is filled with numerous manufacturers and marketers. In many cases, pro skaters develop their own product and manage their own companies. Longboarding, a once forgotten art featuring large boards, has begun to make a comeback, and downhill skateboarding has entered a whole new dimension thanks to street luge. In California, public skateboard parks are beginning to be built once again, thanks to a change in legislation. The hard work of Jim Fitzpatrick and the International Association of Skateboard Companies has ensured that other states will follow, and more parks are scheduled for construction over the next few years.

Over the past 40 years, skateboarding has had its peaks and valleys of popularity. Poor product, issues of safety, and economic recessions have all contributed to the valleys. However, skateboarding technology has vastly improved since clay wheels. In terms of injuries, the sport remains much safer than football, Rollerblading or hockey (when you look at percentage of participants injured). Despite safety concerns or economic recessions, the sport endures simply because it is so much fun!

Jim
Fitzpatrick
Skateboard
Ambassador
(Part II)

In an earlier section, Jim's career as a skateboard ambassador, bringing American skateboarding to Europe, was discussed. But Jim has also used his diplomatic skills back home in the States to address the perennial problem of skate space.

After working with the Bones Brigade's European tour, Jim got the idea to start the equivalent of SIMA (the Surf Industry Manufacturers Association). He had been on the SIMA board as the skateboarding representative, and suggested that skateboard companies create a similar association.

Over time, an organization came together: the International Association of Skateboard Companies (IASC). One of the most important things IASC has accomplished was to ensure that skateboarding was legally classified as a hazardous activity. This classification basically means that participants in the hazardous activity accept the risks and cannot sue if they are injured while pursuing it at a public facility.

Prior to IASC, California State Assemblyman Bill Morrow had been working alone trying to get skateboarding classified as a hazardous activity. Morrow wanted skateboarding reclassified because he was receiving calls from parents with children who skate. The skaters were getting in trouble for skating in illegal places (mostly downtown cores in Morrow's district). "Assemblyman Morrow was trying to solve the problem for his constituents and really had no idea of the scope of the skateboard world," recalls Jim.

Since skateboarding was not legally classified as a hazardous activity, it meant that cities would have no immunity against lawsuits resulting from skateboarding accidents on public property. Without being classified as a hazardous activity, cities could be sued if someone got hurt in a public skatepark. This was precisely the problem that skatepark owners had faced in the 1970's — the liability insurance was crippling.

Eventually, a series of events led to Jim meeting with the politicians. He presented his testimony to the Assembly's Judiciary Committee and this was the first time the politicians heard just how large the skateboard industry was. "They had no idea," recalls Jim.

After numerous presentations and committee deliberations, AB 1296 was finally passed by Governor Pete Wilson in October of 1997. Now that AB 1296 has amended Section 115800 of California's Health and Safety code and cities cannot be sued, new public skateboard parks are being built all over the state. This has led to other states amending their Health and Safety Codes and beginning the process of building public skateboard parks. No doubt the changes in California will have enormous repercussions for skateboarding for many years to come.

Jim Fitzpatrick continues to skate daily and promote the sport as best he can. Now a school principal, Jim's energy and passion for skateboarding remain as intense as they were back when he was banging rollerskates on to wood some 40 years earlier.

When I first saw a skateboard, I knew deep from the heart that it was something I should do. I didn't know why, but looking back, 20 years on a skateboard has given me so much fun, making me investigate and use my creativity, given me great friends from all around the world. Competing and demoing has helped me develop more of my human potential.

Whenever I just cruise down an empty road or sidewalk, doing nothing but feeling the wind in my face, I realize that this is why I do it . . . It's a feeling of total freedom and perfection which is the goal of life.

—"Lillis"

Standup
Street Luge

Over the years, standup racing has produced its share of superstars: John Hutson, Roger Hickey, Guy Grundy and Chuy Madrigal. Most skaters will tell you hitting 30 miles an hour on a skateboard can feel pretty intense; adding another 20 to 30 miles an hour is a whole other experience. As X Game gold medal winner Biker Sherlock says, "The luge is just fun. Standup is big wave surfing, it's the biggest rush I get in my whole life."

Most standup racers hit anywhere from 45 to 55 miles an hour; George Orton has hit 61.87 mph. At this speed, it's all or nothing. Wheel wobbles won't just flip you off the board and cause road rash — you're looking at potentially life-threatening damage.

Street luge is different in that the skaters are lying down as they bomb down hills on boards specially modified for luging purposes. At one time, street luge was a purely underground activity, but thanks to the publicity of events like the X Games, the sport is growing rapidly. Since the riders have less wind resistance than the standup skaters, the speeds reach an even higher level. Street lugers can hit in excess of 70 miles an hour.

Although most skaters are drawn to either street or vert riding, there is certainly a growing interest in hitting the hills. As any skater over 25 will tell you, the knees pretty much dictate where you'll ride your board for most of the day!

The Chocolate Alien Girl from Zoo York

It is not surprising that skateboarding, with its youthful, rebellious streak, would see a backlash against large companies trying to corner or dominate the skateboard market. In the 1980's, the skateboard industry had only five key players that garnered most of the revenue. Over the past decade, numerous new skateboard companies have emerged. Now the industry comprises hundreds of smaller companies trying to compete in the skateboarding marketplace. Riders jump teams or start their own companies within weeks. Board graphics change even faster. It is next to impossible to keep up with this dynamic industry, so here are just a few of the many skateboard companies that started life in the 1990's.

Chris Carter had spent a good deal of time in the skateboard industry, and by the time the 1980's had finished, he was the team manager for Tracker Designs. In 1990 a friend of his, Mike Hill, was working at Gordon & Smith and he offered a job to Chris. Chris immediately took the job but within a year decided to change course. Chris and Mike teamed up to form a new company. "We wanted to have our own business," explained Chris, "a place where we didn't need to ask permission."

The name **Alien Workshop** came from friend John Johnson. In the days before the World Wide Web, John ran a bulletin board that discussed alien conspiracy theories. One of the theories surrounded the Stealth Bomber. It was believed that the bomber was not a product of the 1980's, but rather had been built in the 1940's with technology made in "alien workshops." So compelling were John's conspiracy stories that the name stuck.

California is the home of most of the world's skateboard manufacturers, but **Alien Workshop** chose to set up shop in Ohio, since Mike was originally from the area. Being in Ohio also meant that start-up costs and general expenses were much lower than in California.

Joining Chris and Mike in their eastern adventure was pro skater Neil Blender. "Neil's career was winding down and he wanted a change," says Chris. "He was willing to move." Neil made an immense artistic contribution to **Alien Workshop**.

When **Alien Workshop** started, the skate industry along with the worldwide economy was going through a painful recession. It was a tough go for a lot of companies. "We were eating a lot of pasta," recalls Chris. One problem that plagues many new businesses is undercapitalization and **Alien Workshop** was no exception. However, over time their dedication and original ideas started to pay off.

In explaining the success of **Alien Workshop**, Chris says, "We were unhappy with the whole marketing vehicle. In the early 1990's it was three ideas: 1) rip off logos 2) sex 3) violence. **Alien Workshop** marketed with original ideas." **Alien Workshop** was one of the first companies to start merchandising "alien" products. No doubt there were a number of UFO enthusiasts who purchased a "Visitor" t-shirt or sticker not realizing that they were supporting a skateboard company.

As things began to roll, changes were made to the company. Mark Erikson was brought in as a new partner, and an old warehouse was purchased. This warehouse became half production workshop and half skatepark.

145

New Deal was formed in the spring of 1990 by Steve Douglas, Andy Howell, and Paul Schmitt. It was named after a skateshop in England owned by a friend of Douglas. The New Deal name would symbolize a change in the business aspects of skateboarding.

One of the company's first innovations was to have a promo video out in the skateshops even before their products were available. This resulted in instant demand for New Deal products when they did appear. Using this kind of tactic, New Deal busted out onto the scene and became one of the major board companies in the market by late 1990. Up until then, Powell, Vision and Santa Cruz had dominated the market, primarily by promoting vert skating. New Deal had its share of vert stars, but focused mainly on street skaters. Its pros included Ed Templeton, Danny Sargent, Andy Howell, Steve Douglas, and Andrew Morrison.

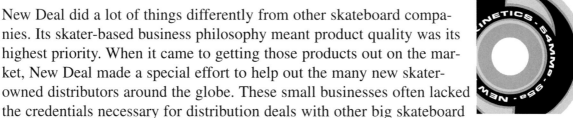

New Deal did a lot of things differently from other skateboard companies. Its skater-based business philosophy meant product quality was its highest priority. When it came to getting those products out on the market, New Deal made a special effort to help out the many new skater-owned distributors around the globe. These small businesses often lacked the credentials necessary for distribution deals with other big skateboard companies; New Deal's support and faith no doubt gave them a boost.

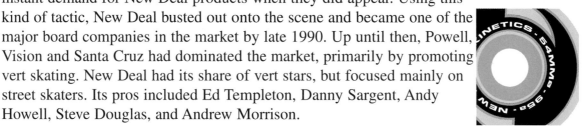

New Deal's somewhat risky distribution arrangements paid off, and the company expanded at a rapid pace, moving beyond skateboards. In 1992, along with its videos, New Deal made a splash in the clothing side of the skateboard marketplace with its Big Deal Jeans. But for some the New Deal team was growing too big; Andy Howell got restless and decided to start Underworld Element (later to be known as just Element) as a sister company.

With all the different branches of the company growing, Giant Distribution was formed in 1993 to be the central source for all of these products and many more to come. That same year, Steve Douglas and Josh Friedberg established *411 Video Magazine*. Chris Ortiz joined soon after to take care of filming aspects and the music. The bi-monthly video 'zine features profiles of companies and riders, and reports on new trends in the industry. For skaters, *411VM* was a breath of fresh air at a time

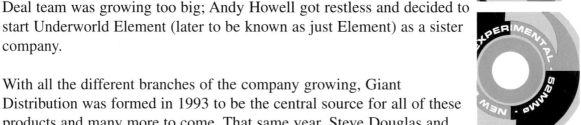

when much of the skate media and advertising had a negative, backbiting tone. The magazine's positive outlook and presentation has made it a worldwide success.

In 1994, New Deal entered the skateboard wheel business when team rider Justin Girard started the Golden State Wheel Company. Andy Howell left the company and Johnny Schillereff was brought in to head up the artistic side of Giant's many different products. In the years that followed, Giant worked to consolidate its position in the skateboarding industry. Summer , 1997, saw the intrduction of Destructo Trucks. With the creative direction of Gary Parkin and Schillereff and a powerful pro team, the trucks have gone on to become hot sellers, challenging the established truck companies.

As the millennium approaches, Giant has established itself as an industry powerhouse, carrying on its founders' tradition of innovative skateboard products and videos. Its worldwide distribution network ensures that at any given moment, someone somewhere is either riding a truck, board, wheel or watching a video that has come from the Giant warehouse.

147

od Swank started Foundation in 1989 with the encouragement of Steve Rocco. Tod had made a name for himself in the skate world as both an impressive photographer and a skater. He was the originator of the "feeble grind" and had worked as a staff photographer at *Transworld Skateboarding*. One of Tod's prized possessions was a Harley Davidson motorcycle that he had spent a considerable amount of time fixing up. He sold this bike for $5,000 dollars and started Foundation Skateboards.

Tod started working out of his bedroom and eventually moved to a 1,000-square-foot warehouse. In what is surely a first for the skateboard industry, Tod put out his own model under a pseudonym — Justin Lovely.

At first, Foundation did not have a team of pro riders, but slowly, through dedicated touring and promotion, word spread and people started to take notice, and a team was formed. Like many of the new generation of skateboard companies, Foundation involved its riders in all aspects of the development and implementation of new ideas. The rise of Foundation has been impressive. From yearly sales of $8,000 in 1992, they have grown to become one of the largest skateboard companies in the business.

The roots of Toy Machine date back to 1992 when Ed Templeton was a pro rider for New Deal. Ed wanted New Deal to create a new line of boards, but things didn't work out. He left New Deal and teamed up with Mike Vallely to create a company called TV. Unfortunately, this didn't work out and the company folded. A new company called Television was started, but due to creative differences with various parties, this too closed. Finally, after 18 months, Ed decided to start his own company and named it Toy Machine.

In early 1994, he approached Tod Swank of Foundation with the idea of joining forces. The timing was good for both parties, since Foundation was about to move to a larger warehouse. By the summer of 1994, Ed had found a home for Toy Machine. When the two companies joined forces the name Tum Yeto was born. Tod Swank explains that the name comes from "Ancient Odtnautious" and means "more than one."

Zero was created by Toy Machine pro Jamie Thomas. In late 1995, he had come up with an idea for a clothing company. The original name was Zero Division, but the last part was dropped due to another company having a similar name. For many skaters, one of the best skateboard videos ever created is Toy Machine's *Welcome to Hell* which was released in the summer of 1996. Jamie, ever the smart promoter, put a commercial for Zero in the video. This set the wheels in motion for Zero's success and it is now one of the biggest brands that Foundation has.

zoo york

This New York City-based company has its roots in a manufacturing operation called Shut Skates, founded by Rodney Smith and Bruno Musso. Shut Skates made skateboards for people in the city and surrounding areas. In the early 1990's, a number of riders left Shut Skates when they were offered more lucrative sponsorships from West Coast manufacturers. Soon after, Rodney and Bruno closed the operation. In 1993, Rodney Smith teamed up with graphic artist/skater Eli Gesner and businessman Adam Schatz to create Zoo York.

There were several factors that led to the creation of Zoo York. As Eli explained in an interview in *Skateboard Business*, "Over the years I've watched so many people who I thought were really talented skateboarders who deserved some recognition just go into obscurity. And I really felt we had a lot to offer here in New York. I just wanted to create some sort of industry here that was self sufficient, so that kids coming up who chose to go the route of the industry and become professional skateboarders would have that option, and not have to look over at something they knew nothing about, like California."

150

birdhouse

1995

1996

1997

1998

willy santos

birdhouse

Per Welinder was a Swedish freestyler/street rider who had made a name for himself on the Bones Brigade at Powell Peralta. "I got into streetstyle at an early time period," recalls Per. "I tried to apply technical tricks to streetstyle and did okay in a few contests. When people started skating handrails, I realized that it was over for me." Per retired from contests in 1989 and went about finishing his college education. He graduated from Long Beach State with a degree in marketing and went to work at Powell. "I was involved in new product management and worked on the development of clear urethane wheels."

At Powell, Per was witness to the dramatic third bust of skateboarding. Things were rough worldwide for many businesses during the 1990–92 recession and skateboard companies were not immune to the economic downturn. But Per faced other issues besides economic problems: "At Powell I was ready to spearhead new things, but I met with some resistance."

As a result of meeting this resistance, Per spoke with fellow Bones Brigaders Lance Mountain and Tony Hawk. "I suggested we try something from scratch," recalls Per. Lance declined the offer, preferring to be either an employee or owner but not a partner. Lance then went on to start The Firm. Per and Tony did join forces, however, and in January of 1992, Birdhouse Projects was formed. The name originated in Tony's nickname — "The Birdman."

The first pro models shipped in March of 1992 and featured a Jeremy Klein and Willy Santos. "We did not release a Tony Hawk board since vert skating had become much less popular compared to street," Per explained. "Eventually, we convinced Tony to start competing again." Tony was still able to place high in contests, and slowly vert skating regained its status.

In summing up the company, Per remarks, "I have always wanted to stay true to skating. At Birdhouse we give our pro riders what they are looking for."

151

planet earth

Chris Miller had spent a number of years as a top vertical pro. His skate roots go back to the days of late-70's skateboard parks like Pomona Pipe & Pool and The Pipeline. During the 1980's Chris had ridden for Santa Cruz, Gordon & Smith, and Schmitt Stix. Chris had experienced a great deal of success at all these companies. Towards the end of 1989, Chris's contract at Schmitt Stix was expiring. Although he had a good relationship with Paul Schmitt, he was unsure of where to go next. "I had an offer to ride for Vision, but I felt this was unfair to Paul." (At the time, Vision distributed Paul's brand of boards called Schmitt Stix.)

Chris talked to others in the skate industry. "I wasn't happy with some of the images in skateboarding and I wanted to do something different," remembers Chris. He came upon the idea of starting a new line of products at a company called H Street. H Street was run by Mike Ternasky and Tony Magnusson and had encountered a great deal of success as a new start-up company. But what to call the brand? He asked his young son Zach what he thought of Planet Earth and Zach replied, "That's a good name for a skateboard company." In 1990, he signed a distribution agreement with H Street and began the hard work of building his own brand. Six months into the relationship, Chris realized things "were not so rosy."

"H Street was becoming a non-functional company. Mike would often threaten to leave H Street and Tony would try and keep the peace." Eventually Mike did leave and in 1993 started Plan B with Steve Rocco. Although Chris was not involved with the breakup of H Street, he was left with a difficult situation. "I was left holding the bag and wondered if I should just start something new."

In 1992, Chris began the process of restarting Planet Earth. Within a month, he had teamed up with his father-in-law, Jim Bahringer, and entered into a manufacturing agreement with Paul Schmitt. From this beginning, Chris took a new approach to marketing the Planet Earth name.

"I had seen what had happened in the surf industry — it had moved from surfboards to clothing." Chris felt the same thing was going to happen with skateboarding and that consumers would move from hard goods like skateboards into soft goods like clothing. Although he admits he didn't see how large the skateboard shoe industry would become, Chris's attention to quality apparel ensured that Planet Earth would gain a loyal following.

Chris attributes this eye for detail and quality with his past affiliation with surfboard apparel giant Billabong. Interestingly enough, Planet Earth wasn't just gaining attention from consumers of skate product, but from other manufacturers as well — very large manufacturers. In October of 1997, Planet Earth was purchased by K2, one of the world's largest makers of ski equipment.

Jim Gray started out skateboarding in 1973 at the age of 10. "I bought my first board from a drugstore — it had clay wheels." As Jim's older brother became more interested in skateboards, so did Jim. He purchased better boards and started going to skateboard parks. Within a short while, he had picked up his first sponsorship — Pro Am. After this, Jim started entering contests; Gail Webb, the "Skateboard Mama," took notice of his abilities and asked him if he wanted to join Powerflex, a dominant player in the wheel marketplace.

After Powerflex, Jim joined up with Gordon & Smith Skateboards and stayed with the company for seven years. When skateboarding's third boom hit during the mid 1980's, Jim was also working with publisher/Tracker Truck head Larry Balma selling advertising for *Transworld Skateboarding* magazine. "I was able to get a good overview of the industry and see who the players were and where I could compete." In 1990, Jim joined Vision to work with Brad Dorfman. After six months of working at Vision, Jim decided to form his own company. "I called it Acme because I thought it was a classic, timeless name. It also had a certain whimsicalness to it," recalls Jim.

In 1993, downhill legend Beau Brown joined Acme. Over the years, Acme has marketed a number of products unique to their company. Jim is passionate about what skateboarding represents and the kinds of product Acme should be involved with: "I believe in the heart and soul of skateboarding and Gordon & Smith is one of those companies that represent this. I called up Larry Gordon and asked him if he would like to start up the brand again. Within a few weeks, we had entered into a licensing agreement." Acme is now producing and marketing Fibreflex skateboards, originally made by Gordon & Smith over 20 years ago.

The Formula One wheels evolved from the first set of wheels that Acme produced. The name "Formula One" was silk-screened onto the side of the wheel. Pro skater Omar Hassan is actively involved in managing the Formula One product.

The Scarecrow product was developed by Russ Pope who started Creature Skateboards at Santa Cruz. Scarecrow was eventually incorporated into the Acme family and adds a very gothic image to the overall lineup of product.

SUPPLY

SHORTY'S SKATEBOARD PRODUCTS

The story of how Shorty's became the biggest skateboard hardware distributor in the United States is a lesson in thinking big with a small product. The company was started in 1991 by Tony Buyalos in Santa Barbara. Tony was originally from Texas and had been skating for many years. He had worked at a skatepark and with a few skate companies before starting up Shorty's.

Tony and his girlfriend April Hammerick along with four other friends started out in an apartment. The idea was simple: In the late '80's and early '90's skateboarding changed and skaters no longer needed riser pads under their trucks. There was a need for shorter mounting hardware, and skaters would usually try to do this themselves with a saw. Tony's idea was to provide shorter mounting hardware (hence the name); he and his friends put together bags of bolts and nuts in plastic bags and started selling to skaters. Shorty's was promoted by pros Chad Muska and Steve Olsen. Over time, Shorty's has added additional products to their roster, including their own line of skateboards, but they are still best known for their nuts and bolts.

Real/Thunder/Deluxe

The roots of Real go back to Fausto Vitello, the owner of *Thrasher* magazine and manufacturer of Independent Trucks. Besides Independent, Fausto's company, Ermico Enterprises, developed a new truck called "Thunder" and special bushings called "Supercush". During the mid 1980's a music lover called Brian Ware was brought in to run Thunder. Since Brian was so into music he started Beware Records (Odd Man Out, Drunk Injuns) and Deluxe Distribution was founded. Deluxe not only handled skateboard product (i.e., Thunder Trucks), but music as well.

In 1987, Spitfire Wheels was launched by Deluxe and achieved some success. However, since Brian was more into music and there was a downturn in the skateboard industry in the late 1980's, he left the company.

In 1990, Fausto went out to visit a number of skateboard shops on the east coast. "I went into one particular shop," remembered Fausto, "and the guy said, 'Every Thursday I order a pizza, the skaters come in to my shop, and they tell me what to order from World Industries. All I carry is World Industries.'" Concerned about one company having complete control of the marketplace, Fausto moved Deluxe away from distributing strictly trucks and wheels and into boards. The name of the resulting new company was Real Skateboards, and its first two riders were Tommy Guerrero and Jim Thiebaud. Real's tremendous success was due in no small part to the contributions of erstwhile board artist Jeff Klindt. Real was followed by Stereo with pro rider Jason Lee and then Anti Hero skater Bob Burnquist.

Girl Skateboards was started by skater Rick Howard and videographer Spike Jonze. Rick had been a top pro at Plan B, but was running into creative difficulties with Steve Rocco, one of the people who ran the company. Spike had shot a number of skate videos for World Industries (also run by Rocco) and both he and Rick wanted to take skateboarding in a new directions.

In August 1993, Rick along with most of the Plan B team left and formed Girl Skateboards. In April of 1994, Chocolate was formed and a number of riders from other teams left to join Rick and Spike.

Skateboarding is all about being yourself, doing your own thing.

It's about having fun.

It's about keeping yourself moving while trying to keep your balance.

And when you understand that, while doing this, not taking the easy way out

is the only way to go, you have touched the soul of skateboarding. It's just like life.

—Paul S.

By Peter "Dietsches" Diepes

Der Münster Mosh
Skateboarding in Germany

Assi Liedke

160

The 1970's

Around 1975, the first skateboards were imported into the country by American citizens living in Germany. By 1976, the first skateboards hit the market. They were mostly made from plastic with crappy wheels and trucks. A year later, skateboarding became a big business and skateboards became a favored birthday or Christmas gift. Skateboarding was embraced by the media and it received an enormous amount of coverage. The biggest skate scene was in Munich where Lulu Magnus organized the first skate contests. He also led the German Banzai team with skaters like Michael Wolf, Thomas Khahn and Michael Hocht.

In 1977, two German skate magazines hit the market, and *SkateBoarder* was sold at all skate and surf shops. The first indoor parks opened in Belgium and Germany. The Hobie team, comprising Ed Nadalin, Bob Skoldberg and Mike Weed, toured throughout Europe and in the process blew everyone's mind. By 1978, the first European Open was held in Germany, bringing in skaters from numerous countries. The first half-pipe was also featured at the Open, but no one was really too sure how to ride it. The main disciplines were freestyle, slalom, high jump and barrel jump. Over time, skateboards improved in quality and the level of skating progressed. However, by 1979 the big skate boom was over. The scene got smaller and both German skateboard magazines ceased publication. In Frankfurt, Gunther Zucholt started up the Pepsi Skateboard Team. Skaters like Martin Wagner, Thomas Hierling (RIP), and Christian Seewald began touring Germany with the first mobile halfpipe. The first German Masters Tournament was held in 1979, but by the end of the year, skating had gone totally underground. There was intensive competition between Dusseldorf and Frankfurt during the Masters Tournament (this still prevails today!).

The 1980's

By the beginning of the decade, a lot of attention was focused on Swedish freestyler Per Welinder who stoked everyone at the European Open. By 1981, a soon-to-be-world-renowned promoter of skateboarding, Titus, opened up the first outdoor park in Münster. In 1982, Titus organized the first halfpipe contest. The winners were Claus Grabke from Germany and Ruben Snitzler from the Netherlands.

The first issue of *Monster* skate magazine appeared in Münster and gained a loyal readership. In 1983, a national skate series was held and Claus took first place again. Also in this year, Titus founded Titus Skates and gave Claus a pro model. It was also during this period that the first German skaters got sponsored by American companies. Skateboarding remained underground with a punk rock attitude.

By 1984, there were a number

of skate scenes throughout the country. Gradually, through informal meetings and contests, a second boom began to build. Skaters like Martin van Doren, Florian Bohn and Ralf Middendorf became the new vertical skate stars. By 1985, the boom was in full swing and pros from the United States were touring and entering contests.

In 1986 the Münster Contest morphed into the European Cup and streetstyle was the new discipline. German skaters converged on Vancouver, British Columbia, for the first truly international skate contest at Expo 86. Over the next year, the media hyped skateboarding to new levels, and Claus Grabke and Florian Bohn turned pro for American companies. By 1988, streetstyle had become the main focus and kids were practicing ollies. Ironically enough, thousands of skaters popped through the streets even though the city councils had provided public skateparks. In 1989, the World Cup was held in Halle Munsterland for the first time and ten thousand spectators showed up to watch skaters from all over the world compete.

The '90's

At the start of the decade, two indoor skateparks were built: Hamburg and Muchengladbach. During 1992 and '93, older pros left the skate scene or found work within skate companies. New names like Sami Harithi, Jahn Waage, Anders Pulpanek, Ingo Frohbrich and Dirk Wehnes

entered the scene and ripped in both street and vert.

By 1994, the German skate scene shrank, but a dedicated core of streetskaters remained. All over the country, the skating turned technical and handrails and curbs got thrashed. A World Cup was held in Münster and it turned out to be one of the largest skate contests ever held. As board shapes changed, so did the pros. A new crop of talent emerged with skaters like Marcus Jurgensen, Fabio Fusco, Nu Heinzel, Mehmet Aydin and Christian Pelz. It has become the norm now for most German pros to be sponsored by American companies.

However, older skaters from the original '70's skate scene have not been forgotten. The Old Man Skateboard Association was founded by myself in Dusseldorf. In 1996 we celebrated 20 years of German skateboarding at a concrete park while skating to punk rock the whole night.

Like their North American counterparts, German skaters are treated to events like the Warped Tour and television shows like The X Games and MTV. These have certainly added to skateboarding's popularity all over Europe. In Germany alone there are now over 60 skateparks and more are being built. Although the third boom will eventually turn into a bust, I know that my friends and I are determined to be the first 60-year-old skaters in Germany. That's in about 25 years!

The Notorious *big brother*

Big Brother *magazine hit the skate world in 1992. Sean Cliver was one of the original people who worked on the publication. These are his thoughts on the history of one of the most notorious skateboard magazines ever published:*

If you happened to be involved in the skateboard industry circa 1991–1992, you're well aware of the fact that it needed a good swift kick in the seat of the pants — the magazines in particular. At the time, Steve Rocco, the head of World Industries, was becoming increasingly frustrated with *Transworld Skateboarding* and *Thrasher* magazines. This was mainly because they were refusing his ads due to content, both political and controversial. (One particular ad *Transworld* refused to print showed a skater committing suicide because he couldn't land a trick.)

The magazines were also catering to their own self-serving interests, i.e., the obviously biased coverage of their own affiliated company's riders . . . Rocco conceived the idea to create a magazine that would be entirely free from the constraints of censorship; one that would expose the behind-the-scenes idiocy in the industry; to inform the kids [about] what was "really going on" in skateboarding (if memory serves correctly, one of Rocco's quotes from this period was, "The kids have a right to know."); and, in a sense, create a "thunderdome" atmosphere where advertisers could spar with one another in a wide open community forum . . . A few of the people involved with Rocco and World Industries at the time, primarily Walter Sims and Natas Kaupas, expressed an interest in working on the magazine, so Rocco handed the project over to the two of them with a wad of cash for computers and whatnot. Marc Mckee and I were both employed as graphic artists for World Industries at the time as well, and the two of us considered the magazine to be a new toy and decided that we wanted to play also.

When the first issue of *Big Brother* arrived back from the printer and landed on his desk in mid '92, Rocco couldn't believe his eyes: it looked like complete crap. Consequently, there was a falling out between he and Walter, and one of those mutual "I quit/you're fired!" deals soon followed. As for the 20,000 copies of *Big Brother* #1, Steve treated them like a red-headed stepchild: he sent every single one of them out for free to kids on the World Industries mailing list. Hence, the first issue was chalked up as a total financial loss. In fact, the cover contained the following sticker: "WARNING — TEST COPY . . . Due to the fact that no one here had any idea what the in hell they were doing, this issue has been declared a total failure. Therefore we have decided to give it away for free."

big brother

warning:test copy
Due to the fact that no one here had any idea what in the hell they were doing, this issue has been declared a total failure. Therefore we have decided to give it away for free.

$3.00
1
Collectable

Soon after this initial debacle, Rocco hired Jeff Tremaine as the new art/editorial director and a 'zine kid from Lawrence, Kansas, named Tom Schmidt, aka Earl Parker. Jeff had previously been involved with a BMX magazine, *Go*, and Tom was responsible for a 'zine called *Polyurethane Monthly*. Marc and I both stepped up our efforts from then on out as well, and *Big Brother* soon became one of the most notorious, volatile and entertaining things in the skateboard industry. People either hated it or loved it — there was no grey area — and regardless of which side of the fence you sat on, everyone made a point of reading every issue.

Right from the get-go of the second issue, it was pretty clear that *Big Brother* was going to be unlike any other skateboard magazine — or any other magazine directly targeted at youths — and several of the shops initially refused to carry it on moral grounds. Rocco remained undaunted and in turn wielded the popularity of the World Industries brands like a sledgehammer, employing "strongarm" tactics to force the shops into carrying the magazine.

Stores would receive the ultimatum that if they didn't order 12 to 24 copies of each new issue they would be "blackballed." In other words: if they wouldn't carry the magazine, they wouldn't be allowed to carry any World products. The shops acquiesced.

Rocco remained involved with the magazine intermittently for the first seven to eight issues, and was primarily responsible for instigating the gimmicks which surrounded each issue. Marketing gimmicks were his forte. For example, issue #2 came in an extra-large format size; issue #3 came in a spiral binding; issue #5 came with trading cards; issue #6 came in a cereal box; issue #7 had eight different covers; and issue #8 came with an audio tape to accompany the magazine's content. These marketing gimmicks proved to be highly successful in generating interest and excitement about the magazine, but they also served to permanently

sink *Big Brother* into a tremendous world of debt (mostly due to the cereal box) which it would never recover from.

One of the little-known facts about *Big Brother* is that following issue #8, Rocco had absolutely nothing to do with the magazine anymore. He allowed *Big Brother* to continue, despite numerous internal rifts and disputes created between the magazine and a few of the companies' sponsored pros, and a continually

mounting debt. The only time Steve ever saw the magazine was when a new issue happened upon his desk.

Once Steve lost interest in the magazine, we remained resolute in our intent to make a magazine free from political interest or bias, not to mention one that celebrated the absurdist philosophy of life. We were often castigated by several "upstanding" members of the industry, who believed that we were doing a great disservice to the sport of skateboarding, but we only

163

sought to reflect what was really going on in skateboarding, whatever it may be, wholesome or not, and above all — just have fun.

In terms of outrageous content, "The How to Kill Yourself" article, which appeared

skaters and god

Big Brother

NUMBER 17 $3.95

in issue #3, garnered the magazine a spot on several news broadcasts, most notably in Ohio and California. Another article that springs to mind would be the "field trip to Hustler," which appeared in issue #9, because it prominently featured a substantial amount of nudity in a

magazine directly sold to minors. This again managed to attract the interest of the news stations. Issue #15 (aka #666), featured Steve Olson heelflipping over a stack of genuinely burning Bibles. This upset many a reborn Christian in the skateboard world as well as many just plain superstitious types. The majority of the articles printed in *Big Brother* were composed or constructed with themes of sex, drugs, religion, midgets, alcohol and rock 'n' roll . . . Our "road trip" articles gave play-by-play accounts of very poor behavior; and we sponsored/hosted the "bong olympics," where skateboarding's premiere pot smokers flaunted their skills with the green instead of the wood. It should also be noted that our advertisers took full advantage of our censorship-free policy and were responsible for a good deal of controversial matter themselves, which significantly added to *Big Brother*'s notoriety.

One of the reasons I've always respected Steve Rocco is the fact that he never let anyone tell him what he could or could not do. And if they did, it was a direct challenge to him which he forthrightly stepped up to accept. As a result, pretty much anything and everything was fair game in the magazine.

Although I honestly don't know who first came up with the name "Big Brother," in all likelihood it was Steve. Of course, there's the obvious reference to George Orwell's book, *1984,* and, in a sense, I suppose this was accurate in regards to *Big Brother*'s role in the skateboard industry. I tend to look at it more like the magazine is a surrogate "big brother" to all the little skateboard kids out there. Like the older sibling who shows the younger one the ropes to growing up and occasionally slips 'em the naughty stuff that you're not able to get on

164

your own. It was kind of funny, but the initial icon for *Big Brother* made it look more like a full-blown pederast organization than anything else: the silhouette of a young boy within that of a grown-up male within the aperture of a camera lens.

Due to the enormous expense of production, the magazine was firmly grounded in a world of debt. By issue #25 of the magazine, I believe we had achieved a dead "breakeven point" on each issue that was produced, and even then I'm sure there was a great deal of financial loss incurred. One of the main problems which consistently plagued the magazine was that it didn't have a knowledgeable publisher behind it, someone who knew how to work with the newsstands and distributors. Consequently, the magazine never achieved an adequate distribution through newsstands and other outlets. The average print run per issue ranged from only 20,000 to 30,000 copies, and people had a hard time in general just trying to find it. A lot of this also stemmed from the fact that our content was still highly controversial at times, and shops wouldn't carry it on those grounds (many shops kept them behind the counter and only sold them to kids 16 or 18 years or older).

Larry Flynt, the publisher of *Hustler* magazine, came into the picture when his company, Larry Flynt Publications (LFP) were researching the possibility of acquiring a snowboard magazine.

At the time, Dickhouse Publications, our "proper" publishing name, was responsible for producing *Blunt* snowboard magazine as well. *Blunt* was having similar problems, espe-

cially in the areas of sales and distribution. In late 1996, LFP contacted World Industries with a proposal, and later an intent to buy. The sale was finalized in March of 1997 and the two magazines moved up into the palace of porn in Beverly Hills in April. The funny thing is, *Big Brother* was merely a "consequence" in the sale. LFP primarily wanted *Blunt*. Since then, *Big Brother* has gone on to become the more successful of the two magazines.

Many people feared the worst when they heard that Flynt had acquired the magazines, expecting their content to become even more controversial but, in fact, the exact opposite happened. Due to Flynt's high profile, we were forced to impose new editorial guidelines (sort of). Though the sale was some time ago, to this very day we regularly receive letters condemning us for "selling out," but in all truthfulness, the choice wasn't ours to make: it was Steve's sole decision to sell the magazine. We really didn't even have any say in the matter whatsoever, but we knew what it meant to go under the corporate thumb. The purchase would free us of many trivial responsibilities we had (there was only a total of six people on the payroll, all of whom pitched in on every aspect of making the magazine, from the creation to the final production) . . . In the end, Jeff Tremaine, Rick Kosick, Dimitry Elyashkevich, Dave Carnie and myself all made the decision to remain involved with the magazine, because the basic thing is that we still have a great deal of fun working on it, and it allows us to keep the skateboard dream alive as we all roll headlong into "adulthood."

Rockin' the Rainforest

by Bob Burnquist

While I was growing up in Brazil I always got to skate a lot of cement parks, the majority of them being public skateparks. Skateparks always were and still are a big part of the skateboarding scene in Brazil. The reason being that most of the streets aren't skateable and the traffic is a little crazy, although skaters still end up finding street spots and there are a lot of dedicated street warriors out there.

Many of these parks have come and gone. Some have been around for 15+ years and are still skated to this day by the new and old generation. I could name a bunch of these parks but I'll name only the ones that were most influential to me and important to the history of the sport: Campo Grande, Barramares and Rio Sul. All three were made from concrete and were located in Rio de Janeiro. Guaratingeta Country Club was located in between Rio and São Paulo. This park was the place to be in the '80's. It was where all the nationals took place. Ultra skatepark (wood), São Bernardo do Campo, Polato and Prestige were all located in São Paulo. Prestige was the park that kept vertical skating alive in Brazil, breeding skaters like Rodrigo Menezes and bringing back into action Lincoln Ueda who was gone for a while due to a shoulder injury.

Rodrigo Menezes, with his dedication to the small cement vert ramp, got people to come to the park and session. The sessions consisted of Cristiano Mateus (owner of the vanished Ultra skatepark), myself, Anjinho, Geninho, Ruda Lopes, Lincoln Ueda. Every once in a while some old school skaters would show up and have fun with us. Some of those skaters were Sergio Negao (national champion three years in a row — '85, '86, '87), and the most inspiring of them all, Georginho (who is now building vert ramps for events and parks in Brazil), Tio Liba and Edsinho. These skaters and a few others were the vert warriors in Brazil. It was a small scene since vert had been banned from the American mag-

Skateboarding in Brazil

azines and therefore it wasn't cool anymore to be a vert skater. The parks that had vert ramps in them could no longer get by every month and as a result, shut their doors. This was the case with the Ultra Skatepark, the only good wooden vert ramp around. When it closed down, a lot of vert skaters just gave up and found something else to do.

Meanwhile, there was a way around it: face reality and skate what we had, which was the small cement vert ramp. It wasn't an easy change — if you've ever hung up on cement you know what I'm talking about. We were used to skating wood and it was a lot easier to learn tricks and less harsh on your body when a slam came your way.

I mostly skated vert when I was growing up; the Ultra Park was only three blocks from my house. It had an indoor vert ramp and a spined mini-ramp and a few street obstacles, all wood. When the cement phase came in, I started to skate street a lot more. But always getting a vert session with the boys — that's where my heart is, and vert skating is something that I couldn't and still can't live without. In the late 1990's vert skating is back (never going away for some of us) and you actually see some kids going for it in Brazil.

Lincoln Ueda, stalled invert, Madrats contest, São Paulo

Brazilian companies are increasing their product quality and kids are able to buy cheaper equipment without having to resort to the expensive imported American goods. This quality search was triggered by the increase in American product brought into the country after some Brazilian skaters got sponsored by American companies. It's too bad that some Brazilian brands don't make an effort to take care of the professional skateboarders that ride for them. They always leave the skater in second place. Without the skater there is no company. Things are changing though, and I see positive progress already taking place. We Brazilians are traveling a lot more and marking our presence on a global perspective, and that makes the young ones in Brazil believe in their country and fight for the sport they chose.

Bob Burnquist, kick flip indy, Prestige Skatepark, São Paulo

Carving, Cruising, and Bombing

— The Story of **Longboarding**

The history of longboarding goes back to the roots of skateboarding itself. Longboards are large skateboards that were originally made for cruising or downhill speed. They range in length from 38 inches to 60 inches. The name comes from long-board surfboards, which are much larger than traditional surfboards. Longboarding has always been around in various forms, but until recently garnered little attention from the skateboard press. Perhaps this is because its appeal is not so immediately apparent as the stunts performed by streetskaters. But more and more skaters are giving it a try and becoming converts.

As with other types of skateboards, efforts have been made to improve and refine longboard design. In the 1970's a number of people got involved with longboards, but perhaps the greatest proponent of the sport was Tom Sims. Tom was known for his extremely fluid style with a long-board. He originally started with water skis and experimented with a variety of wood and wood laminates.

Other longboard pioneers of the 1970's were Ed Economy and Brad Stradlund. Brad recalls the roots of his longboard career: "The way I looked at it was my influences on skateboarding were surfers. When I started riding skateboards in 1975, there were no real skateboard heroes. I tried to style my skateboarding after surfers like Jerry Lopez, Buttons and Larry Bertleman. All I wanted to do was skate like them. I wanted to be relaxed and smooth — just like Lopez was when he surfed the Pipeline."

Over time, Brad would adopt a more aggressive style with his longboarding due to the influence of Jay Adams. However, he kept a smooth style as a result of skating with Tom Inouye. Ed Economy feels that skateboarding is just another form of expression — "going fast, carving lines and pretty much like I'm pretending that I'm surfing on the pavement."

In 1978, *SkateBoarder* magazine featured a story entitled "Cult of the Longboard" which profiled some of the top longboarders. Other than this piece however, longboards weren't prevalent in the 1970's.

In the 1980's, Madrid Skateboards manufactured a few models and *Thrasher* magazine covered a number of downhill events. For the most part, though, longboarding was only practiced by a select few. It should be noted, however, that Schmitt Stix did manufacture and sell a fair number of 36-inch Yard Stix. These boards were fun to ride, but they were very stiff.

In the early 1990's, friends Steve Lake and Dennis Telfer from La Jolla, California, formulated an idea that has led to the revival of longboarding. Their goal was to build a product that rode more like a surf or snowboard. Starting in

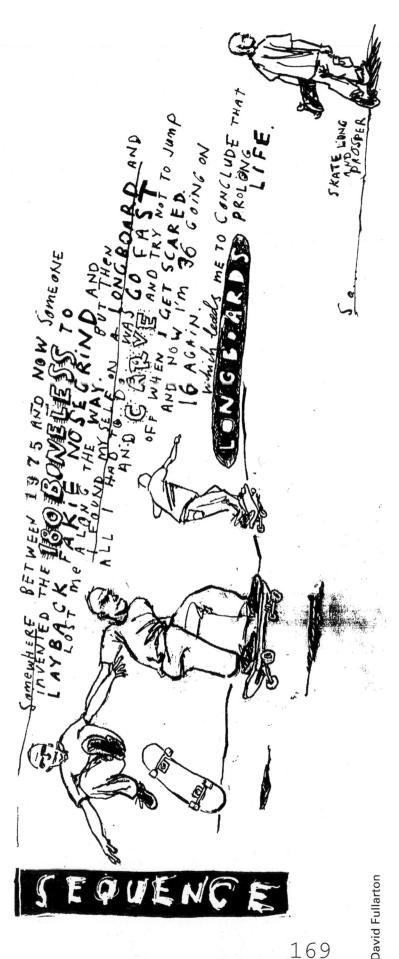

SEQUENCE

David Fullarton

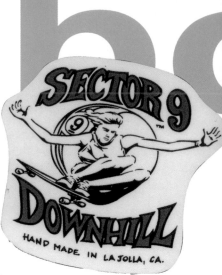

their backyard and quickly progressing to a full blown factory, Sector 9 has made a dramatic impact on the world of skateboarding.

Along the way, others have joined in on the process. Gravity Streetboards have added hand-painted graphics to their boards, along with the option of a speedometer. Envy Skateboards' Mike Shanahan was a one-time champion snowboarder who experienced a painful injury that effectively ended his career. He decided to change direction: "Everybody's thought about putting skateboard trucks onto a snowboard — but it doesn't work. Basically what I did was to design the holes into the board so you wouldn't get any wheel bite." Compression Technologies creates longboards made from hemp which adds to the boards' durability and strength.

Besides their larger shape, longboards have one other feature that makes

them quite different when compared to today's regular-sized skateboards: the wheels are much larger and softer. While most skateboard wheels are between 50 and 60 mm with a durometer of 98 to 101, longboard wheels are 60 to 80 mm with a durometer of 78 to 82. This ensures a smooth ride and less hangup on cracks in the sidewalk.

Even the traditional, regular-sized skateboard manufacturers now include longboards as part of their offering. Although most longboarders are content to cruise and carve, new school skaters are adding their own signature to the sport with insane ollie variations on 48-inch boards.

While it remains to be seen just how large a movement longboarding will become, there is no question that it is starting to build as a popular cross-training exercise for surfers and snowboarders. Longboarding is also bringing more women, surfers and former skateboarders into the sport, which should have a positive effect on the overall sport of skateboarding.

The Permanent Wave

In these pages I have chronicled how skateboarding has risen and fallen in public favor over the last four decades. As skateboarding enters its fifth decade, there are hopeful signs this ebb and flow is becoming less pronounced, and that skateboarding may be finally riding a "permanent wave" of popularity. I have also shown that this is the result of the enthusiasm of a core of dedicated skaters who have stuck with the sport through thick and thin and kept it alive while the mainstream has been temporarily distracted by some flashy fad.

I hope this book drives home (to those who don't already know) that skateboarding is a sport worthy of serious attention. I would like to close with some thoughts and skateboard memories from a few of those devoted skaters who have always and will always take skateboarding seriously.

"We should be ahead by twenty points right now, but we can't make layups and we can't complete a damn pass! We don't bust our asses in practice to play as horribly as this, do we!?!?!?"

The tremulous voice echoed through the entire quad, as a dozen or so teenage girls sat and stared at their coach, the one who is supposedly there to help improve their enjoyment of the game.

"How glad I am that I skateboard," I thought to myself as I rolled around the halls of the school, finding my own lines and creating my own ways of playing. I began to revel in the fact that as skateboarders, we have no coach grilling us over whether or not we win.

I looked on as he swore, yelled at, and insulted his team for not living up to his standards, just like an irate preacher condemning unbelievers to the depths of hell. I began to give thanks that I, as a skateboarder, would never be subjected to such intolerable and degrading idiocy from a "coach" or, a little more accurately, critic.

Then an idea hit me, as they usually do, that in skateboarding, we do have a coach who can be our worst critic, and that person is ourselves. How many times have you seen kids throwing their boards around, cussing, yelling, and hollering because they can't make their 360 flip nosegrind to nollie hardflip out? I've done it plenty of times, and chances are you have as well. Matter of fact, we're all guilty of not enjoying skateboarding to the fullest at one time or another, from the pro to the amateur and everyone in between, which brings us to the moral of the story, so to speak.

Now more than ever, skateboarding has been more enjoyable for me than it's been for a long time. I'm thankful and stoked to get the opportunity to go out and skate three or four days a week, if that many. I've had times where I've said, "This is stupid, my board isn't doing what I'm telling it to," and then got all pissed off, starting to complain. Everyone does this.

As I got older, circumstance and necessity forced me into the tumult of the workplace, and I had to get a job. It was only part time, and I could skate after work or before work or pretty much whenever I wanted. I had a lot more money from my job, which meant boards, wheels, etc., a lot more often. It was great!! Then I turned 18, and consequently moved out from home. This was even greater!! No parents telling me to do some schoolwork instead of skating, no leaving spots early to do this or that; complete and total freedom to do whatever, whenever. Or so I thought. Once "the bills" began to mount up (a completely new concept yet to be grasped by all you grommets out there) I realized what it actually takes to support yourself in our beautiful system, "by the people, for the people," and that is one thing and one thing only: MONEY!!

Lots of it, too, which means lots of work, unless you were born rich. Working two jobs to make ends meet doesn't leave a lot of time to skate, along with all the other crap society wants you to do once you turn 18. I began to dislike the unfamiliar feeling of not having the option to go skating for two weeks at a time because of work. For the first time in my life, I couldn't skate all day, every day, whenever I wanted.

As skate days became more sparse, I realized how rad skating really is and how lame the nine-to-five world is. I felt like a fool for ever becoming frustrated or unhappy with skating, and realized that my love had been taken for granted.

So the old adage is true: "One man's trash is another man's treasure." The freedom of skating at will is a treasure, yet a lot of us act like it's not. So if you really love skating, find a way to shape your life or career around it, whether it's turning pro, working in "the industry," or having a "real job" and enjoying skating when you're not at work. Whatever you do, be content with your skating, and don't ever take it for granted because I can guarantee you, if neglected and unappreciated, it will not always be there.

— Chris Long

173

90's Legends

Salman Agah

"Sally" pretty much single-handedly brought switch stance skating to the level it is at today. Because of Salman, today's top skaters are generally expected to have an extensive switch repertoire. Known for his close association with the Christian faith, Salman continues to be an inspiration in the world of skating.

Cara Beth Burnside

An impressive vert skater who was the first female get a shoe sponsorship. Cara started skating in the 1980's and became a pro skater in 1990.

Bob Burnquist

Bob comes from Brazil and has an innovative style when it comes to riding vert. He has taken switch stance tricks to new levels. Included in his runs are switch stance lip slides, blunts, nose blunts, airs and very technical flip tricks. "I can't remember a time when I didn't skate. I love doing it."

Kareem Campbell

Kareem is known as a very technical streetskater and has been associated with World Industries for a good many years. He currently runs Axion, a skateboard shoe company.

John Cardiel

One of the only pro snowboarders that has stayed true to his skating roots. "Cards" is a gnarly skate maniac willing to tackle any terrain. A card-carrying member of the Northern California Thrasher crew, John can bust a backside 540 on vert just as easily as he can slide a slick rail.

Mike Carrol

"Mc" was just a kid when he gained fame with H-Street in the early 1990's. He emerged as one of the brightest stars in the sport. Mike has a super smooth style and can rip street as well as vert.

Mike Crum

Mike is a super technical skater from Texas who stuck with vertical riding all through the era when vert was dead (early to mid '90s). When vert started to come back he found a home with the World Industries posse. On the progression front, Mike has taken frontside nollies to new heights on vert. "Skateboarding to me means skating with friends, fun and scars!"

Rob Dyrdek

Streetskater from Ohio. Has spent his entire career on the Alien Workshop team. Rob been on top of solid technical streetskating since the early '90s. Always the guy to watch if he's at a contest.

Rune Glifberg

Rune is from Denmark and is known for his technical ability and lip tricks. He has become one of the most accomplished vert riders of all time. He rides for Flip Skateboards. "Skateboarding is an individual sport. You can pretty much do it anywhere. It's a thing you can do on your own and you don't need anyone to tell you what to do. It's all about fun, really pushing your own limits and riding everywhere."

Matt Hensely

In the late 1980's, Matt came up through the ranks as a next-generation streetskater. By the time the 1990's rolled around, he was at the top of the sport. Best known for his progression of stylish modern street-skating, Matt retired from professional skateboarding in 1992, only to make a comeback a few years later.

Eric Koston

An icon in the world of '90's skating, Eric is an inspiration to many skaters worldwide. He is known for his abilities and quiet demeanor. Eric makes the impossible look effortless and has single-handedly propelled skateboarding forward in the mid 1990's.

Jason Lee

Jason has had a tremendous influence on the mid to late '90's generation of pro skaters. He pioneered such tricks as the backside 180 kickflip, the backside tailslide and the backside kickflip tailslide. In addition to having a unique style, Jason is, along with Chris Pastras, a co-founder of Stereo Skateboards.

Kris Markovitch

When everyone else doing triple kickflips two inches off the ground Kris was throwing himself off double-sets and flipping big gaps. Kris looked to be powered by pure adrenaline at a time when skating became slow and technical. Definitely a standout at any session and a true mad man. A fine example of this crazed skating can be found in the early 101 videos where Kris is doing flip tricks at super fast speed.

Guy Mariano

Guy is one skater who is way ahead of his time. He was just a young skater when he had his first feature-length video part in Mark Gonzales' *Video Days.* Although he has a tendency to stay out of the limelight, when he does come forward, his skating genius is readily apparent.

Chad Muska

Chad hails from Las Vegas and has had a major impact both on and off a skateboard. Known for his big stairs and big rail moves, Chad was responsible for developing the ghetto-homeboy-white-trash look.

Tom Penny

Hailing from Oxford, England, this '90's sensation is known as somewhat of an excessive party goer. However, this does not deter Tom from showing up at a session or contest and pulling the biggest, smoothest most technical moves without the normally required practice or warm up time. Tom currently rides for Flip Skateboards.

Geoff Rowley

Straight out of Liverpool, this young Brit believed that all American pros were as good as their video parts suggested. Geoff arrived in North America and, to his amazement, proceeded to kick all their butts. This guy is not afraid of much and can slide a double kicked rail and flip a 15 set of stairs in the same line. Geoff is known as a very technical and precise rider and is sponsored by Flip.

Daewon Song

Daewon enjoys the status of being the technical king of the late '90's. The trick combinations he puts together could be done by virtually no one else. Many believe that he has unseated even Rodney Mullen. Daewon sports a very smooth style combined with solid ollie skills. He has been riding for World Industries since its early years

Ed Templeton

From the start of his skate career in the late 1980's Ed was known for his adaptations of the ollie impossible and one-footed ollie. He is known for his sense of humor, artistic flare and, most important, all-around skateboarding abilities. Ed was the founder of Toy Machine.

Danny Way

A full blown vert madman, Danny is simply too outrageous for words. The pictures tell the whole story. He dropped out of a helicopter onto a halfpipe and hit 16 feet of air. Known as "The Terminator."

Just like I said before, if you are an older skater out there, you're over 30 and you don't ride anymore, you just got to get out there and do it. You have to have the right attitude. I think that it's all in your mind; basically if you have a good attitude and you're lucky enough to be in good health to get out there and bang your body around, get out there and skate. All these older guys need to get back out there and discover the thrill. If you can't handle skateboarding try snowboarding, or paddle out and try and catch a few waves. Just do something that's in tune with an individual type of expression. I think that's what's so important about skateboarding. There's no rules, there's nobody telling you what to do, you don't need a team or any special place to do it. Just get on your board and ride and that's the most important thing. Let your spirit and let your soul get into it and that's where you'll get the enjoyment that's accessible through skateboarding. That's about it.

— Tony Alva

Skateboarding Is

By Dave Hackett

Skateboarding is many things to many individuals. Pure and simple, it's a healthy, radical art form. Skateboarding is the positive release of undirected explosive youthful energy. Skateboarding utilizes the ever-expanding environment of steel, concrete, plaster, or wood as its canvas. For pure spontaneous action, skateboarding is unequaled. The skater becomes one with his board, while the board in turn translates the language of the terrain.

Like all great pastimes, skateboarding is a succession of stimulating experiences. It's sensations and impressions; a remembrance of early radical lines thrown down in a private empty swimming pool; laughter, friendship and camaraderie shared by all after an intense session. Skateboarding is waking up at noon after raging all night, dancing and celebrating your last session. It is also waking up at 5:00 am to drive 300 miles, rockin' all the way with your bro's in search of a secret pipe, pool or ditch. Or better yet, the neighbors down the street drain their perfect keyhole swimming pool so you can skate because they think it's neat to watch.

If you're mellow, skateboarding is the joy of carving soulful surf-like moves down long banked streets. Skateboarding is freestyle, streetstyle, vertical, bankriding, surfskating, slalom, downhill, stand-up and luge. It's also high jump, barrel jump, obstacle course racing, and rails. When you're gnarly, skateboarding is done inside a 25-foot cement pipe, where every move must be carefully calculated, as one mistake could be fatal. This is the ultimate test medium for a man's ability to pit flesh and bones against the laws of gravity and thick cement. Skateboarding is hitting 11 o'clock on the ceiling of that pipe. This weightless second of exhilaration and release represents days, months . . . years of experiences.

Skateboarding is being scared and doing it anyway. It's hanging on and making it. It's hangin' and slamming. When you are a sponsored amateur, skateboarding is the excitement of seeing your picture in a magazine for the first time. It's being asked to do your first demo, getting to travel to foreign countries, competing in your first contest, winning your first trophy, and receiving free equipment because you're hot. When you're a pro, skateboarding is getting a signature model, royalty checks, ads, signing autographs, groupies, interviews, travel, movies, television, stunt work, responsibility, and finally, forgetting why you started in the first place.

Then you remember that skateboarding is a unique kind of madness. It's a combination of balance, technique, power, knowledge, love, hate, respect and fear — instinctive perception gained only through repeated action. Skateboarding is a moment of glory, of achievement, of unsung triumph. For the man, skateboarding is freedom and youth rediscovered; for the boy, a means of self expression vital to his being. For you see, skateboarding is the blood, rolling through his veins.

"No handed pipe to pipe transfer at eleven o' clock"

by David Hackett, summer of '79

177

Skate Pros Over the Last 40 Years

(A very subjective and incomplete list!)

Micke Alba (Malba)
Younger brother to Steve, but no less accomplished. Malba won numerous contests and ripped vertical terrain.

Pierre Andre
One of the most talented freestylists to emerge from Europe in the 1980's. Pierre competed at an international level and finally settled in California. He rode for Sims and now heads up the skate shoe company Etnies.

Ray Barbee
Ray's flatland tricks impressed a lot of people in the 1988 Powell Peralta video "Public Domain." Over the years, he has developed numerous ollie variations including the ollie blunt. Ray is one the true pioneers of technical skateboarding.

Brian Beardsley
An extraordinary high jumper, "Flyin'" Brian is best remembered for his leaps over sports cars. Brian rode for Ty Page/Freeformer skateboards.

Ellen Berryman
Know for her gymnastic moves and graceful style, Ellen was sponsored by Bahne Skateboards.

Larry Bertleman
Another surfing superstar who crossed over into skateboarding. Bertleman's carefree, flowing style influenced many skaters. The "Bertleman" or "Bert" for short, was his signature move and was successfully transitioned to vertical environments.

Bob Biniak
Bob started skating with the original Zephyr (Z team) around 1974. He went on to ride for Logan Earth Ski. Besides riding vert, Bob was also an accomplished downhill skater, and in 1976 achieved the fastest time in the standup division at Signal Hill.

Rick Blackhart
One of the greatest skaters to emerge from Northern California, Dr. Rick was instrumental in the development of Independent Trucks. Rick also wrote a skateboarding advice column for Thrasher called "Ask the Doctor."

Bobby Boydon
Bobby was a freestyle competitor who moved into vert riding. He was known for his kickflip variations including triple kickflips.

Tom Boyle
Tom is one of the 90's strongest most consistent vertical riders, hence the nickname "the Rock." "Skateboarding means creativity. At this point in my life, it is my whole life. Skateboarding means freedom — the never-ending freedom to do new things. It's just an awesome device."

Tim Brauch
Top 90's skater: "Skateboarding is a way to express myself. A way to leave all my troubles behind. It's guaranteed that you'll have fun when you do it."

René, Ritchie and David Carrasco
Three brothers who performed as part of the Pepsi Skateboard Team. Ritchie is one of the best 360's spinners in the world and hit

over 130 revolutions in the 1970's. As a result of this achievement, Hobie introduced "Spinners" — wheels made especially for doing 360's.

"The Flying Carrasco Brothers"

By René Carrasco

What a privilege to be part of one of skateboarding's most famous skate families — the Carrasco Brothers. I started skateboarding in the early 1960's when I was eight years old. This was during the first wave of skateboarding, the era of cut-off steel roller skate wheels nailed to a 2x4. In my case, it was a board off an orange crate.

I was already training my younger brothers Ricky and David to skateboard. Little did I know that someday we would win our lion's share of skateboard championships and become members of the legendary Pepsi Pro Skateboard Team!

In 1976 we won our spot on the team at the Concrete Wave Skateboard Park when we demonstrated the skateboard safety program in front of the Pepsi Cola company executives. At the time my brothers and I were stoked!

As part of the Pepsi Pro Team we performed over 2,000 skateboard demos for schools, churches, amusement parks, TV shows, movies and major skateboard publications and newspapers. I even appeared on the first-ever all-pro skateboard bubble gum cards in 1978.

We had the distinction of having the first-ever skateboard backyard ramp article to appear in any skate publication. If we weren't demonstrating, you could find us at skateboard parks, judging contests, racing at La Costa and riding every vertical ramp or pool we could find.

My brother Dave won both downhill and slalom championships, Ritchie was a top 360 specialist, and I won a number of downhill and freestyle contests.

Kim Cespedes
Kim's skating was influenced heavily by surfing and her aggressive style paved the way for other females to get into bank riding. A profile of Kim in *SkateBoarder*'s February 1977 issue remarked that she "is possibly the only female to power slide at speed." Kim rode for Hobie Skateboards.

Desiree Von Essen
1970's freestyle standout. Desiree rode for R.A.C.O

Scott Foss
One of the first Bones Brigade riders. Best known for burly backside air.

Mike Frazier
A 1990's skater with an intense determination. Mike pushes everything to the max. An exciting skater to watch, Mike appears to always on the verge of losing control and yet doesn't let many tricks get away from him.

Jim Gray
Jim was an eighties pro known for effortless bionic backside footplants and Lien to frontside footplants, as well as burly backside airs. He skated for G&S as a pro and has since gone on to run ABC Skateboards.

Tom Groholski
Originally from New Jersey, Tom skated for Vision in the 1980s and was an accomplished vert rider.

Dave and Paul Hackett
These brothers came to the attention of *SkateBoarder* readers through their astounding use of skateboard suspenders. The suspenders were made of Velcro and enabled Paul and Dave to achieve incredible air without holding the board. Dave also became a legendary skater of the 1980's and had a successful career with Skull Skates.

Omar Hassan
A standout on any terrain, Omar began riding in 1990. "Skateboarding to me just means fun. Hanging out with my friends that skate — that's it."

Frank Hirada
Frank grew up next to Matt Groening (creator of *The Simpsons*) and was to be the inspiration for Bart's skateboarding stunts. These stunts included riding on his aunt's beat up car and ollieing over fences, etc.

Paul Hoffman
A member of the Z-Flex team, Paul was an accomplished freestyler. His signature trick was the one-footed nose 360.

Brian Howard
One of the smoothest vert skaters ever. In addition to going for big airs, Brian doesn't mind getting technical in the air or on the lip. One of the first vert skaters to consistently do technical moves like frontside blunt slides.

Rick Howard
One of the founders of Girl Skateboards, Rick has an extremely smooth style and is known for his innovative tricks. Before most people had perfected backside kick-

flips and tailslides, Rick had them wired switchstance (using his opposite leg)

Mike Hynson
A surfer who appeared in the legendary film *The Endless Summer,* Mike got heavily involved with skateboarding. He joined the Hobie Super Surfer team for a tour out East.

Jason Jesse
Jason rode for Consolidated and was a pioneer of super high airs to fakie along with numerous revert tricks. Jason was also known for his intense attitude.

Rodney Jesse
Sponsored by Brewer Skateboards, Rodney took an aggressive approach with his skating.

Tony Jetton
Tony rode for Pepsi, G&S, Tracker Trucks. He also was also one of the stars of *Skateboard Mania*, a spectacular "skateboard show" that was produced in the 1970's.

Rudy Johnson
A real street pioneer who had a strong and innovative video part in Blind's *Video Days*. Rudy was a founding member of the Girl team.

Lester Kasai
Big air innovator from the '80's. Super stylish, super rad vert skater. The Sims "Lester" board was immensely popular.

Jeff Kendall
Jeff was a top rider for Santa Cruz in the 1980's. "When you are skateboarding professionally, you can't beat it. A lot of my friends went on to college — I don't regret the fact that I didn't get to do that because as I look back now, I could go back to college any time. I remember my life as a pro as being some of the best times in my life. I look back now and I really appreciate it."

Ron Knigge

Sponsored by New Deal in the early to mid 1990's, Ron was influential in the growth and popularity of extremely technical skating.

Gary Kocot

In 1976 Gary was profiled in *Circus* magazine — probably the first time a skater had been mentioned in a music magazine. He rode for R.A.C.O. and was an accomplished freestyler and barrel jumper.

Curt Lindgren

Sponsored by California Freeformer, Curt is known as the originator of the kickflip. This trick was done by hooking one foot under the board and pressing down with the other. The kickflip was one of skateboarding's first "technical" type tricks.

Jim McCall

Freestyler Jim McCall came out of Florida and was known for some very impressive gymnastic moves like one-handed handstands. Jim rode for Fox skateboards and had one of the first pro models (1976).

Colin Mckay

Coming from Vancouver, Colin is a street and vert pioneer. Many tricks that were done in the early 1990's by Colin in videos like Plan B's *Questionable* video are now standard moves today.

Andy Macdonald

Superb '90's vert rider. "Skateboarding to me means freedom and expression. There's no one there telling you that there are rules. It means self motivation, creativity and it's the funnest thing that I know to do."

Tony Magnusson

Impressive Swedish skater who competed strongly against all the California pros. Rode for Uncle Wiggly which then led to the development of H Street (with Mike Ternasky). After H Street, Tony started

Evol. Tony was a featured competitor in the 1997 X Games.

Ernie Martin

Hailing from the East, Ernie had an incredible ability to jump. His crowd pleaser was jumping over cars — specifically Corvettes. He was able to clear two at a time. Ernie was also able to high jump five feet and do massive leaps over barrels.

Chris Miller

An accomplished vert rider who rode for Santa Cruz, G & S and Schmitt Stix before starting his own company Planet Earth.

Conrad Miyoshi

Slalom champion of the '70's who perfected a unique parallel ski stance position.

Bob Mohr

Bob placed fourth in the 1965 Anaheim Nationals. He rode for the Kips Team and led them to victory in a contest that was televised on the Los Angeles television show, "Surf's Up." In the 1970's, Bob rode for Bahne and was known for his impressive gymnastic moves and incredible skill at high jumping. Sadly, Bob took his own life in 1996.

Ed Nadalin

Ed was known for his showmanship and would wear a suit and tails during his freestyle routines. He was one of the first to utilize music in freestyle contests during the 1970's.

Monty Nolder

Strong vertical skater from the 1980's who rode for Gordon & Smith. Monty was one of the first (if not the only) deaf skate star.

Ellen Oneal

One of the top female freestyle skaters in the 1970's, Ellen rode for Gordon & Smith. She can be seen in the film "Skateboard." Known for many two-board moves (called daffy's), Ellen took first and second place in a number of professional freestyle contests.

George Orton

"The Wildman" was one of the greatest aerial innovators and technicians of the 1970's. Seventeen years after he became a vert champion, George got back on a board and became a downhill champion. He has hit 61.87 mph on a skateboard.

Mathias Ringstom

"Skateboarding used to mean everything to me when I was younger. It was what I dreamed, thought and lived for. Now it's still almost the same, except it's also my living which makes it a bit different."

Billy Ruff

Late 70's and 80's vert master. Billy was sponsored by G & S.

Mike Santarossa

Mike first came to light as a standout at the Powell Skateboard Park in Santa Barbara in the early 1990's. He is a versatile skater who is equally talented in the street and on transitions. "Skateboarding for me means just being able to do what comes naturally. Not that I'm some natural skateboard wizard or anything, but growing up around skateboarding for me was a natural thing. When I realized what could be accomplished between myself and the board, I was hooked. I found my first love."

Willy Santos

He may be small in stature, but Willy's skating ability speaks volumes. His Hawk-like ability to throw technical street and obstacle course tricks back to back has earned him many contest victories and top placing. Willy is sponsored by Birdhouse.

Tim Scroggs

A Florida skater who developed an arsenal of impressive freestyle tricks in the late 70's. Tim rode for Powell Peralta and was famous for his toques which he would wear completely over his face. Tim was one of the first skaters ever to do an acid drop (leaping up with the board and then landing on it).

Chris Senn

To put it bluntly, Chris Senn is a wild animal. As *Thrasher* stated, "Chris rides a skateboard like a rabid dog: foaming, thirsty, and demented. He has dominated the pro street contest circuit during the mid 1990's. Being one who enjoys throwing caution to the wind, Chris likes to skate incredibly fast and precise and has a wide assortment of technical and burly tricks."

Jay Smith

Another early Bones Brigade rider. Used rubberband-like body to maximize flat wall laybacks.

Elyssa Steamer

One of the most progressive women ever to get on a skateboard. As far as tricks go, Elyssa has all the bases covered and she's not afraid to take a painful slam.

Jamie Thomas

Hailing from Alabama, Jamie started out riding for a number of companies including Toy Machine and then went to start Zero. He is known as a death-defying skater who will try anything.

Lonnie Toft

Lonnie rode for Sims and was instrumental in redesigning skateboards. He is best known for his "Outrageous" Eight Wheeler and for being one of the first skaters to embrace and promote snow-boarding. The eight-wheeled skateboard was quite difficult to ride, but Lonnie was able take it to vertical terrain with no problem. Lonnie also originated the G-turn with Gordy Lienemann.

Robert Valdez

First guy to pull off an invert on vertical in a major competition (at Big O Skatepark) — with his arm set in a cast! Sponsored by Powerflex.

Primo Desidero and Diane Veerman

Eighties freestylists with incredible sharp footwork. Primo and Diane took their synchronized freestyle skate act on the road for God. While toe-tapping and spinning their decks to disco, they would not only get cash but recite little biblical lessons at the same time. The couple eventually married.

Sergie Ventura

Known for his vertical riding. He has a similar style to Christian Hosoi.

Vicki Vickers

One of the top female vertical riders of the 1970's. Vicky gained a huge following among both female and male riders.

Bruce Walker

Coming out of Melbourne Beach, Florida, Bruce Walker carved a name for himself on both the east and west coasts. A skater since 1963, Walker's style was based on his surf roots. In the 1970's Walker co-owned surf shops and setup Fox Skateboards. This company eventually became Walker Skateboards and was one of the first skater-owned and -operated companies.

Mike Weed

One of the most accomplished vertical and freestyle skaters of the seventies, Mike rode for Hobie and toured around the world.

Bill Weiss

Bill comes from Toronto and is known for his completely outrageous moves on and off a skateboard.

"Skateboarding takes care of pleasure, anger, everything. It keeps my head straight."

Woody Woodward

Although known for his skating ability, Woody is best remembered for his profile in *Surf Guide*. Writer Bill Cleary featured Woody as a cigar-smoking, "titan of the skateboard industry." Woody was nine years old at the time.

Simon Woodstock

1990's rider known for being somewhat eccentric. Simon rides some rather unusual boards including "Double Trouble" (with trucks on the top and bottom of a board) and a skim board with trucks and wheels. Dresses up as a clown occasionally.

Jeremy Wray

Jeremy has been taking technical street and rail tricks to new levels ever since he first broke onto the scene in the early 90's with Blockhead. Was recruited by Kris Markovitch for Color Skateboards in 1993 (this team later became Prime). His video part from then is still innovative by today's standards.

Skateboards at the Movies

Many skateboard films were produced in the same style as surf and ski movies. Directors like Bud Brown and Warren Miller had quite an influence on how skateboard films were made. Before there were video players, people had to wait until films arrived at their local theatre or auditorium to see surf movies. From small coastal towns to major metropolitan areas, people would line up to get their fix of the latest surf action. Production quality could range from fair to unreal. The skateboard films of the 1970's followed in the same pattern of the surf films — action and plenty of it!

Skater Dater (1965)
Winner of Best Short at the 1965 Academy Awards. This film illustrated the problems of peer pressure using skaters as the backdrop. Probably being shown in some classroom as you read this.

Super Session (1976)
Directed by master surf film maker Hal Jepsen. Mostly features surfing, but skateboarding is in there! In the words of Steve Pezman of *Surfer* magazine, "Explosive surfing — exciting skateboards . . . I was climbing and dropping in my seat." Original music by Smoghorn.

Freewheelin' (1976)
Directed by Scott Dittrich (his first feature film). Starring Stacy Peralta as a young skater about to turn pro. Features incredible slalom action from Bobby Piercy, along with some great scenes of downhill riding.

Spinnin' Wheels (1975)
Mike Weed riding pools, Ty Page doing freestyle and Skitch Hitchcock as the "Airborne Kamikaze."

Five Summer Stories-Plus Four (1975/76)
Originally a surfing film, the producers decided to add four skateboarding stories.

Hard Waves/Soft Wheels (1977)
Pool Riders, Puerto Rico Hill Sliders and Bone Breaking Stunts — if that's not enough, how about a surf-skateboarding duel?

Skateboard (1978)
Teen idol Leif Garrett has the lead role, but movie really stars Tony Alva (as Tony Bluetile) and Ellen Oneal. Improbable story line — a loser bets it all on a skateboard team to pay back loan sharks. Sometimes shown on late-night TV; rated either turkey or one star by most film guides.

Thrashin' (1986)
A "Romeo and Juliet" love story between rival skateboard gangs, starring Josh Brolin. As Kevin Thatcher (editor of *Thrasher*) wrote, "While the fact that *Thrashin'* even made it to the big screen is worth applause, it doesn't exactly rate as a triumph for skating, or movie making for that matter." Features some of the

biggest skateboard stars of the time: Christian Hosoi, Chris Cook, Lance Mountain (both stunt doubles), Eddie Reategui, Steve Olson and of course Alva. Rated a "turkey" in most video review guides.

Gleaming the Cube (1989)
Most watchable of all skateboard-themed movies (that is, it can be enjoyed with non-skater friends). Stars Christian Slater and features the skating of Tony Hawk, Mark Rogowski, Mike McGill and Rodney Mullen (Mark, Mike and Rodney all are stunt riders for Christian). A murder mystery involving a faked suicide and the search for the real killers; not really focused on skateboarding. Stacy Peralta was second-unit director on this film. Rated three stars by most film guides.

Other Notable Skateboard Moments in Film:

Back to the Future (1985)
Who could forget Michael J. Fox blazing through the air on his "hoverboard"? Believe it or not, there are a number of enthusiasts promoting the concept of a hoverboard. Suggested retail price: $200.

Police Academy 4: Citizens on Patrol (1987)
Featuring the "crazy antics" of the Powell Peralta Bones Brigade.

Kids (1995)
This film has very little skateboarding; rather, it follows a gang (most of whom skate) and the trouble they get into. Director Larry Clark caused quite a stir with this film, especially in the scene where the skaters attack a guy with their boards.

The following is a list of some of the many thousands of contests held from 1963 to 1993. Although some may be more significant than others, the skaters who competed were all equally passionate about winning.

While coverage of contests in the skateboard magazines exists for skaters to enjoy, a whole new level of awareness of skateboarding competition has entered into the general population. This is primarily due to the Extreme Games, which were first broadcast in 1995. The X Games, as they are now known, has brought skateboarding to a whole new audience. The skateboard community is still coming to grips with the ramifications of this new-found publicity. So many elements go into the staging of a contest — from ramps, to speaker systems to security — holding a contest is a major undertaking. Thousands of organizers over the years have worked hard putting together contests. To these people, the skateboard world says "thank you."

Thirty Years of Skateboard Contests

1963
Pier Avenue Junior High School, Hermosa, California
Won by Brad "Squeak" Blank; 100 spectators in total. This was the first skateboard contest ever held.

1964
International Surf Festival, Hermosa Beach, California
Overall Winner — Bruce Logan. Subsequent competitions in 1965, '66, '67, '68.

1965
National Skateboard Championships, La Palma Stadium, Anaheim, California
Featured teams from all over the US, Mexico and Japan. Originally, a 20-foot high ramp was constructed, but this was lowered to 11 feet due to so many skaters having difficulty with the height. Covered by CBS, NBC and ABC, along with a multitude of national newspapers. Scholarships of $500 were awarded to the winners.

1965■66
Numerous contests between skateboard teams including South Bay, Makaha, Dewey Weber Team, Palisades Team, Gordon & Smith Team, Hobie Super Surfer Team.

1966
Santa Monica Sports and Arts Festival

1974
Bahne-Cadillac Ocean Festival, Del Mar, California
This was the contest that featured the arrival of the Z-Boys who caused quite a stir with their surf-based moves.

1975
Hang Ten World Contest, Los Angeles Sports Arena
First place overall team was Dial-A-Flex. Tony Alva won cross country/obstacle race. Youngest competitor — George Wahl, age four. Also held in 1976. Freestyle division won by Bruce Logan for both years.

Southern California Skateboard Championships, Orange County Fairgrounds
Henry Hester took first in slalom.

Oceanside Contest
This contest held in Oceanside, California, has run throughout the '70's, '80's and '90's.

Steve's X-Caliber/South Bay Championships, Torrence, California
Over 125 skaters competed in freestyle and slalom. Prizes included a motorcycle, bicycles and surfboards.

Signal Hill Downhill Competition
Subsequent contests held throughout the '70's. In 1976, Guy Grundy hit 53 mph, blacks out during his run and bails. Also in 1976, Sam Puccio hits 54 mph and wins contest.

La Costa Races, California
Downhill and slalom races every weekend during the summer; $2 entry fee for pro's, $1 for amateurs.

1976
Hang Ten World Contest, Los Angeles Sports Arena
Tony Alva won cross country/obstacle race. Freestyle division won by Bruce Logan for both 1975 and '76.

Professional Colorado Skateboard Circuit
Presented by the group Another Roadside Attraction and held in the Colorado Rockies by promoter Peter Camann. Subsequent contests took place in '77 and '78.

Magic Mountain Masters Contest
Held at an amusement park in California. Bob Mohr cleared the high jump at 4' 5" (an unofficial world record); Bob Skoldberg became Master's Grand Champion.

Northern California Pro-Am Skateboard Championship, Cow Palace, San Francisco
One and only contest sponsored by R-M Enterprises (the venture lost a pile of money due to poor attendance). Paul Engh took first in slalom competition; Bob Jarvis cranked out 11 360's.

Summer Skateboard Contest, La Costa, San Diego
Featured slalom, cross country and freestyle competitions. US Marines lent officials field phones and a generator — no cellular phones in '76!

California Free Former World Professional Skateboard Championships, Long Beach, California
Featured six events: freestyle, slalom, speed racing, high jump, barrel jump and consecutive 360's. Two-day combined attendance reached almost 20,000 people. $20,000 in prize money. Woody Woodstock cleared 16 barrels, Alva cleared 17 barrels, Ernie Martin high jumped 4' 7", and Bob Jarvis cranked out 15 ½ 360's.

1977
Signal Hill
4,000 spectators, 41 entries (5 standups and 36 enclosed vehicles). Dave Dillberg had three runs, all at 57 mph, and wins the contest.

California Free Former World Championship Giant Slalom and Speed Run, Akron, Ohio
Held at Derby Downs, the event drew over 13,000 spectators. John Hutson won standup event and D.L. Leonard captured first in skatecar division. Brian Beardsley jumped 4'11" in high jump exhibition.

Catalina Classic, Avalon, Catalina Island (26 miles across the sea . . .)
John Hutson took first in the downhill, Bobby Piercy won Dual Slalom and Deanna Calkins won Woman's Slalom.

1978
Runway/Pepsi Challenge Cup Banked Slalom Race, Runway Skatepark
Charlie Ranson took first place.

Hester/ISA Pro Bowl Series, Spring Valley, Upland and Newark Skateparks
Competition included One Wheelers, Longest Carve, Pipe Pasting (pasting stickers for height) and a Doubles event; four contests in total, put together by Henry Hester. Steve Olson was the overall winner, followed by Steve Alba and Rick Blackhart.

Signal Hill Speed Run
Tina Trefethen wound up bailing and received a lacerated lung, but she took first place. Nick Leonard crashed and required 40 stitches on his nose. John Hutson won standup division at 53.45 mph. Roger Williams took skatecar division with a speed of 56.92 mph.

Oceanside Freestyle Contest
Ten thousand spectators. Doug "Pineapple" Saladino took first place in the men's division. Ellen Berryman won the women's division. Richie Carrasco blasts out 47 360's.

Winchester Pro Bowl, Campbell, California
Frank Blood blasted a 2' 10" air to take first place in Air Freestyle event. Tim Marting took first place in Bowl Riding and Teri Lawrence

won in the women's division.

Oasis Pro Bowl and Half Pipe Contest
Dave Hackett took first place and earned $1,000.

1979
Northern California Pro Bowl, Milpitas, California
New judging system implemented. Tim Marting took first place for the second time.

Lakewood World Pro, Lakewood Center Skateboard World, California
Steve Alba took first place, Robert Valdez hit 3' 5" in the aerial event, and Terri Lawrence won in the women's division.

Oasis Easter Classic, Oasis Skatepark, Mission Valley, San Diego
Thirteen-year-old Bert Lamar took the contest over Doug "Pineapple" Saladino by one point!

2nd Annual Clearwater Sun 'n' Fun Championships, Clearwater, Florida
In the "boys" division, young Rodney Mullen takes first place in the Giant Slalom, Dual Slalom and of course, freestyle events.

The Gyro Dog Bowl Pro, Marina Del Ray Skatepark
Dave Andrecht won and Marty Grimes' "Grimes Slide" was named most outrageous maneuver of the competition.

Winchester Open, San Jose
This contest featured pros competing with top amateurs. Pro rider Eddie Elguera won but was closely followed by amateur Steve Caballero.

Hester Series #4, Skate City, Whittier
Duane Peters stunned the crowd and took first place.

1980

Glendora Mountain Race, Glendora
This race was 9.4 miles down a mountain with four to five skaters racing together hitting speeds of 50 mph. Roger Hickey won the standup event and Jim Lad took the lay-down speed event.

Reseda Pro Am
Eric Grisham took first place and Patti Hoffman beat Carabeth Burnside in the amateur women's division.

Van's/Offshore Amateur State Finals, Del Mar
A number of amateurs at this contest would make a name for themselves later on during

the decade. Skaters who placed in the top 5 (boys 11-13 division) included Mark Rogowski, Christian Hosoi and Tony Hawk.

1981

Skate City Whittier Pro-Am
A number of pros were absent for this contest due to injuries. Duane Peters blew people's minds with his insane riding style and took first place in the pro division. Lance Mountain took first place in the amateur event.

1982

Rusty Harris Series Series
Named after a skate photographer who died at a contest in Pomona. The series eventually morphed into the National Skateboard Association and numerous contests were held throughout the '80's throughout North America and Europe. It was headed by Tony Hawk's father, Frank.

At the first contest Micke Alba took first place in the pro pool contest and collected $150, Frank Blood won in banked slalom and Lester Kasai beat Tony Hawk in the sponsored amateur event.

In the final contest of 1982, Billy Ruff hit five-foot airs, Rodney Mullen won in freestyle, and 14-year-old Tony Hawk claimed his first vert contest.

1983

Del Mar Spring Nationals, Del Mar Skate Ranch, California
Tony Hawk won first place and earned $250. Swedish freestyler Per Welinder beat Mullen and pocketed $250 as well.

Mid Eastern Skateboard Series (MESS), Mike Hills Ramp, Fairborn, Ohio
This was the first MESS contest. Ray Underhill won in the sponsored division.

Upland Pro-Am, Upland Skatepark, California
Steve Caballero won pro pool and Chris Miller won in the amateur division.

Upland Turkey Shoot, Upland Skatepark, California
Contest included pipe pasting and longest rock 'n' roll slide. Lance Mountain won pro bowl and wins $300. Neil Blender managed a 26-foot carve and Kevin Staab won in the amateur division.

1984

Kona Pro Am, Jacksonville, Florida
Randy Barfield won in pool, Reggie Barnes took freestyle event and Buck Smith won the halfpipe contest.

NSA-Del Mar Skatepark
Tony Hawk won the contest. Mike McGill introduced the McTwist (a 540 mute air). Per Welinder won in freestyle event and Jeff Grosso won in the amateur pool division.

European Championships, France
Claus Grabke won in the ramp event and Jean Marc Vaissette took the freestyle title.

1985

NSA World Open, Huntington Beach, California
Winners: Billy Ruff pro street and Rodney Mullen in freestyle. Sponsored amateur Mark Gonzales won street contest.

British Open, Franborough, United Kingdom
Winners: Shane Rouse, freestyle and Danny Webster, halfpipe.

French Open, Fountain, France
Winners: Pierre Andre, freestyle and Englishman Sean Goff, halfpipe.

Tahoe Massacre II, Tahoe City, California Ramp
contest won by Lance Mountain.

NSA Summer Series #5 — Border War, Stanley Park, Vancouver, British Columbia
Held in conjunction with the 10th Annual BC Skateboard Championships. Winners: Pierre Andre, freestyle, Christian Hosoi, pro ramp, Jeff Grosso, amateur ramp.

1986

Transworld Skateboard Championships, Expo, Vancouver, BC
First time a skate contest had been organized with an "Olympic flavor." A $25,000 super ramp was built with a very poor surface. Competitors pitched in and rebuilt it together! Tony Hawk won first place in the ramp competition and received $1,000 (Canadian) in prize money. Vic Ilg spun 112 360's and veteran skater Bob Skolberg took the Giant Slalom. Ludek Vasa cleared 5' 1" in the high jump event.

1987

NSA SkateWave, Toronto
First street contest featuring a jump ramp.

1988

Vision Skate Escape
Major skateboard extravaganza put on by Vision and featuring the Red Hot Chili Peppers. Christian Hosoi emerged as the winner, but Tony Hawk was a very close second place.

Titus World Cup, Germany
Steve Caballero took first in Streetstyle. Christian Hosoi won the halfpipe contest and Pierre Andre was first in freestyle.

1989

NSA Contest, Mini Ramp, Neil Blaisdell Arena, Hawaii
Over 6,000 spectators watched Steve Caballero win first place. Danny Way's first pro contest — he took 7th place.

NSA Contest, Vans Factory, Anaheim, California
Secret contest with no spectators. Paul "The Professor" Schmitt was recruited to help improve the ramp. Chris Miller won first place.

Underground Racing Association, foothills of East Los Angeles
Luge-type racing with six-wheel modified skateboards. Seven-mile run took about 15 minutes to complete. Roger Hickey hit 60 miles per hour plus and took first place.

1990

NSA Backyard Series
Three contests held at three different sites. Major problems with the ramp at contest #1. Masters Event (27+) was held; heard on the PA: "Ray Flores, your wife would like you to call home immediately." Won by Jim Gray. Chris Miller took first place in the pro vert.

1991

Münster Contest, Germany
NSA contest won by Bob Boyle; Danny Way reportedly trying and landing (a few) 900's.

1992

Professional Skateboard League Contest, Powell Skate Zone
The PSL had a number of contests over the years at their indoor skatepark. Mike Santarossa took first place.

1993

Professional Skateboard LeagueThrash-a-thon, Cal Poly
This contest had its roots in the 1980's and was put on to raise money for the American Cancer Society. Omar Hassan won first place in Mini Ramp. Willy Santos was first in pro street.

Appendix D
Memorable Skateparks of North America

Well Known Early Parks
Carlsbad — Carlsbad, California
Concrete Wave — Anaheim, California
Moving On Skateboard Park — San Diego, California
The Runway Skate Park — Carson
Skateboard City — Port Orange, Florida
Skateboard Junction — Trabuco Canyon
Skatepark Montebello — Montebello
Solid Surf — Fort Lauderdale, Florida
Ocean Bowl — Ocean City, Maryland
Aala International Park — Honolulu, Hawaii

Notes on Other Famous Parks
In 1977 **The Pipeline** was introduced to the skate world. Located in Upland, California, it featured a 20 foot x40 foot concrete pipe which emptied into a 18-foot deep bowl. The estimated cost to build the pipe was $15-20,000. Proprietors Stan and Jean Hoffman worked tirelessly to provide a superb skate environment. A number of pros helped in the design of the park, including Steve and Micke Alba, Tay Hunt and Charlie Ransom. The Pipeline was a truly a legendary park that was unfortunately demolished in April 1989. Jean Hoffman has since moved on to a position with the California Amateur Skateboard League (CASL).

Imagine a mogul maze constructed out of concrete — it existed at
Sparks Carlsbad!
The **Kona Skatepark** located in Jacksonville, Florida, featured multi colored asphalt.
Reseda Skatercross had a really interesting design: it was a one-course layout that ran through an old A&W drive-thru restaurant.
Skatopia in Buena Park, California, featured a 15-foot-wide half-pipe which ran for 175 feet. It also had beautiful landscaping.
The **Cadillac Wheels Skateboard**

Concourse, Lighthouse Point, Florida, was put together by urethane wheel visionary Frank Nasworthy. Developed in part with Phil Albright, the park had 12,000 square feet of terrain that featured incredible bowls.
.

SkateBoarder called New Jersey's
Cherry Hill a "skatepark breakthrough." Located in New Jersey, Cherry Hill was 34,000 square feet of sheer joy. An indoor park that brought many west coast skaters to the east, including the resident pro, Shogo Kubo.

Fast Facts:
- First skateboard park built in in the San Francisco Bay Area: Alameda
- First outdoor skateboard park in Long Island: The Concrete Wave of Long Island
- First skateboard park in North Texas: South Bay Skateboard Park
- Waldo Autry helped design Skatepark Paramount.
- The West Vancouver Skatepark was Canada's first skatepark.
- The Fyber Rider Skatepark of Lakewood, New Jersey, was made of molded blue fiberglass.
- One of the last skateboard parks built in the US during the 1970's was Milwaukee's Surf 'n Turf. Interestingly enough, it was spared the bulldozer during the second skate bust of the early 1980's. However, the building where the park was situated was leased to a new company and the site became a strip club. It wasn't until 1988 when Jerry Steuernagel, one of the original owners of the park, was able to find a loophole to break the lease and evict the strip club, that skating began once again at one of the midwest's finest indoor parks.

Additional Parks
We didn't find them all, and most were either torn down or bulldozed. Apologies to those we've missed.

Alabama
Wheel-A-Wave Skatepark, Birmingham,
Alaska
O.T. Enterprises
Anchorage
Arizona
Permanent Wave, Mesa, Arizona
Skate of the Shade, Tempe, Arizona
Arkansas
Skater Town, Little Rock, Arkansas
California
Fountain Valley Skateboard Park
Wild Wheels, Covina,
The Big O, Orange,
The Runway, Carson,
Sierra Wave, Sacramento,
Skateboard Odyssey, Mission Viejo,
Skatepark Victoria, Milpitas,
The Endless Wave, Bakersfield and Oxnard,
Grand Prix of Pomona Skate Park, Pomona,
Boogie Bowl, Glendale,
Badlands Skatepark, Long Beach,
Oasis Skatepark, San Diego,
Lakewood Center Skateboard World, Lakewood,
Heat Wave, Modesto,
Alameda Skateboard Park
Aloha Skatetown, Agoura
Camino Real Park, Ventura
Canyon Country Skateboard Park
Field House Skateboard Park, Thousand Oaks
Glendora Pipeline
Irvine Community Park
Movin' On Skatepark, San Diego
National Skatepark of El Cajon
Paradise Island Skatepark, Lafayette
Rainbow Skatepark, Sacramento
Ride On Skatepark, Newark
Shady Acres, Long Beach
Sidewalk Surf Park, Fountain Valley
Sierra Wave, Rancho Cordova
Skateboard Heaven, Spring Valley
Skateboard Palace, Carmichael
Skateboard World, USA, Bakersfield
Skatepark Montebello
Skater Crater, San Bernadino
Skateworld, Livermore
Solid Wave Skateboard Park, Arroyo Grande
Spinnin' Wheels Skatepark, Concord

Stahl's Skateboard Palace, Carmichael
Soquel Skatepark, Santa Cruz
Surf De Earth, Vista
The Perfect Wave, Pomoa
Winchester Skatepark, Campbell

The Carolinas
The Concrete Connection Skateboard Park, Charotte, North Carolina
Fun Land Skateboard Park, Myrtle Beach, South Carolina
Wizard Skateparks, North and South
Concrete Connection, Charlotte,
All American Skateboard Park, Summerville
Banks and Bowls Skateboard Park, Winston Salem
Barney's Concrete Curl, Nags Head
Carolina Beach Skateboard Park
Cosmic Wave, Columbia
East Cooper Skateboard Park, Mount Pleasant
Freewheelin' Skate Ranch, Wilmington
Mach 1, Columbia
Myrtle Beach Skateboard Park
North Myrtle Beach Skateboard Park
Skateboard Junction,Charlotte
Skatepark of Norfolk
Spartenburg Skatepark
Thunder Road, Virginia Beach

Colorado
Concrete Curl, Denver, Colorado
Up the Wall, Colorado Springs

Conneticut
Climax Skatepark, New Haven
Rock Park, Colchester

Florida
Golf Club & Skateboard Park, Fort Myers
Sensation Basin, Gainsvill,
Skateboard Heaven, Fort Lauderdale
Saturn Skatepark, Titusville,
Groundswell Skatepark, Fort Pierce,
Kissimmee Skateboard Park,
Indian Harbor Beach Skatepark,
Skateboard Safari, West Palm Beach,
Earth'n Surf'n, St Petersburg,
Safe Surf, Fort Pierce
Lakeland Skateboard Arena
Longwood Pipeline, Longwood
Longwood Skatepark, Orlando
Safe Surf, Ft. Pierce
Skateboard City, Port Orange
Skateboard USA, Hollywood
Skate Wave, Tampa
Suferdome, Sarasota
The Paved Wave, Cocoa
The Paved Wave, Pensacola
Tomoko Moonforest Skateboard Park

Georgia
National Skateboard Park, Lake City
Nova Skate Park, Brunswick
Concrete Surf, Decatur
Skateboard Surf, Atlanta

Hawaii
Aala International Park, Honolulu

Idaho
American Skateboard Park, Boise
Chinks Peak Skatepark, Pocatello

Illinois
Country Surf'n, Springfield,
Olympic Skateboard Arena, Crystal Lake,
Rainbow Sports, Chicago

Indiana
Indy Skateboard Inc., Indianapolis

Louisiana
Thunderboard Skatepark, Gretna
Zoom City, Metaire
Solid Surf, Baton Rouge

Maryland
Glass Wave, Gaithersburg
Ocean City Skate Bowl
Salisbury Skateboard Park

Massachusetts
Zero Gravity Skatepark, Cambridge,
Pioneer Valley, Chicopee
Skateboard USA, Peabody
Wooden Wave, Haverhill
Berkshire Skateboard Park, Springfield

Michigan
Astro Speedway Skatepark, Jenison,
Playland Skatepark, Flint
Redford Skatepark, Redford
Skateboard City, Warren

Minnesota
Ride the Glass, Eden Prairie

Missouri
Concrete Surf, Tupelo
Earth Wave, St. Louis
Skateboard Cities of the Ozarks, Springfield
Banzai Pipeline, Kansas City

Nebraska
Concrete Wave, Omaha

Nevada
Las Vegas Desert Surf, Las Vegas,
Mile High Skatepark, Reno,
Skatemaze, Las Vegas
Flow Motion Skateboard Park, Reno

New Hampshire
Great Bay Arena, Newington
Skateboard Center, Manchester

New Jersey
Monster Bowl, Seaside Heights,
Off the Wall, Pleasant Beach,
The Paved Wave Skateboard Park, Oakhurst,
Brave New World Park, Pt. Pleasant Beach
Free Spirit Skateboard Park, Long Beach Island
Fyber Ryder Skateboard Park, Lakewood
SKAbo Casino Arena, Asbury Park
Super Surf Skatepark, Vineland
Verson Valley Ski Area, Vernon
Weber's Wave, Brooklawn
Wonderwave Skateboard Park, Ocean City

New York
Competition Skateboard Center, Clay
Island Skateboard, Staten Island
Darien Lake Skateboard City, Corfu
Island Skateboard Track, Staten Island
East Coast Skate Arena, Huntington, Long Island
Skate-Away Skateboard Arena, Nanuet
Great Bay Arena, Newington
Long Island's Concrete Wave

North Port Skatepark, Long Island

North Dakota/South Dakota
American Sportsman Skatepark, Fargo
SkateAll Park, Inc., Sioux Falls

Ohio
Apple Skate Park, Columbus
Soaring High, Hollan
Hi Rollers, Elyria
Surf's Up Skatepark, Warren

Oregon
High Tide Skatepark, Medfor

Pennsylvania
Paved Wave, Cocoa, Florida, Philadelphia,
Wild Waves Skate Park, Erie,
Thunderdohm Skatepark, York,
Eastern Skateboard Park, Carlisle
Philidelphia Skateboard Park

Rhode Island
Yawgoo Valley Skateboard Park, Slocum

Tennessee
Jetway Skateboard Park, Bartlett
Jetway of Memphis
Orange Wave, Knoxville
Super Bowl Skatepark, Knoxville

Texas
Free Flight SkatePark, Carrolton, Texas
Surf City Skateboard Park, San Angelo, Texas
Gulf Coast Skatepark, Houston, Texas
Desert Surfing Skateboard Park, El Paso, Texas
Earth Surf, El Paso, Texas
Skateboard Slopes, San Antonio, Texas
Jetway Skateboard Parks, Memphis,
Tennessee, Bartlett, Texas
All A Board, San Antonio
Holly Hills Skateboard Park, Corpus Christi
Mid Cities Skatepark, Grand Prairie
NW Skateboard Slopes, San Antonio
Skateboard City, Houston
Skateboard USA, Irving
Skater's Crater, Pasadena
Solid Surf, Houston
South Bay Skateboard Park, Fort Worth
Texas Pipeline Skatepark, Houston
Texas Skateboard Park, Houston
Wizard Skatepark, Dallas

Utah
Nordic Valley Skatepark, Nordic Valley

Virginia
The Skateboard Park of Norfolk
Skateworld, Alexandria,
Flow Motion, Richmond,
Thunderbowl Skatepark, Virginia Beach,
Mt. Trashmore Park, Virginia Beach,
Concrete Pipeline, Virginia Beach
Glass Glider, Roanoke

Washington
E J's Skatewaves, Spokane Washington

Wisconsin
Surf 'n Turf

Canada
Skateboard Palace, Vancouver, British Columbia
Ontario Skateboard Parks, Markham, Ontario

Mexico
Skapistas de Mexico, Tijuana

189

Appendix E
Skate 'Zines

One of the greatest things ever to emerge from the punk/new wave movement was the concept of the "do it yourself" magazine. Whether you wanted to write about skating, politics, music, or who you hated, as long as you had the time and energy, you could run a 'zine. All you needed were some scissors, tape, paper, access to a photocopier, and presto — instant publishing empire.

Hundreds of thousands of skateboard 'zines were put out in the late '70's and '80's. Some are probably still kicking around today. For a lot of people, the amount of energy and time spent putting together these magazines probably equalled the amount of time they skated. On second thought, it's more than likely that putting together the 'zine probably ate up way more time! Did you remember to enclose fifty cents and stamp?

A Select List of 'Zines & Mags
(apologies to the thousands we didn't include)

Big Boys	Spunk	Squid West
Skate Threat	Street Grinder	Midwest Grind
Skate Scene	I Be Sompin	Death Skate
Pool Dust	Ragged Edge	Rolling Papers
Kamikaze Skate Mag	Vertical	PA Skate Vu
Stop Skate Harassment	Skate Session	Mayheem
Speeed Zine	Skater of Fortune	Lapper
Shred	Local Chaos	Street Issue
Free Zine	Skate Madness	VB Thrash
Shred Of Dignity	Dirthead Rat	Down Syndrome
Swank Zine	Skate Brigade	Just for Fun
Interspace	Slam Mag	Edge Out
Jolly Jumper	No Limits	Local Chaos
Skate Rat	Body Slam	Skate Environment
Board Youth	Skaters On Board	Body Slam
	Skate Fate	Trasher
	The Jammer	Street Grinder
	The Monthy Shredder	Indy Airs
	Stuff Mag	Rise Above Skate Rag
	Very Sketchy	Skatecore

Resources

Companies of Interest to Old School Skaters

Alva
1404 Descanso #L San Marcos, California 92069 USA
760-591-3989

Dregs
1666 Garnet Avenue #308
San Diego, California 92109 USA
619-272-3095

Envy
1945 Camino Vida Roble, Suite H, Carlsbad, California 92008 USA
760-431-5545

eXkate
562-634-8492

Flexdex
5535 Ruffin Road, San Diego, California 92123 USA
619-560-2640

Fluid Longboards
949-650-7774

Freebord
3001 20th Street, San Francisco, California 94110 USA
415-285-BORD

Gordon & Smith
4901 Morena Blvd., Building 402, San Diego, California 92117 USA
619-581-5155

Gravity Streetboards
132 E. Cliff Street, Solana Beach, California 92075 USA
619-259-1334

Madrid
17401 Nichol Street #A, Huntington Beach, California 92647 USA
714-848-5959

Makaha
531 Main Street, #422, El Segundo, CA 90245 USA
310-322-3924

Powell
30 S. La Patera Ln., Santa Barbara, California 93117 USA
805-964-1330

Randal Trucks
650-327-5566

Road Rider, Independent
PO Box 2718, Santa Cruz, California 95063-2718 USA

Sector 9
5666 La Jolla Blvd. Suite 99, La Jolla, California 92037 USA
619-552-1296

Seismic Trucks
1630 30th Street #257, Boulder, Colorado 80301 USA
303-440-9449

Skull Skates
2868 W. 4th Avenue, Vancouver, British Columbia V6K 1R2 Canada
604-739-7796

Tracker Trucks
3210-B Production Avenue, Oceanside, California 92054 USA
760-722-1455

Xtreme Wheelz
12528 Kirkham Ct., #5, City of Poway, California 92064 USA
619-679-5599

Z Products
PO Box 5397, Santa Monica, California 90409 USA

Skateboard Museums
Skatopia
34961 Hutton Road, Rutland, Ohio 45775 USA
740-742-1110
An 88-acre farm that already includes an enormous collection of skateboards, gigantic indoor wooden bowl (40' x 60') and numerous ramps. Plans are underway for more expansion. Hats off to Brewce Martin, Carlos Biaza and Wendy Willhoite for creating skate heaven!

Skatelab
4226 Valley Fair, Simi Valley, California USA
805-578-0040
The Skatelab features a large collection of skateboard products and memorabilia. Also on display are scooters from the 1930's — the precursor to modern skateboard. A 15,000-square-foot skatepark sits next to the museum, featuring enormous bowls and ramps. The facility is operated by Todd Huber (CalSk8Lab@aol.com) and his wife Jennifer.

Huntington Beach International Skate and Surf Museum
411 Olive Street
Huntington Beach California USA
714-960-3483

Print Resources:
Glen E. Friedman's books *F*** You Heroes, F*** You Too,* and *The Idealist* (which all contain some classic old school skate shots) all published by Burning Flags Press and distributed by ConSafos, P.O. Box 931568, Los Angeles, CA 90093 1-800-655-4897 or 323-463-6401 (outside U.S.)

Dysfunctional by Aaron Rose is a collection of amazing images and ideas from skate culture. Published by Booth-Clibborn Editions, London ISBN: 1584230029

High Speed Productions (*Thrasher* magazine)
1303 Underwood Avenue San Francisco, California 94124 USA
415-822-3083

Transworld Skateboarding
353 Airport Road Oceanside, California 92054 USA
760-722-7777

Surfer Publications (*SkateBoarder*)
P.O. Box 1028, Dana Point, California 92629 USA

Miscellaneous
Extreme Downhill International
1666 Garnet Avenue #308, San Diego, California 92109
619-272-3095
The premier sanctioning body of downhill skateboarding and street luge. Yearly membership fee.

International Association of Skateboard Companies (IASC)
PO Box 37, Santa Barbara, California 93116
805-683-5676
Dedicated to the promotion and advancement of skateboarding worldwide.

California Amateur Skateboard League (CASL)
Sonja Catalano 909-883-6176
Amateur and professional skateboard events

International Network for Flatland Freestyle Skateboarding
Stefan Akesson,
Abbedissavagen 15, 746 95 Balsta, Sweden
Promoting freestyle throughout the world

World Cup of Skateboarding
www.wcsk8.com
503-426-1502
Don and Danielle Bostick run numerous contests all over the world.

Internet Sites
www.boardpark.com
(Huge skate, surf, and snowboard site)

www.ncdsa.com
(The Northern California Skateboard Association's longboard website)

www.interlog.com/~mbrooke/skategeezer.html
(Old school skateboarding from the site that started it all!)

SOURCES

Works Consulted:

Books

Cassorla, Albert. *The Skateboarder's Bible.* Philadelphia: Running Press, 1976.

Davidson, Ben. *The Skateboard Book.* New York: Grosset and Dunlap, Inc., 1976.

Dixon, Pahl, and Peter Dixon. *Hot Skateboarding.* New York: Warner Books, 1977.

Weir, LaVada. *Skateboards and Skateboarding.* New York: Pocket Books, 1977.

Magazines

(Issues from throughout the publishing history of these magazines were consulted. Some have ceased publication.)

Big Brother
Skateboard
Skateboard World
SkateBoarder (The Quarterly Skateboarder)
Thrasher
Transworld Skateboarding
Wide World of Skateboarding

Photograph, Graphic and Text Sources

The author and publishers wish to thank all those who contributed their words and pictures to this volume. Every effort has been made to give credit to the originators of materials used in this book. Any questions in this regard may be directed to the publisher.

Text:

The following items were originally contributed to the Skategeezer Homepage. Some were edited for inclusion in this book. Some contributors declined to give their full names.

p. 17 — "There are a few old geezers ...," A.W.; "I started skateboarding...," Anonymous

p. 18–19 — "The Day They Invented the Skateboard," by Bob Schmidt

p. 33 — "Contests and Championships," by Paul Fisher; "Guy/girl skaters ...," A.W.

p. 41 — "I'm 35 years old...," by David F.

p. 50 — "I started skating on a steel-wheeled 'sidewalk surfer' ...," by Andy G.

p. 81— "Autotopia," by Anonymous

p. 86–87 — "Swedish Style," by Stefan Lillis Akesson

These items were written specifically for *The Concrete Wave*:

p. 37 — "Four Decades of Skating ... and Still Rolling," ©1999 by Cliff Coleman

p. 42–43 — "Dreaming of a California Sky in the Golden Age," ©1999 by Richard Jones

p. 76–77 — "My Skateboard Story," ©1999 by Tannis Watson

p. 84–85 — "Pepsi Pro Skateboard Team Memories," ©1999 by René Carrasco

p. 89 — "Skateboarding Across America," ©1999 by Jack Smith

p. 114–15 — "The Four-Wheel Wonder Down Under," ©1999 by Richard Jones

p. 121 — "Another Roadside Attraction," ©1999 by Peter Camann

p. 126 — "Profile: Lynn Cooper," ©1999 by Lynn Cooper

p. 127 — © 1999 by Kevin Harris

p. 129–31 — "The Story of World Industries," ©1999 by Steve Rocco

p. 132–35 — "Pooling Your Memories," ©1999 by Darrel Delgado

p. 136 — Excerpt from "Sidewalk Surfing," ©1999 by Craig R. Stecyk

p. 141 — "When I first saw a skateboard...," ©1999 by Lillis

p. 159 — "Skateboarding is all about being yourself,..." ©1999 by Paul S.

p. 160–61— "Der Münster Mosh," ©1999 by Peter "Dietsches" Diepes

p. 162–65 — "The Notorious Big Brother," ©1999 by Sean Cliver

p. 166–67 — "Rockin' the Rainforest," ©1999 by Bob Burnquist

p. 173 — "'We should be ahead by twenty points...," ©1999 by Chris Long

p. 176–77 — "Skateboarding Is," ©1999 by Dave Hackett

p. 178–79 — "The Carrasco Brothers," ©1999 by René Carrasco

The items below were previously published in journals and are reprinted with the kind permission of the authors:

p. 78–80 and p. 175 — Interview with Tony Alva, ©1995 by Tim Chiappetta; first published in *The SkateTrader,* 1995.

p. 83 — "Russ Howell: Gymnastics Meets Freestyle," ©1997 by Dan Gesmer; first published in *The Journal of the International Network for Flatland Freestyle.*

photoCredits

Courtesy Bob Burnquist, 167 *(right)*
Courtesy Curtis Stevenson, 22, 25
Courtesy Darrel Delgado, 132 *(top)*, 135 *(top)*
Courtesy Dave Hackett, 176 *(both)*, 177, 179, 193
Courtesy Gordon and Smith, 34, 35
Courtesy Hobie, 28
Courtesy Jack Smith, 12-13 *(sequence)*, 88, 89
Courtesy Lynn Cooper, 126
Courtesy Mike Rector, 69
Courtesy Paul Schmitt, 116, 117 *(all)*, 118, 119
Courtesy Peter Camann, 120 *(all)*
Courtesy Powell Peralta, 99 *(both)*, 100, 101, 102, 103
Courtesy René Carrasco, 68, 84-85 *(all)*, 178
Courtesy Russell Howell, 82, 180 *(top)*
Courtesy Scott Starr, 44, 45, 51, 70 *(Don Autry, Ty Page, Tom Sims)*, 141, 168 *(bottom)*, 180 *(bottom)*
Courtesy Sector 9, 168 *(top)*, 170
Courtesy Skull Skates, 122
Courtesy Stefan Lillis Akesson, 86 *(bottom)*
Courtesy Wee Willi Winkel, 60, 62 *(both)*, 63
Courtesy World Industries, 128 *(illustration by Mark McKee)*, 131 *(illustration by Mark McKee)*
Courtesy Val Surf, 16

Ace Kvale, 171
Big Brother magazine, 162, 163, 164
Bill Eppridge/*Life* Magazine © Time Inc., 27
Bill Sharp, 65, 67 *(top)*
Brad Bowman, 66, 72-73 *(sequence)*, 87,

Chris Ortiz, 10
Dan Devine, 70 *(John Hutson)*
Daniel Bourqui, 166 *(left)*
Darrel Delgado, 133
Dave Duncan, 86 *(top left)*, 110 *(Christian Hosoi)*
David Fullarton, 169 *(illustration)*
Diordandi Nagao, 166 *(top left)*, 167 *(bottom)*
Eric Harp, 185
Gary Frayer, 135 *(bottom)*
James O'Mahoney, 186
J. Grant Brittain, 134
John Old, 110 *(Steve Caballero)*
Michael Brooke, 16 *(insets)*, 19 *(both)*
Mike Belobradic, 181, back cover *(author)*
Peter Diepes, 160 *(both)*
Peter Ducommun, 20 *(both)*, 21, 81
RAD magazine, 42
Rick Ducommun, 8, 123
Scott Starr, front cover, 2, 5, 6 *(both)*, 7 *(both)*, 17 *(top)*, 39, 91, 106-107, 108-109, 114, 139, 159, 172, 187, back cover *(Chad Muska)*
Skateboard! magazine, 43
Skateboarder magazine, 64, 67 *(sequence)*, 71
Stan Sharp, 58
Tannis Watson III, 76
Thrasher magazine, 92, 94, 95
Tom Browne, 110 *(Lance Mountain, Neil Blender)*
Transworld Skateboarding magazine, 33, 96
Xeno, 132 *(bottom)*

index

960s Skate Gods

Danny Bearer

Danny placed first place in flatland slalom (boys 12 and under division) at the 1964 Anaheim Nationals. He rode for Hobie Super Surfer Team and in 1975 wound up riding for Logan Earth Ski. Quoted in *SkateBoarder* 1980 "I remember Revere and Bellagio during the early days . . . 20-foot, wide open banks. Too bad all the kids now are stuck in those pools and can't get out. I've got a piece of ash wood sitting here for a new board. Skating's a good, healthy sport."

Brad "Squeak" Blank

"Squeak" was the first person to ever win a skateboard contest-1964 Anaheim Nationals. He rode for Makaha and influenced a generation of skaters.

Joey Cabell

A member of the Hobie Super Surfer team. Credited by Mike Hynson as the developer of slalom skateboarding in the early 1960's. Joey and Mike used sandals as markers for the course. Soon after they were found by a cop and told to stop.

Phil Edwards

One of the world's most famous surfers, Phil also got heavily into skateboards in the 1960's. Phil had an enormous impact on the skateboard world and aided the successful transition of the image of skateboarding from that of a toy to a sport.

John Freis

John won first place overall at the 1965 Anaheim Nationals. Rode for both Makaha and Super Surfer Teams. Developed many tricks including the nose wheelie.

Skip Frye

Long time surf legend, Skip Frye was part of the first wave of skateboarding in the early 1960's. Skip rode for many years on the Gordon & Smith team and promoted their classic Fibreflex boards. He currently runs a surf shop in Pacific Beach, California.

Dave Hilton

Dave was the youngest member of the Hobie Super Surfer team. He was the first person to appear on the cover of *SkateBoarder* magazine (1965). Dave was also a frequent skater at a pool located in Foxtail Park (near Santa Monica). This pool is considered to be one of the first ever ridden by skateboarders. Dave's brother Steve was also a very talented rider.

Torger Johnson

One of skateboarding's greatest legends, Torger invented many freestyle tricks, including the "space walk" (a rider will balance on the back wheels and move the board sideways in the air). He had a solid surfing background and won many contests. Tragically, Torger died in a car accident in 1988.

Bruce Logan, Brian Logan, Brad Logan, Robin Logan

The three Logan Brothers were fixtures of the 60's and 70's skate scenes. Bruce was known as "King of the Nose Wheelie" and was the dominant freestyler in the 1960's and part of the 1970's. He invented a number of tricks including the "headstand spinner." From 1964 to 1977, Bruce took first place in over 22 contests. He originally rode for Makaha and went on to ride for the family company — Logan Earth Ski. Brian and Brad were accomplished riders in freestyle, downhill and slalom. Their sister Robin was reportedly the first woman ever to do a kickflip. Together with their mother, the Logans were known as skateboarding's first family.

John Milius

John is known as "The Father of the Kickturn." He was an early skater/surfer pioneer from the Pacific Palisades area. John went on to write screenplays for Hollywood films including *Apocalypse Now.*